Duck Season

Duck Season

Eating, Drinking, and Other Misadventures
in Gascony—France's Last Best Place

David McAninch

HARPER

An Imprint of HarperCollinsPublishers

DUCK SEASON. Copyright © 2017 by David McAninch. All rights reserved. Printed in the United States of America. No part of this book may be used or reproduced in any manner whatsoever without written permission except in the case of brief quotations embodied in critical articles and reviews. For information, address HarperCollins Publishers, 195 Broadway, New York, NY 10007.

HarperCollins books may be purchased for educational, business, or sales promotional use. For information, please email the Special Markets Department at SPsales@harpercollins.com.

FIRST EDITION

Designed by William Ruoto

Illustrations by Alexis Seabrook

Library of Congress Cataloging-in-Publication Data has been applied for.

ISBN 978-0-06-230941-9

17 18 19 20 21 LSC 10 9 8 7 6 5 4 3 2 1

For Michele and Charlotte

Gascon-headed man, will you have done?

—ALEXANDRE DUMAS, PÈRE

Contents

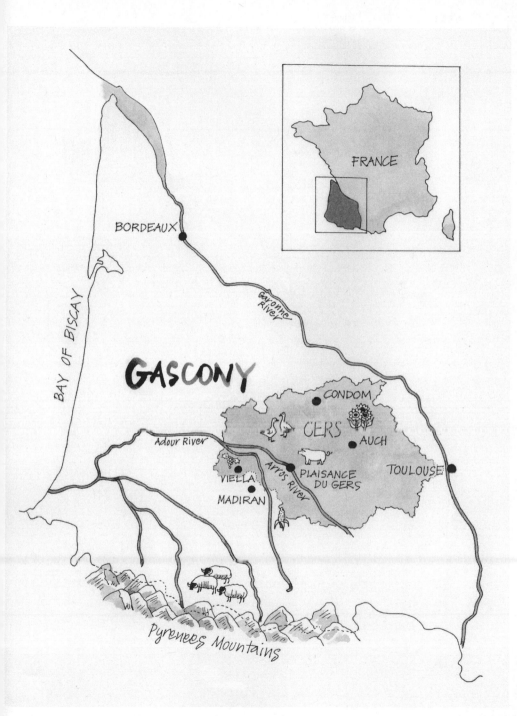

1

Fire

The making of dinner began auspiciously enough. Having stumbled onto—rather, into—a small barbecue pit in the backyard of our new home, I decided to kick off our eight-month epicurean journey in the Southwest of France with a dish as elemental as it was delicious, a dish that would root us firmly in the local culinary idiom, a dish that, not for nothing, was hard to screw up: grilled duck breasts. As if to endorse my decision, the rain clouds that had been dogging us since our arrival a few days ago were finally breaking up. Tonight, I would cook under the open sky and we would eat like Gascons.

At a nearby duck farm, I purchased two *magrets*, as duck breasts are called in France, from a woman in rubber boots and a white smock smeared with blood—a duck's, I presumed. The two heavy red ingots were topped with a layer of fatty skin as thick as my finger. They looked as if they'd belonged to a creature larger than a waterfowl—say, a creature with hooves. For a few euros, I also bought a mason jar filled with rendered duck fat, an ingredient as indispensable to Gascons as olive oil is to Sicilians: "a balm for the wounds of the soul," as I'd sometimes heard it referred to. The fat, in which I intended to roast some potatoes, looked like white cake frosting.

Gascons like to grill duck over dried vine cuttings. I had to settle for damp firewood left over from the previous winter, but eventually I got the flames going. While the logs popped and hissed, I swirled my wine and took stock of my surroundings. Looming above me was our rented house, a 200-year-old converted textile mill. It was an austere-looking edifice, of a style common to early-nineteenth-century water mills in this rural corner of France: plastered-stone façade, red tile roof, tall casement windows, and stout dimensions that called to mind the plastic houses from a Monopoly game. To one end of the structure a small balcony had been tacked on. Perched on it at present, enjoying a pre-dinner snack of goose rillettes on toasts, were my wife, Michele, and six-year-old daughter, Charlotte, who was peering at me through the balcony railings. I looked up and waved.

The most interesting thing about our dwelling, in my estimation, was that a river ran through it, or at least a stream. From where I was standing, I could see where it emerged from dense foliage on the south side of the house, trickled under three arches cut into the mill's foundation, flowed beneath the roof of the old wheel shed, and emptied into the greenish-brown waters of the Arros River some twenty yards on. The meeting of the stream and the river created the grassy wedge of land, shaded by walnut trees and garlanded with stinging nettle, that served as our yard.

This private eden—a robust habitat for insects, it must be said, and also river rats, which I'd seen lumbering along the stream's pebbly shoals—offered a fine view of the sand-colored stone bridge that spanned the Arros and led to the heart of the village, which was named, agreeably enough, Plaisance. An old stone bridge being a fine thing to gaze at while sipping a drink, I watched idly as a tractor rumbled across, followed by an old man on a woman's bike, then a dog that appeared to have taken a dip in the river. If I looked east, past the shallow ravine that edged our property, I could see a grove of oak trees and a muddy cornfield. Beyond that, just out of sight, gentle hills and rolling vineyards rose up from the alluvial plain. If I climbed atop the stone retaining wall near the stream embankment, stood on my tiptoes, and looked south, I could make out the serrated silhouette of the Pyrenees. On the other side of those mountains lay Spain.

Had I been a pin on a map, I'd have been sticking out of the lower-left edge of the Gallic hexagon, halfway between Toulouse and Bordeaux, in a Delaware-size swath of countryside devoid of highways, major train lines, and big cities—about as close to the middle of nowhere as you could get nowadays in mainland France. This was the Gers, the most rural of France's 101 *départements*, a place where ducks outnumbered people twenty to one. This was the verdant heart of Gascony.

I swatted at a bug and glanced at the fire. It was ready. After three jet-lagged days of supping on bread and pâté, it was time to put heat to meat.

I'D BEEN A CARD-CARRYING FRANCOPHILE for most of my life. I felt the first stirrings in high school, in a French classroom adorned with paper tricolor flags and furnished with a wastebasket on which the teacher, Madame Liesman, had taped a sign reading INTERDICTION

DE CRACHER ET DE VOMIR—"No spitting or vomiting." But the love affair really blossomed in my early twenties, when I lived in the South of France as a student for a year and then for another year in Paris, working as a teacher and, like so many feckless expats before me, leading a life of splendid dissipation, hopping trains and hitch-hiking all over the country every chance I got. I traveled wide and deep. I had my first tastes of magret and foie gras and cassoulet. I became a habitué of cheap, chalkboard-menu bistros. I fell in whole-heartedly with the French conviction that meals should be long and relaxing, that *they* were the day's focus and that work was merely a necessary intermission. I learned to speak the language well enough that French people sometimes thought I was Belgian, or at least not American. I went back home and got a master's degree in French literature. I honeymooned in France with Michele. I started cooking coq au vin and boeuf bourguignonne regularly. I pursued a career as a food writer largely so I could return to France as often as possible on someone else's dime. Indeed, as is the case with so many Fran-cophiles, food became the lens through which I viewed my travels, and life in general.

I don't recall precisely when Gascony slipped onto my radar—I'd passed through the region a few times as a tourist, not pausing long enough to really see or taste the place—but I do remember when I first fell hard. It was 2012. I was on assignment for the food mag-azine I worked for, researching a story on duck, an ingredient I'd always loved but which got short shrift in the United States, usually taking a backseat to the exalted beefsteak or the oh-so-fashionable pig. Driving around the region, I discovered a land where duck is king—four and a half million were being raised each year in the Gers alone, twenty-five million across the greater Southwest of France. Duck got top billing on virtually every restaurant menu from Toulouse to Bordeaux. Cooks in Gascony used every part of the bird—the breasts, the legs, the wings, the neck, the feet, and, of course, the fattened liver—and they cooked its flesh every which way: They grilled it, roasted it, sautéed it, braised it in wine, and, most famously, cured it lightly in salt and simmered it in its own fat to make confit, that pillar of farmhouse canning cellars all over southwestern France.

This had all duly impressed me, but my come-to-Jesus moment didn't occur until the last day of that duck-filled visit, after a string of rich meals that included, in no particular order, Armagnac-flambéed duck tenderloins, skewered duck hearts with chanterelles, duck carpaccio, and a duck-confit shepherd's pie strewn with shavings of foie gras. At dinner that night, somewhat the worse for wear, I asked the server at my hotel for a green salad. A bewildered, slightly hurt expression flickered across his face. He nodded curtly and returned minutes later with a plate containing a few leaves of Bibb lettuce topped with confited duck gizzards, six slices of cured duck breast, duck-skin cracklings, and a quartered hard-boiled egg. It wasn't what I'd had in mind, but, my God, was it good.

Once back home in Chicago, I immediately started angling for another Gascony assignment, and within a few months I got one: to cover a wine festival in a village called Viella. On the first night of my trip, the founder of the wine cooperative, a genteel older man named André Dubosc, invited me to a dinner at the home of a matronly widow named Nadine Cauzette, who was the president of the Friends of Pacherenc Society—Pacherenc being a little-known white wine made in this particular sliver of Gascony. The meal started in a sitting room with duck rillettes, duck sausage, and glasses of chilled Pacherenc; progressed to the dining table with pan-seared foie gras, duck confit, cabbage-and-white-bean soup, potato gratin, wine-braised wood pigeon, several bottles of inky Madiran, four kinds of cheese, and a sheet-pan apple tart; and wound down, several hours after it began, in front of the fireplace with chocolate truffles and snifters of very old Armagnac. Every dish brought to the table had been made from scratch, including the sausage, the confit, and the truffles. It was an excessive, magnificent meal. I was sure Monsieur Dubosc had put Nadine up to it, insisting she pull out all the stops for a visiting journalist. And yet, toward the end of the evening, when I said something to the effect of "Nadine, you really shouldn't have," she flashed me the same perplexed look I'd received from the hotel waiter—as if to say there was simply no other way to do things.

The dinner at Nadine's upended whatever notions of balance and restraint I'd hitherto associated with French cooking. And yet there was something about the over-the-top-ness—the sheer *more-ness*—of that meal, and of the other meals I'd eaten in Gascony, that appealed to me in a deep and emotional way. Here was a cuisine that modern gastronomic trends—Nouvelle Cuisine in the 1970s, the diet crazes of the '80s, the small-plates fad of today—seemed to have passed over completely. Whereas in other parts of France, the sacred institution of the two-hour lunch was in decline and bottled water was overtaking wine as the midday drink of choice, in Gascony nothing much had changed. The Gascons I met drank wine with lunch every day. They ate what they craved. They always ordered cheese or dessert and often both. They sang a lot. On my trip to Viella, I went to a winemakers' lunch where everyone was calmly eating their soup one moment, and the next they were standing up, waving their napkins in the air, and belting out a song in the old Occitan tongue: *"Qu'aimi lou men oustau, las bios e la lano / Quand boulho lou Boun Diu, aquiu que mouriréi."*—"How I love my home, its fields and vines / When God sees fit to take me, it is here that I shall die."

What's more, people in Gascony seemed more open-minded than many of their compatriots. I never once heard a Gascon complain about "freeloading immigrants" or witnessed a Gascon throw money back at an American tourist who offered the wrong bills. The Gascons were French through and through, and yet not—there was a hint of the Spaniard about them, an easy warmth and boisterousness.

On top of it all, Gascons lived a long time—longer, in fact, than the residents of any other part of France. The Gers had more than twice as many men over the age of ninety as the national average. Gascons were the paradox within the French Paradox.

They had their duck and ate it, too.

Soon, I was reading everything I could get my hands on about the cuisine of this tremendously fertile patch of France—at one time a duchy and now a fuzzily bordered cultural area. To my surprise, there wasn't much out there, especially when compared with the glut of cookbooks and culinary memoirs about Provence, to Gascony's east. What few books I could find—most of them in French—tended to be small-press publications of the "recipes from my grandmother" variety. Elizabeth David, the British-born gastronome, dipped into southwestern France, if not Gascony in particular, in her now-classic 1960 omnium gatherum *French Provincial Cooking*. Some twenty years after that, Paula Wolfert gave Gascony's signature foods lengthy consideration in *The Cooking of South-West France*, alongside specialties from the Quercy, the Languedoc, the Bordelais, the Limousin, and Basque Country. A towering achievement of culinary scholarship and recipe sleuthing, it remains the only definitive English-language cookbook—and the only truly exhaustive and authoritative book I've been able to find in any language—on the cuisine of the region.

I took from those books what I could, and over time a clearer picture began to emerge. It depicted a land moored fast to tradition, populated by cooks at once overflowing with generosity and yet resistant to change, painstakingly creating dishes of immense depth from a limited palette of local ingredients that hadn't expanded in generations and, with the exception of a dab of Iberian influence, seemed impervious to intrusions from other countries or even neighboring regions.

I grew fascinated with the old farmhouse practices that still underpinned Gascon cooking: confit making, first and foremost, but also the annual *tue-cochon*, or pig slaughter, and *gavage*, the ancient technique of force-feeding ducks and geese in order to engorge their livers for foie gras, and to generate more precious fat. I studied the history of Armagnac, Gascony's aged grape brandy, which mellows in casks of Gascon and Limousin oak, sometimes for many decades. I read about Madiran, the Southwest's blackish, tannic wine (and drank it whenever I could find a decent bottle). I learned about peasant dishes like *garbure* (the confit-studded cabbage soup that is still a Gascon staple), long-braised stews known as *civets* and *daubes*, and tangy sheep's-milk cheeses, fermented at high elevations by Pyrenean shepherds and sold in every outdoor market from Agen to the Spanish border. Other peculiarities intrigued me, too: Spanish-inflected dishes like *piperade* and *paella*, brought into the Gascon fold by the neighboring Basques; age-old preparations for obscure game birds and wild boar, hunted in the remnants of Gascon forests; rustic cakes and tarts, like *croustade* and *gâteau à la broche*, that required the better part of a day to make.

As curiosity sometimes does, mine blossomed into an obsession. This hilly region of duck farms and vineyards began to shimmer in my imagination like France's Last Best Place, a kind of Brigadoon. The unabashedly rich food, the long meals, the fanatical devotion to tradition, the indomitable joie de vivre—not only did these things intrigue me as a writer, but I began to believe they might be an excellent cure for some ills in my own culinary life. Which, suffice it to say, was no longer living up to the spirit of my youthful

Francophilia. An insidious expediency and—even worse, at least from a Francophile's perspective—abstemiousness had crept into my cooking and eating. So had a certain jadedness. I'd grown weary of urban food trends, of chefs' obsessions with novelty, of strenuously artistic dishes that were more titillating than satisfying—what Paula Wolfert had called "front of the mouth food"—to say nothing of the theatrical repackagings of traditional comfort-food cuisines: Alsatian brasserie! Japanese izakaya! Italian enoteca! Jewish deli! It had all started to feel slightly ridiculous.

Gascon cuisine was immune to trends. It relied on simple preparations and ingredients. It defied shortcuts. It insisted on slowness. It adamantly required wine. In short, it was like the concentrated essence of all the pleasures that had caused me to fall in love with France in the first place. Even better, the entire Gascon way of life was, as far as I could tell, predicated on the belief that those pleasures were nothing less than a right—a right to be exercised not just on special occasions, but every day.

One evening, after a late supper of broiled salmon fillets devoured in front of the TV—see above about expediency and abstemiousness—I picked up Wolfert's *The Cooking of South-West France* again and happened on a passage I'd skipped over. Halfway through the introduction, the author remarks, "One could write a rich and anecdotal book about the region, the people, and the land, the sights and smells and moods."

It felt like a personal call to action.

After convincing Michele that moving to rural France would be both doable and life-changing—in a good way—I made a four-day house-hunting trip to the Gers. After visiting a dozen summer rentals lost in the hills, I made a handshake deal on Plaisance's old water mill, enthused by the idea of living above a river and being able to walk to the bakery in the morning. The principal of the village school informed me that enrolling Charlotte in classes would be as simple as filling out a few forms—and assured me that she would pick up French in no time. Soon, the other puzzle pieces started falling into place. I obtained visas and residency permits. I found renters for our condo. Michele got a sabbatical from the music school where she worked—the director happened to be a Francophile, too, and a sentimental one at that. Michele and I went over our budget again and again—sometimes, perhaps not wisely, while drinking wine—and determined we could pull off a sojourn of half a year or so.

In the end we decided to give ourselves eight months, from May to December. This way, we'd avoid the coldest and rainiest part of the year—this wasn't the Côte d'Azur, after all—but still get a taste of all four seasons. We'd arrive when the best spring produce was hitting the markets and stay through summer's village festivals, the fall harvest, and the early-winter rituals of gavage and confit making. We promised Charlotte we'd be home by Christmas Day.

I had every hope that this would give me enough time to immerse myself in the Gascons' *art de vivre*. At the very least, I had to believe some Gascon-ness would rub off on all of us, one way or another.

IT WAS ALMOST TIME TO EAT. I went inside the house to fetch the duck breasts, which, in the interest of quicker grilling, I'd cut into dainty, heart-shaped steaks, each side generously rimmed with fat—this was a trick I'd seen at a cookout on one of my earlier trips to Gascony. I brought out the duck on a fancy serving platter and placed a metal grate over the fire pit. Not without a respectful sense of moment, I laid the duck steaks onto the grill. They made a satisfying sizzle.

Michele and Charlotte were still on the balcony. Charlotte was gnawing on the end of a baguette. She looked down at me and grinned. Michele pushed a breeze-blown strand of hair behind her ear and raised her wineglass. We made an air-toast.

An orangish glow flared in the corner of my eye. I turned to see my steaks engulfed in flames. The fat was melting off them in great glops and igniting. Kneeling in the grass, I frantically flipped the steaks and moved them around, but the fire pit was so small that there was no cool spot where the meat could take refuge. My maneuverings were just releasing more fat into the inferno. I batted at the smoke and cursed.

Charlotte yelled down to inform me that the fire was too big.

"I know!" I yelled back.

The hairs on my fingers singed.

By the time I got the steaks off the grill, they had blackened and curled up like tulip bulbs. It was a dispiriting sight. I brought the duck to the table anyhow, along with the rest of dinner. At least the potatoes looked good—I'd cooked them in the duck fat until they'd turned deep golden brown and, to my delight, had filled the kitchen with the smell of roast duck.

Michele and Charlotte sat down.

"What happened out there?" Michele asked.

I poured myself another glass of wine, took a swig, and stared at the charred meat. "Rookie error," I said. The longer answer was that I'd broken the cardinal rule of cooking duck: Manage the fat. What I'd failed to recognize is that with Gascon ducks, there's a whole lot more fat to manage.

We started in on dinner. The duck actually tasted okay, with a touch of rosiness left in the center. You just had to get past the carbonized flavor on the outside. The wine helped.

2

Market Day

like hundreds of small burgs in the Southwest of France, Plaisance du Gers, as our village was officially called, had been constructed around a *bastide*, which is a central market square bordered by arcaded sidewalks. Today bastides are to Gascony what covered bridges are to Iowa and New England—quaint examples of the local vernacular—but in the socioeconomic history of the French countryside, they were a big deal, as their rise signaled the moment (beginning in the thirteenth century, by most accounts) when trade started to replace mere survival as a reason to build villages. Instead of evolving pell-mell as an agglomeration of houses and workshops in the shadow of a church or a feudal château, like scared children huddling around their mother, bastides were boldly laid out on a grid, with a few wide main streets converging at the arcaded square, where all manner of buying and selling and fraternizing could be conducted in the light of day.

Plaisance, though not the prettiest of bastide villages, had the rare distinction of having not one but two arcaded squares. This owed to a quirk of history. By the early nineteenth century, Plaisance was a boomtown, its riverfront lined with tanneries and ateliers, its streets clogged with all kinds of conveyances and livestock. The village was quickly outgrowing its medieval bastide. So, in the mid-nineteenth century, the town fathers, full of bullish optimism, built a bigger bastide just west of the old one, and, for good measure, erected a pointy-spired neo-Gothic church to go with it, creating a second node of commerce and civic life for the town.

This had resulted in a curious circumstance. Plaisance, which you could drive through in about ninety seconds, had two of everything: two pharmacies, each with its green neon sign and sexy window advertisements for butt-slimming creams; two *tabacs*, each with its lozenge-shaped shingle; two café-bars, each with its sparse clientele of men sipping beer and pastis; two bakeries; two butcher shops; two newsstands; and so on. Plaisance also happened to be a *chef lieu du canton*—basically a county seat—which meant that the inhabitants of a small constellation of surrounding hamlets drove into town in puttering Citroëns, Renaults, and, occasionally, farm vehicles to mail letters, deposit checks, fill prescriptions, exchange gossip, and provision meals. All this gave Plaisance a pleasing hustle-and-bustle, especially if it happened to be a Thursday, which is when the village held its weekly market.

RURAL FRENCH MARKETS HAD ALWAYS filled me with a kind of manic, electric energy. Often when traveling I'd work myself into an acquisitive frenzy and end up buying way more food than I could reasonably consume in a hotel room or carry home on a plane. Now, as I followed a small stream of villagers toward Plaisance's market, I had the calming realization that I could slow down and take my time. I could focus just on what we needed for the next few meals. The market would be back the following week. And there'd be a half dozen other markets on the days in between, in villages just a short drive away. The Gers, which contains fewer people than the farmers' market–less suburb where I grew up, boasts more than fifty weekly village markets—including several *marchés au gras*, or fat markets, devoted exclusively to the buying and selling of fattened ducks and geese and their tasty constituent parts.

And so I kept my wallet in my pocket for a while and wandered among the tented stands that filled the wide square of Plaisance's new bastide, catching the odd sidelong glance from a local here or there, but generally feeling comfortably invisible. I noticed some interesting things that had little to do with food. One was that while I saw money and merchandise being exchanged, mostly what people were doing was cheek kissing, shaking hands, and gabbing—in pairs, in trios, in quartets, clustered in front of the church or over by the tabac or the bank or the hair salon, the talkers discoursing on subjects that, from what I could pick up in passing, ranged from rugby matches and crop yields to rainfall and hip replacements. While Gascons have for much of their history been a people apart—with their own dialect, their own customs, their own insular culinary predilections—it seemed they nonetheless shared one salient trait with rural French folk everywhere: They consider the *marché* to be the supreme social event of the week.

Most everyone at Plaisance's market was speaking in the bouncy patois of the Midi, as the South of France is collectively known, but to my ear their accent was lavished with even more extra syllables than that of the natives of the Languedoc and Provence, to the east. And unlike the denizens of Mediterranean France, the Gascons seemed to comport themselves with a decorousness that felt out of sync with the antic nature of their repartee. Hands, for the most part, were thrust into pockets, or wrapped around the handles of a market basket, or, occasionally, held up with a finger extended, when a point was being made.

As is the case across much of rural France, which has been bleeding its youth to the cities for several generations, a good number of the market-goers were old. Of the men, many wore hats. In a pleasing intersection of stereotype and reality, many of those hats were berets. Of the women, most favored short, sensible hairdos, and there appeared to be a partiality for a certain style of cheap designer eyewear, characterized by severely angled frames and ornate temples. The faces were decidedly Gallic, expressing feeling with the time-honored tics common to French people everywhere: pursed lips, outthrust jaws, raised eyebrows. But these weren't the polished, aquiline countenances that I'd regarded with mild envy while living in Paris or traveling in France's big cities. These were the rustically handsome, bold-featured faces of *paysans*—people who had grown up on farms—or of the sons and daughters of same.

Plaisance's market was a good one, its stands well stocked with all kinds of produce and fresh fish and tasty-looking charcuterie, as well as an impressive profusion of preserved ducky things like confit and foie gras. I started where I always tend to start at a good French market: at the meat and charcuterie stand. I got in line behind a woman who was peering over her bifocals at a calf's liver, held before her in the butcher's hands like a newborn baby. The two of them were spiritedly conversing about how best to cook it. The conversation went on for a very long time, during which the line grew behind me considerably. No one looked particularly put out as they waited for the lady to conclude her inquiries. Finally, I bought a length of dry-cured sausage and three confit duck legs to crisp up in the oven for dinner. Like the magrets I'd bought the day before, these legs were bigger than what I'd been accustomed to in the States—not because their erstwhile owners had been pumped with hormones but because, like most farmed ducks in Gascony, they'd been fattened on grain at the end of their free-roaming lives for the making of foie gras. These legs were still coated with some of the fat, now chilled to the consistency of soft butter, that they'd been preserved in. Thick, generous flaps of excess skin hung off them. I admit that a better man, if he wanted to dive headfirst into Gascon farmhouse cooking, would have bought fresh duck legs, salt-cured them overnight, and poached them for several hours with garlic and onions in duck fat. But I gave myself a pass. Diving headfirst wasn't my style. Plus, given my poor handling of Gascony's sacramental fat in our backyard, making my own confit seemed premature. Prepared duck legs would do for now. Baby steps, I told myself.

I needed cheese. I saw people queuing up at a cart in front of the church. It was tended by a sprite-like girl in a too-big army jacket and black-and-white keffiyeh. She had a Mao cap pulled tight and low over her head so that it hid her eyes. Her cart contained a few wheels of cheese from the Pyrenees in varying stages of ripeness, plus some cylinders of fresh chèvre. Ceramic goat, sheep, and cow figurines had been placed on the shelves of the display case, and a small chalkboard was affixed to the front, advertising the day's selection in a frilly script: VACHE, BRÉBIS, MIXTE, CHÈVRE FRAIS.

I waited my turn. Like the butcher, the cheese monger took an extravagantly long time with each customer. Even after painstakingly negotiating the desired size of the customer's wedge of cheese by laying her two-handled knife atop the wheel and inching it this way or that, even after meticulously wrapping said wedge in pink-and-white-checkered waxed paper and labeling the package with a ballpoint pen in the same frilly script, even after tallying the purchase on a notepad the size of a golf scorecard, and even after counting out the customer's change coin by coin, the young cheese monger was not finished. Only when the bubbly conversation that had begun many minutes earlier had reached the end of its full and natural life did she deign to utter the words I'd been panting to hear: *"Allez, au revoir, et bonne journée."* Then it began all over again with the next customer.

This, I realized as I shifted from one foot to the other and looked at my watch, was going to take some getting used to. The long wait, however, did prompt an interesting observation: The smaller-scale vendors were doing better business than the big ones. Not ten yards from the keffiyeh-sporting cheese monger's modest cart stood a fancy-looking truck equipped with wood-trimmed vitrines that contained a greatest hits of French cheese making: Époisses, Salers, Brie de Meaux, Camembert, Comté, Gruyère, Roquefort, Rocamadour, a Mont d'Or meant to be eaten with a spoon. The market-goers were largely passing it by. The same was true of the immense produce stand, stocked with everything from Israeli oranges to Mexican avocadoes to Spanish onions, which took up a whole corner of the square. By contrast, over by the church, no fewer than five impatient-looking ladies were massed near the folding table of a beleaguered young man with dirt-crusted fingers who was selling organic vegetables grown in the Gers: green cauliflower, eggplants, skinny radishes, beets with iridescent orange flesh.

Finally it was my turn. Feeling I'd more than earned the right to engage in some lively market banter of my own with the cheese monger, I felt dejected when my attempt failed to achieve liftoff.

After pointing to what I wanted—a nice-looking round of chèvre—I mentioned to her that I'd just moved to Plaisance with my family.

She didn't look up. "Oh, yeah, where from?"

"Chicago."

She wrapped and labeled my order without a word. I handed her some money. She handed me my change.

"Chicago," she said finally, chewing over this piece of information as she pulled a pack of cigarettes from her coat pocket and lit one. Then she made a pistol with her fingers. "Al Capone. *Bang bang.*"

I made another sortie, telling her that we were living in a house down by the river, opposite the bridge at the edge of town.

She narrowed her eyes, which, I could now see, were almond-shaped and quite beautiful, and blew smoke from the side of her mouth. "So you live in the old mill?"

"That's right."

"Must be damp down there, with all that water everywhere."

I told her it wasn't so bad.

"And the bugs? *Ouf.*"

I was unsure how to wrap up our chat. In an untempered burst of midwestern friendliness, I extended my hand and introduced myself, and then asked her name.

"Amandine," she said reluctantly.

"*Enchanté,*" I replied, and picked up my bags to leave.

I visited a couple of other vendors and started for home, feeling a bit at sea in the face of what should have been an obvious reality: Procuring one's food at the weekly village market doesn't make one a villager. We were outsiders here, for the time being at least. We were from *very* outside. I considered the possibility that most Gascons' knowledge of where we came from might begin and end with old gangster movies.

I strode home briskly along Plaisance's main drag, the Rue de l'Adour, which sliced arrow-straight through the village—east to the stone bridge and the hills beyond, west out of town and into the broad, flat valley of the Adour River, into which the Arros emptied.

I passed a shuttered beauty salon, a couple of vacant storefronts, and a clothing store with mannequins in Adidas tracksuits in the window and a sign on the façade that read VÊTEMENT. The *s* that should have been at the end had fallen off, leaving a faint outline on the concrete. I turned right and crossed an empty esplanade with a lonely looking war memorial on one end and a weedy *boules* court on the other. It had begun to rain. Like many a rural market town, Plaisance wasn't exactly postcard material.

I HEATED UP THE CONFIT duck legs for dinner. Before putting them in the oven, I snipped off the excess skin, cut it up, and roasted the pieces to make cracklings, something I'd been served as a snack during my first visit to Gascony. I called upstairs for Charlotte. She came down, and I put one of the crunchy *fritons* in her mouth like a communion wafer. She let it melt on her tongue and pondered for a moment.

"It's like bacon," she said, "but better."

I threw some of the cracklings onto a salad and put the rest in a snack bowl, then poured kirs for me and Michele and an Orangina for Charlotte. The sun had peeked out, so I toweled off the table and chairs on the balcony and the three of us went outside for our evening aperitif.

I brought out the fresh chèvre and spread some on slices of baguette. It was satiny, snow-white, and somehow both dense and airy at the same time. I handed a slice to Michele.

"Damn," she said with her mouth full, then managed to add, "That's some kick-ass goat cheese."

As for the duck confit, the skin of which had magically turned golden and crisp after a short spell in the oven, I'll just say this: If you let someone else do the curing and preserving, it's a spectacularly easy dish to get right.

3

The Country Life

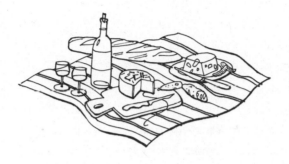

I have no doubt that sparkling trophy kitchens with granite-topped islands and multiple sinks exist somewhere in the Gers, but to date I've not seen one. In a land where meals are as sacred as life itself, the typical Gascon kitchen is surprisingly small and old-fashioned. Indeed, many farmhouses and even some *maisons bourgeoises* in the farther-flung reaches of southwestern France retain a deep genetic link to the era of open-hearth cooking, with older dwellings often featuring a fireplace and a wood fired bread oven in the kitchen, as well as cramped dimensions, the better to keep in warmth. I've even heard stories, from various Gascon friends, about old-timers in the Gers still living in houses with dirt-floor kitchens, though I've never seen this with my own eyes. Even in homes of newer construction, a certain thriftiness prevails. In *Peasants into Frenchmen*, his magnum opus about the modernizing of rural France, the historian Eugen Weber alluded to this state of affairs by invoking the old paysan aphorism: "It isn't the cage that feeds the bird."

No surprise, then, that one of the things I had to get used to when I started cooking in the old mill was having to do more with less. The sum of our kitchen's amenities—which, to my disappointment, did not include a wood-fired bread oven—was as follows: an electric range, a small microwave, a refrigerator no wider than a pizza box, a toaster, a few sauté pans, a well-used Dutch oven, a drawer crammed with utensils, several of which served purposes I couldn't discern, plus a trio of cheap prep knives, an extraordinary collection of corkscrews, a plastic salad spinner, an orange Moulinex food processor with a blade I couldn't remove, and just enough counter space to accommodate a splayed-open cookbook and the kitchen's small cutting board, which was in the shape of a pear.

Somewhat mystifyingly, our living-dining room was as vast and lavishly stocked as the kitchen was small and spartan. Against the far wall stood a formidable antique buffet filled with pewter serving platters, domed cake trays, cut-glass pitchers, a vintage raclette set, and a variety of decanters. The room was also furnished with two handsome wood sideboards that held porcelain plates and demitasses, Laguiole cutlery, a dozen brandy snifters, and enough champagne flutes for a small wedding. Occupying pride of place in the middle of the space—which had an immense stone hearth on one end and a set of French doors leading to the balcony on the other—was a heavy, varnished-wood dining table the size of a barn door. Finally, consigned to a kind of Siberia in the far corner of the room, near a TV that didn't seem to get any channels, sat a few frayed easy chairs and a coffee table on which a handful of outdated guidebooks had been stacked. The overall feel of the place suggested the tastes of someone with an abiding love of estate sales and only a passing acquaintance with the living habits of a modern family.

We'd met the mill's owner, Henri de Rességuier, a retired schoolteacher, on the night we arrived. He and his wife, Monique, had welcomed us with homemade pâté and tomato salad, and then Henri had shown us around our new home, demonstrating how to operate the windows' archaic rod-and-latch mechanisms and instructing us to close the shutters on the windward side of the house during inclement weather. Small in stature and compactly built, with a full head of wavy gray-and-black hair, Henri had a courtly air and walked with a fluid gait, his body slightly canted to the right. Throughout the tour, Monique, a pretty woman with thick black eyeliner and a warbly voice, delivered an interesting soliloquy about the history of the *le moulin*.

Henri came by the house frequently, making the ten-minute drive from his home in a neighboring village to address a variety of concerns. He always arrived in the same attire: crisp khakis and a natty button-down shirt. Always, he greeted me with a barely there handshake and a cordial *bonjour*, and responded to my description of the problem with the same reassuring phrase: *Je m'en occupe*—"I'll take care of it."

And he usually did, sort of. When I inquired about procuring better-seasoned wood for our outdoor grilling, he insisted that the muck-coated logs in the mill's musty storage room were perfectly fine, and to prove it, he dashed off to the butcher, returned with some fresh pork sausages, built a fire in the pit out back, and, showing a bit more panache than necessary, delivered us a hot lunch on a plate. A few days later, when we told him we had an ant infestation, he came over promptly, sprayed insecticide around the front door, and concluded the visit by saying, "They come every spring. The best strategy is simply not to look at them." When we told him we didn't have enough hot water, he made a few adjustments to the emulsion heater and, on his way out, said, "I wouldn't worry. You won't need it so much when summer comes."

To his credit, Henri attacked other problems with impressive determination and know-how. When the house's sewer pump failed, he rushed over, slipped a pair of knee-high rubber boots over his khakis, and, for the better part of an hour, wrestled with pipes and valves while standing in a foot of foul-smelling water inside a cement-walled hole at the base of the house. After reassembling the pump motor and getting things up and running, he rinsed his boots under an outdoor spigot and, as a parting salutation, offered his forearm for me to shake, in the classic manner of French butchers and plumbers.

One day, after he'd spent the morning weed-wacking the thick overgrowth that had colonized the banks of the stream, Henri, his face flecked with bits of vegetation, appeared at our front door with a stack of books in his hands. "Given your curiosity about *la Gascogne*," he said, "I thought these might be of interest."

When I thanked him, he offered the standard French nonplussed eyebrow-raise and took his leave.

I carried the books out to the balcony. One was about the historic water mills of the Gers. Who knew there were so many? Henri had bookmarked a page that contained a small black-and-white photo of Le Moulin de Saint Pierre Lesperet—as our mill was mellifluously named—in its turn-of-the-century heyday: The enormous mill wheel could be seen beneath the roof of the shed; some men with bushy mustaches were standing next to it. Another book was titled *Les Gens de Gascogne à Travers la Carte Postale* and contained reproductions of hundreds of postcards from a century ago showing Gascon *paysans* in traditional garb doing things like hunting pigeons, harvesting grapes, and washing their clothes in communal *lavoirs*.

Henri had also included a book prosaically titled *Le Département du Gers*, written in 1997 by one Renaud Camus. It had the austere matte cover favored by literary presses in France. An arts-and-letters-minded guide to the Gers, it was filled with wordy commentary about the region's churches, châteaux, and ruins. I skimmed the introduction and paused at this observation: "To live in the Gers, to decide to live in the Gers, is to cast one's lot with, to deliberately choose, a great deal of absence." The author went on to state—a bit self-defeatingly, given he was presumably trying to entice readers to the area—that the Gers suffers from a chronic lack of cinemas, theaters, museums, and good pastry shops. He concluded on a slightly sunnier note. In the Gers, he wrote, "you can simply *be*."

There was a small recipe book, too. Its pages were brittle and had turned the color of toast. The cover bore the title *La Cuisine du Pays: 500 Recettes de Cuisine, Pâtisserie, Confiserie—Recueillies par Simin Palay*. The volume was a collection of old Gascon and Basque dishes compiled three-quarters of a century ago by—to judge from what little I was able to find on the author—a poet-linguist from the Béarn, the ancient province on the mountainous frontier of greater Gascony. Each chapter contained a few folksy proverbs in the old Béarnais dialect. I found one I particularly liked: "*Dab boune sauce, machant tros que passe*"—"A good sauce helps the tough morsel go down." I perused the recipes, which were peppered with phrases like "Ask your tripe seller for his cleanest veal tripe, as well as the cheeks and rumen." Or "Nail the lamprey's head to the wall, cut off the tail, and let the blood drain into a bowl." One specialty was a fried pastry called *pets-de-nonne*, or "Nun's Farts." The recipes—written in an archaic style, with less than exact measurements—weren't really inspiring me to wet my toes in Gascon cuisine.

The truth was, little of what I'd been cooking since our arrival belonged strictly to the local culinary canon. I cut myself a break, considering we'd just made a 4,000-mile move and I was now having to do all my chopping and mincing with a plastic-handled, dollar-store–quality knife. Mostly I'd been making simple meals cobbled together from produce, meat, and fish from the weekly market. Yet this in itself was an education: The ingredients were fresher, tastier, and all-around better than what I was able to get regularly back home. Lamb chops were sold unfrenched and cut thin, with an extra rib bone attached, and were edged with the most delicious fat. Another of our favorites, Basque brook trout, was very fatty, too; its skin became cracker-crisp in the skillet while the pink flesh stayed perfectly tender. The chickens and guinea fowl, sold with their heads on, were long-legged and rangy, with less meat but more flavor. The fresh sausages, which I took to serving atop Puy lentils, were coarsely ground and super-savory. The strawberries, of a local hybrid variety called *gariguette*, were no bigger around than a penny, but exploded with candy-like sweetness and dissolved on the tongue. Then there were the magnificent pâtés and *salaisons*— Basque chorizo, skinny *saucissons*, smooth duck-liver terrines, and the silky dry-cured ham known as *jambon de Bayonne*.

Arguably the most Gascon aspect of our meals was how long they were. Suddenly we were spending more time at the table than we ever did in Chicago. It just felt like the natural thing to do. For one thing, we were a lot less busy. Michele didn't have an office to go to; I didn't have pressing deadlines; and while Charlotte hadn't started classes yet, I knew that once she did, there wasn't going to be a packed dance card of after-school activities. There didn't seem to be any on offer. Distractions after dark were few: maybe a coffee at Le Plaisantin, the seedy café near our house, or a post-dinner walk on empty village streets prowled by house cats. Such walks confirmed my assumption that the world occupied by the residents of Plaisance, and by Gascons in general, shrunk to the confines of the kitchen and the dinner table after seven thirty or so. That said, to judge from the flickering blue light I'd seen emanating from dining room windows here and there during my evening strolls, watching TV after dinner, or even during the meal, wasn't frowned upon. But for us, at least, it wasn't an appealing option. One night, upon discovering that in clear weather our television actually got a couple of channels, we tried to watch for a while, but after toggling for ten minutes between a dubbed episode of *Stargate* and a talk show featuring French book critics in rimless glasses, we switched it off.

Also, Michele and I were drinking more wine than we used to, which tended to make our meals altogether more relaxed affairs. We could get through most of a bottle of low-octane white or rosé at lunch, and kill a brawny Madiran at dinner. For a time, my doctor's admonition—"No more than two glasses a day"—rang in my ears, but eventually the ringing stopped. Also, we discovered that our local wine co-op packaged a respectable table wine made from tannat grapes grown in the hills north of Plaisance. A five-liter, sous-vide container fitted with a plastic spigot, it cost about as much as bottled mineral water. I pulled out one of the etched-glass decanters from the buffet, and in the evenings I got in the habit of filling it from the wine tap. Using the decanter gave our suppers a fancy, upstairs-downstairs feel.

In short order, meals became the organizing principle of our daily life. This was partly out of necessity. Like other newcomers to rural France, we were quickly discovering that the preparation of lunch and dinner required a good deal of forethought. If we didn't get our shopping done in the morning, we were out of luck come lunchtime, as all commercial life ceased promptly at 12:30 p.m. and didn't resume until two or three hours later. Nowhere outside of Gascony had I seen the sanctity of the lunch hour observed with such zeal. As early as 11:30 a.m., there was a change in the cadence of villagers' comings and goings. Cars breezed past stop signs, their drivers speeding home for the midday meal, and in the main square, one could observe a frenzied ballet as people zigzagged about, conducting any final items of business at the bank or the pharmacy or the hardware store before all human endeavor turned to the sacred ritual of lunch. By 12:15, the streets in Plaisance were empty, except for the pitiable straggler making a desperate dash for the bakery, which by then was mostly cleaned out anyhow. If you walked around Plaisance on a warm day between 12:30 and 2:30 p.m., the only sounds to be heard through the open windows were the clinking of silverware or the crackle of some fatty thing frying in a skillet.

THE DAY BEFORE CHARLOTTE STARTED classes at Plaisance's *école primaire*, we decided to take a drive and have a picnic—the gentle hills of the Gers being very conducive to both activities. The morning had dawned bright and warm, with a scrim of haze hanging in the sky that gave the landscape the white-tinged brilliance of an overexposed photo. I piloted our rented Peugeot hatchback along a tortuous *route communale* that climbed from the Adour River Valley into the hills. The road entered a patch of woods and emerged into the open to reveal a vista of grazing pastures bordered by hedgerows and populated by cream-colored cows. Farther on, vineyards alternated with fields of sunflowers that hadn't yet bloomed. We passed signs for places with funny-sounding names, like *Monplaisir* (My Pleasure) and *l'Église de Croûte* (the Church of Crust). Charlotte was in back with the window down, her hair whipping around her head. It didn't seem possible on such a lovely day, but we were the only car on the road.

After a while, we crested a ridge and passed a hamlet called *Bières* (Beers), at which point the road doglegged around a wood-steepled chapel and a cemetery. I pulled over. Beside the church, in a clearing partly shaded by an immense oak tree, sat a picnic table. The grass around it had been freshly mowed, and some thoughtful person had planted geraniums in hollow tree stumps arranged along the clearing's edge. Across the road, the quilted landscape sprawled to the horizon.

I spread out our *déjeuner champêtre*: thin slices of Bayonne ham, a loaf of bread, *brandade de morue* with crackers, *pâté de tête*, fresh cherries, and a cucumber salad dressed with olive oil and fresh mint. I'd also bought more of Amandine's chèvre at this week's market. She'd remembered me from my first visit and offered the suggestion of a smile when I complimented her cheese. Progress.

To drink, I'd packed a label-less bottle of rosé, filled from our "tap" and chilled that morning. It wore a fine pelt of condensation and sparkled in the sun. The whole scene was so pretty that I almost didn't want to mess it up by eating.

After lunch, I walked around the tiny graveyard next to the chapel. A squat date palm stood just inside the rusted gate, giving the place an exotic feel. Some two dozen gravestones in varying states of decay were crowded inside the cemetery's stone walls. Many were adorned with fresh flowers. Some were decorated with polished-stone tablets engraved with a poem or words of endearment: "To our nana," "To our friend," "To our comrade in arms." Many bore testament to long lives that began in the nineteenth century and ended well into the twentieth.

Down the road, we paid a visit to Lupiac, a hilltop village with a vast, sun-hammered central square surrounded by narrow, tile-roofed houses with closed shutters. The place appeared to be evacuated of all human life. According to a sign we'd seen as we drove into it, the village was the birthplace of none other than Charles de Batz-Castlemore, better known as D'Artagnan, Gascony's most famous son. This caused me some excitement, as I'd just been reading *The Three Musketeers*, Alexandre Dumas's nineteenth-century fictionalization of D'Artagnan's seventeenth-century exploits.

Over by the church, I noticed a plaque directing visitors to Le Musée D'Artagnan. While Michele sought a shady spot where she and Charlotte could have a rest, I walked over to the tiny museum, which occupied a former chapel next to the church, and paid my admission fee to a friendly woman who informed me I was her first visitor of the day. The museum featured, among other things, mannequins in the tricolor livery of a seventeenth-century musketeer, a life-size statue of D'Artagnan carved from linden wood, pages of the first serialized excerpts of *The Three Musketeers*, and vintage movie posters bearing the likenesses of some of the many actors who'd played D'Artagnan over the years.

Though the museum skewed toward the myth of D'Artagnan, there were some texts and engravings concerning the real-life musketeer, too. He'd been born into the family of a recently ennobled merchant by the name of Bertrand de Batz, who was the owner of a château called Castlemore and had married a woman from a noteworthy family that went by the considerably more musical name of De Montesquiou d'Artagnan. When he came of age, Charles adopted his matronymic. Like a lot of young Gascon men, D'Artagnan left home to join the military, in this case the king's guards. The rest of his life, as far as I could tell, played out as a series of brawls, skirmishes, and intrigues, first in the service of Louis XIII and then under that monarch's more famous successor, Louis XIV, and the king's scheming adviser, Cardinal Mazarin. Aside from passing through the region as part of the wedding procession of Louis XIV in 1660, D'Artagnan never came back to Gascony. Not that this last fact had prevented locals from claiming D'Artagnan as the very paragon of Gascon-ness itself, at least if one was to judge from how freely they traded on his name.

I SERVED CHARLOTTE A SPECIAL breakfast for her first day of school: a chocolate croissant from the bakery, a bowl of fresh raspberries, and a soft-boiled egg, which I presented to her in one of the porcelain egg cups from our dining room's vast collection of tableware. Our eggs were from the weekly market; they'd cost pennies apiece, and their yolks were a deep sunset-orange.

Charlotte was too nervous to eat. I was, too. The assurances of Plaisance's school principal notwithstanding, I knew that Charlotte wasn't the type to handle change easily. She loved her routines, and resisted embracing new things until she was convinced she'd mastered them. Today, we were tossing her routine out the window, and drowning it in the river while we were at it.

Before we left, I handed Charlotte a gift that Henri's wife, Monique, had dropped off the day before. It was wrapped in a large brown envelope bearing a handwritten note: "*Bon courage* on your first day of school! And remember, cooking is a great way to learn a language!" Charlotte opened the package and pulled out a red-and-white apron with a recipe for crêpes embroidered on the front.

The school was just a short walk from our house. Charlotte, her plaid backpack from Target slung over her shoulders, was holding back tears as we approached the front gate. All around us, parents were chatting and kissing their kids good-bye. The principal came out and introduced us to Charlotte's teacher, a slim, unsmiling woman with her hair in a Parisian updo: Maîtresse Nathalie. I asked the Maîtresse if she spoke any English; looking slightly embarrassed, she confessed that she could recall only two phrases: "water closet" and "I don't understand." At that moment, Charlotte started to cry, upon which Maîtresse Nathalie gently pried Charlotte's hand from mine, drew the girl toward her, and looked at me and Michele with an expression that was both tender and tough.

"*Ça va aller*," she said. "It'll be fine."

Then she led Charlotte across the school's gravel courtyard to the blue wooden door of her classroom.

Michele hooked her arm through mine and we walked home. "She'll thank you for this when she's older," she said.

Later, at lunch, I drank more wine than usual.

That night, I decided to make ham-and-cheese crêpes for dinner using the recipe from the apron Monique had given us. Charlotte had made it through her first day without any disasters; there'd been some tears because she didn't know how to ask for the bathroom, but after that things had gone fine.

I measured out the milk and flour and grated some Emmentaler. For want of a mixing bowl I used the receptacle from the salad spinner, and, unable to locate a whisk, I beat the ingredients with a dinner fork. On assessing our kitchen's ascetic inventory, I'd considered buying some new knives and tools, but instead I decided to do my best with what we had, partly because I didn't want to spend the money and partly out of a determination to be more *débrouillard*. To be débrouillard is to be resourceful, in a MacGyver kind of way.

I showered the crêpes with black pepper, Parisian-street-vendor style, and tossed a salad. Then I poured some wine and we sat down to dinner.

Charlotte, I observed with some relief, finished every bite.

4
Old School

oday the Gers, which constitutes Gascony's geographic, cultural, and spiritual core, is not exactly an A-list destination for
epicures of the Michelin-star-chasing ilk. The département has only
two starred restaurants: Le Puits St. Jacques, in the village of Pu-
jaudran, and La Table des Cordeliers, in a town that goes by the
misbegotten name of Condom. By comparison the Gironde, just to
the northwest, has sixteen *restaurants étoilés*. The Bouches du Rhône,
in Provence, has twenty-four. A little to the east of that département
is the Alpes-Maritimes, with forty. Take from those numbers what
you will, but it's safe to say that in the Gers, the home cook reigns
supreme.

This is not to say that the Gers doesn't have its own peculiar
haute-cuisine pedigree. In the 1970s and '80s, a league of amply
starred chefs who called themselves La Ronde des Mousquetaires

presided over a brief golden age of Gascon gastronomy, traveling around France and overseas to promote the food and wines of the Gers and its neighboring départements, rallying—no surprise here—under the musketeers' famous "One for all, all for one" credo. Roger Dufour of Le Relais de l'Armagnac, Joseph Sanpietro of La Bonne Auberge, Bernard Ramounéda of Le Florida: These were the *grands gourmands* of Gascony's postwar generation, cooks who had apprenticed at the knee of a mother or grandmother, and whose names had once enjoyed currency well beyond the Southwest of France. These were the same chefs who, in their prime, had offered recipes and wisdom to Paula Wolfert as she made her five-year odyssey across the region while compiling *The Cooking of South-West France*.

The most famous and laureled member of La Ronde des Mousquetaires was André Daguin, the chef at the Hôtel de France in Auch, Gascony's historic capital. He was considered the godfather of French duck cookery, the man credited with, among other things, the rather game-changing feat of being the first professional chef in France to cook duck breast rare, like a steak. (Most cooks had long believed that ducks weren't clean enough to eat unless roasted or confited to total grayness.) I'd interviewed Daguin back in 2012; he had a Legion of Honor medal on his wall, a practiced spiel for journalists, and a piercing gaze. Daguin's daughter, Ariane, was famous, too; she'd moved to the States in the 1980s and became a successful purveyor of foie gras and specialty meats. She named her company—no surprise again—D'Artagnan.

What I hadn't known until after we arrived in Gascony is that Plaisance du Gers boasted its own Ronde des Mousquetaires chef. Maurice Coscuella, a contemporary of Daguin's, had for a number of years run a Michelin-starred restaurant under the arcades of Plaisance's new bastide. Called Le Ripa Alta, it had closed years ago, though the old sign for the place was still there, above a real estate office.

I learned all this from Henri, who stopped by the moulin to drop off a flier he'd saved for me. It was a laser-printed announcement for weekly cooking classes being taught by Coscuella. The chef was getting on in years, Henri explained, and had a bad stammer, but his classes were popular among *le troisième âge*, as retirees are affectionately referred to in French.

"Coscuella was quite famous in his day," said Henri, in an elegiac tone. "Everyone knew Le Ripa Alta. Locals used to go to the square on Saturday nights just to watch the fancy cars with Paris plates pull up."

I did some research on the chef, but turned up little. All I was able to learn was that, beyond cooking at Le Ripa Alta, Coscuella had worked for a while on a transatlantic luxury liner. I found an archived article in *La Dépêche du Midi*—a hagiographic profile of a type common to French regional newspapers—that claimed Coscuella had been invited to stay in New York City to start a restaurant, but had heeded the "siren call" of his native Plaisance. That seemed hard to fathom, but whatever the case, Plaisance is where Coscuella ended up.

Classes were held on Saturday mornings in a cramped communal kitchen, only slightly bigger than the one in our house, that was rented out by Épisode, the local seniors' association. I showed up for the first class at nine thirty. A dozen men and women, all older than me by at least a couple of decades, were already seated at a plastic-covered table crowded with ingredients, bowls, knives, and cookware. Everyone seemed to be talking at once. At the stove stood a rotund, gnomish man in thick glasses and a chef's tunic. He was placing bricks of butter into a saucepan.

I paid my fee to a woman seated behind a desk near the door. She placed the money in a cash box and marked something in a ledger. Then she looked me up and down. "You didn't bring an apron?"

I told her I hadn't.

She turned toward the table. "Alphonse!" she called out, "can you find an extra apron for Monsieur?"

A wiry man who had to be Alphonse handed me a maroon apron with the silhouette of a bull appliquéd onto it. He shook my hand and asked where I was from. I told him, and his face lit up. He led me over to Coscuella.

"Momo!" Alphonse shouted, leaning in so close to the chef that I thought he was going to kiss him. "We have an American with us today!"

Coscuella turned slowly in my direction and extended a plump hand. I gripped it but received no squeeze in return. The chef mumbled something I couldn't quite make out.

Alphonse paraphrased. "Momo says he visited New York nearly a hundred times when he worked aboard the liner."

I asked the chef what we were making today.

"*Gras double*," he said, pointing to a cutting board next to the stove. On it was what looked like a length of terry cloth.

"It's tripe," said Alphonse, patting his own midriff. "Cow's stomach!"

Alphonse handed me a printout of the day's dishes, which could have been culled from a French restaurant menu circa 1965. In addition to tripe, there would be white asparagus with a *sauce Maltaise*, a salmon terrine, and a strawberry mousse.

Alphonse introduced me to his wife, Lorette, and then to a tall man named Bernd, who had a long scar running down the side of his neck and spoke in the hoarse, sawing-wood voice of a dedicated smoker. I shook hands around the table and found a seat between a man named Thierry and a terse woman called Lydia. I was given the task of peeling asparagus.

Coscuella had remanded the care of the saucepan to a nervous-looking gentleman named Philippe, who began stirring the butter vigorously.

"*Trop vite, trop vite!*" Coscuella snapped. He shooed Philippe aside and took over.

"Sauces are not my forté," Philippe said sheepishly.

Thierry called out to Coscuella, "Demote him to dishwasher!"

Lorette swatted Thierry with a dish towel.

At ten thirty we took a break. Alphonse opened a couple of bottles of rosé and poured the wine into plastic cups. Bits of gossip were traded.

"I hear the wife of the grocer is sick," said Lydia.

"Crohn's disease," said Lorette.

"*Horrible*," said Alphonse.

Conversation turned to the recent D-Day commemorations, which had been covered extensively in the morning papers. President François Hollande had been criticized for sucking his teeth like a bored schoolboy while Queen Elizabeth stood at a dais speaking of sacrifice and heroism. Around the table there was a spirited round of Hollande-bashing, followed by reminiscing about *Les Trente Glorieuses*—the thirty years of prosperity in France that followed the war—and then about France under Mitterand, whom Lydia referred to as "*un vrai socialiste.*" It seemed that on the whole Gascons, unlike so many of their counterparts in other parts of the Midi, are leftists of the old school.

Coscuella, who had been slicing the tripe, spoke up. "I cooked for Mitterand. He knew how to eat, that one."

I asked Coscuella if it was true that Mitterand ate ortolan—the banned delicacy of southwestern France consisting of tiny songbirds drowned in Armagnac and fried whole—as his last meal before dying of cancer.

The chef waved off the question. "That was a long time ago."

Coscuella's evasiveness caused me to wonder for a moment whether *he* had been the anonymous chef who'd prepared that famed meal. But I decided to let it drop. Instead, I mentioned that I'd been reading about La Ronde des Mousquetaires, Le Ripa Alta, and André Daguin.

At the mention of Daguin's name, Alphonse looked as if he'd smelled a fart. He took a seat opposite me and leaned in conspiratorially. "Daguin stole recipes from Coscuella. Momo was doing grilled duck breast before Daguin. *C'est vrai!*"

Alphonse glanced behind him at the chef, who was now poking desultorily at the strawberries that Lorette and Lydia had trimmed, and then leaned in even closer. "But Momo was never a good self-promoter like Daguin," said Alphonse, his face a mask of concern. "He didn't know how to market himself. His stammer made it hard."

I wanted to press Alphonse for more details, but Coscuella was summoning him to the counter to help out with the salmon terrine. As the two of them worked together, Alphonse talked to the chef with a mix of deference and affection.

The terrine went into the oven in a *bain-marie*, and Coscuella instructed Bernd to fold big dollops of *fromage blanc* into the strawberries, which Lydia had just puréed, to make the mousse.

Then Alphonse and Coscuella began frying pieces of *gras double*. The kitchen filled with the thick, sweetish scent of cooking offal—a comforting aroma if you grew up with it and, as a rule, an off-putting one if you didn't. Bernd stepped out for a smoke. I could see him standing just outside the kitchen's open window, sucking at a cigarillo and looking like a delinquent schoolboy.

"Frying isn't the proper way to do it," Coscuella said to me over his shoulder, "but it's fast. Proper gras double is cooked for six hours." I tried to imagine how the kitchen would smell after *that*.

When the tripe was done and set on paper towels to cool, Coscuella brought the bowl of strawberry mousse to the table. Fingers swiped the sides of it and were sucked lustily.

Alphonse poured more wine, and Coscuella handed me a piece of the tripe. It was salty, fatty, and quite good.

The next couple of classes were much like the first, fueled by gossip and cheap wine and featuring menus—some more Gascon than others—that harked back to a bygone era: sweetbreads in Madeira, *caviar d'aubergine*, melon balls marinated in sweetened eau-de-vie and served in hollowed-out melon halves, the edges of which Coscuella had instructed us to cut in a crenellated pattern. The chef was a harsh taskmaster, but, with the exception of the perpetually browbeaten Philippe, his students treated him with affection, referring to him as Maurice or Momo and ignoring his fits of pique. Lydia would sometimes say, "Oh, Maurice, you're a *piment*"—"a hot pepper." Coscuella was no Daguin, but he was Plaisance's culinary mascot, a treasure to be looked after and cherished.

Not long after the classes ended, I ran into the chef at the bakery. He insisted I accompany him to his house, around the corner. He had some books he wanted to lend me. I waited as Coscuella padded about his cluttered library, pulling various volumes off the shelves. He handed me a stack and said I could keep them until I returned to the States. I decided to peruse the books on a bench facing the arcades of the new bastide. Like Henri's library loan, Coscuella's contained an odd mix. There was a coffee-table book from the '80s showcasing the architectural creations of the Gascony-born chef Jean-Louis Palladin, whom Coscuella had referred to as a "dear friend." There was an equally hefty tome grandiosely titled *La Grande Messe de l'Armagnac* by Abel Sempé, a master distiller who, Coscuella had told me, went on to become a senator representing the Gers. To my surprise, at the bottom of the stack was a first edition, in somewhat better condition than the one I had, of *The Cooking of South-West France*. A yellowed courtesy card from Wolfert's first editor at The Dial Press was still paper-clipped to the dust jacket: "For M. Coscuella, with compliments."

THOUGH I WAS MORE INTERESTED in Gascon home cooking than in restaurant food, eventually curiosity got the better of me, and I persuaded Michele to join me for lunch at La Pergola, an unprepossessing plat-du-jour joint at the edge of town. I'd been eyeing the place for some time, noting that it did a brisk business at lunchtime.

At 12:15, the restaurant was already packed. Michele and I stepped into a garish, mirror-walled bar area crowded with men in worker's coveralls drinking a pre-meal beer or pastis, making the most of their state-mandated lunch break. Just beyond the bar, I could see an enormous dining room with a drop-ceiling. Some patrons were choosing cold hors d'oeuvres from a refrigerated case. More men with weather-chapped faces were squeezed shoulder to shoulder at four-tops set with paper placemats. Still others sat around a huge communal table in the middle of the room, sawing into steaks and duck legs. Unlabeled liter bottles of red wine sat on every table.

I liked the place right away. Michele looked less enamored. I should note here that on matters of eating out, she and I differed. Having grown up in Los Angeles, weaned on fish tacos, sushi, bibimbap, Chinese chicken salad, and the occasional In-N-Out Burger, she favored quick and casual meals over two-hour repasts anchored by cured and braised meats. When she did go out to proper sit-down restaurants, she preferred ones where the server would happily oblige her request to taste a few of the wines before she decided on one, and where she could choose lots of small, fresh-tasting things to eat, preferably in a room generously endowed with blond wood and natural light. Such establishments, alas, were few and far between in provincial France, and virtually nonexistent in Gascony.

After we'd waited for a minute or so at the threshold of La Pergola's dining room, a harried-looking man caught our eye and looked at us with an urgent and inquisitive expression. I held up two fingers. He motioned for us to follow him. He led us to the big shared table and brusquely pulled out two chairs.

When I asked if he had a table for two, he tapped his watch. "*Ah non*. You have to get here early for that."

And so we sat. Each of the men at our table lifted his face long enough to give a perfunctory *b'jour* before returning to the midday feeding. Moments later the proprietor returned, pen poised over pad. "*Alors*," he said, eyes darting between Michele and me, "*onze ou treize?*" After a brief exchange, I understood what he meant: Did we want the 11-euro menu or the 13-euro menu? There were no other options. The pricier menu got you soup, appetizer, and your choice of three different plats du jour, plus dessert. The cheaper one got you soup and a plat du jour, but you had to choose between appetizer and dessert. We splurged on the *treize*.

I asked about wine. The proprietor leaned between me and Michele, reached for one of the open bottles that were distributed across the table, and plunked it down in front of us.

"*À volonté*," he said. "As much as you want."

The soup was a garbure—the standard opening act for every cheap prix-fixe menu from the Pyrenees to the Garonne River—and a hearty one at that. It came family-style in a large metal tureen, and consisted of potatoes, turnips, cabbage, carrots, and ruby-colored chunks of duck confit swimming in a murky broth that had been fortified with a ham hock or two, and quite probably some other non-premium parts of the pig. A few confit duck wings were poking out of the tureen.

Michele remarked that the soup on its own would have been enough for her. I told her to loosen her belt—Gascons don't do doggy bags.

When we'd finished, a server cleared away our bowls and gestured toward the cold case. We got up and scanned the selection of prepared salads and charcuterie. Michele went for shredded carrots in a vinaigrette with hard-boiled eggs, and I chose a slab of pâté garnished with cornichons. The appetizers seemed superfluous after the garbure, knowing we had a main dish with sides on the way, to say nothing of dessert, but this was a French worker's lunch of the old order.

The *plats principaux* arrived. I got a half chicken braised in a tomatoey ragoût, with green beans. Michele had ordered a skirt steak in a mushroom sauce; it came with sautéed potatoes possessed of a roasty aroma and lacy crispness that strongly suggested a romp in the pan with some duck fat. We returned to the cold case for dessert: a rice pudding for me, chocolate mousse for Michele. Then coffee.

A lot of restaurants bank on some version of the claim "home-style cooking." Not many deliver on the promise. But this lunch really did remind me of a homemade meal. The food was simple. It wasn't garnished with frilly herb sprigs or squiggles of sauce. Some of it had been prepared ahead of time and tasted faintly of refrigeration. The chicken was slightly overcooked and the steak was a little tough; I couldn't think of two more common home-kitchen pitfalls. But the soup, the sides, and the sauces were good—excellent, even. Someone back there was cooking with love, or at least with savoir faire. *Dab boune sauce, machant tros que passe*—"a good sauce helps the tough morsel go down."

5
Magret

Virtually every farmed duck in Gascony is a moulard, also variously known as a mullard, a mulard, or a mule duck. This sterile hybrid breed is not to be confused with the mallard, which is a wild waterfowl, the one with the iridescent green head. By contrast the moulard, a cross between a Pekin duck and a Muscovy duck, is usually white-feathered. Also, it has a knack for putting on weight quickly, making it ideal for gavage. These *canards gras* (fat ducks) have more of everything: more fat, more flesh, and—at least when compared with other kinds of domesticated ducks I've tasted—more flavor.

The magret, or breast, of a Gascon moulard, as I had already discovered firsthand, is an imposing specimen. (The word *magret*, somewhat deceivingly, comes from *maigre*, for lean or thin.) In addition to being topped with a prodigiously thick layer of fatty skin, the moulard breast is roughly twice as big as that of a standard American Pekin, and thicker than a porterhouse. Its flesh is firm and deep red.

Unlike the tough legs, which must be slow-roasted, braised, or confited, the tender magret of a moulard takes beautifully to fast, high-heat cooking, as André Daguin so boldly demonstrated to his countrymen and to the world. What makes searing or grilling a moulard breast trickier than searing or grilling, say, a steak or a chop is—as might be guessed—the fat. Not only does it have a tendency to catch fire when the magret is laid over hot coals, but, when the breast is cooked in a skillet, the fat must be given time to gently render out. If a cook sears the skin side too quickly, not enough of that subcutaneous fat will liquefy and the skin will come out tough and chewy. Conversely, if the cook sears the magret too long, the skin will blacken and burn. When faced with this delicate proposition, and occasionally owing to matters of taste, some people strip away and discard the skin altogether before cooking. This, I put to you, is heresy. When a magret is cooked right, that crisp, thin, savory apron of skin is the dish's raison d'être.

I took all these things into consideration as I prepared to welcome our very first dinner guest with a main course of pan-seared duck breasts in a port wine reduction. Our honored invitee? Nadine Cauzette, the widow from Viella whose home-cooking had fanned the flames of my Gascony-love a year and a half before. It had taken some cajoling to convince her to let me cook for her instead of the other way around, but I'd finally won her over. Michele, on learning that Nadine was coming for dinner, pointed out that a native-born Gascon with duck fat for blood who made her own confit and rillettes was perhaps not the ideal candidate on whom to test out a Gascon duck recipe. But the die was cast.

The magret preparation I'd chosen was from Wolfert's book, which, given the dearth of clearly written, user-friendly Gascon cookbooks out there, I'd come to regard as something of a sacred text. I'd decided on the magret in port wine after much deliberation, having ultimately dispensed with the notion of making anything that required standing vigil over a three-day braise or pickling a calf's tongue or deboning a pig's foot. I'd flirted with the idea of doing a garbure, but Wolfert's recipe for that elementary Gascon dish ran to three pages, was portioned for eight people, and called for more than twenty ingredients. The recipe for duck breasts called for seven. Salt and pepper were two of them. That was more my speed. I'd tackle a garbure soon enough, but magret would do nicely for now.

After mulling over the menu for a few days, I decided that to accompany the duck, I'd go for something just as straightforwardly Gascon: a *salade Gersoise*. This was the dish, also sometimes known more generically as a *salade Gasconne*, I'd been served on my first trip to Gascony years earlier: the one with the lettuce leaves topped with preserved duck products. It probably won't come as a surprise that Gascons and North Americans have somewhat different expectations when they hear the word *salad*. It's not that a Gascon wouldn't recognize a plate of lettuce, sliced cucumbers, and tomato wedges as a salad—that genre of light side dish isn't unknown in Gascony. It's just that he'd probably be disappointed by it. For a Gascon, the word *salade* holds a certain promise. Within the wide salad rubric is the potential for many savory and often meaty things mingled together atop a layer of greenery. I had a cheap and delicious restaurant meal on my second Gascony trip that included a dish the menu referred to as a "*salade saison*." The requisite bed of lettuce was almost completely obscured by tender hunks of brisket and boiled potatoes that had been bathed in broth. When I asked the proprietor what was seasonal about the salad, she told me the beef and potatoes were left over from the previous night's special: pot-au-feu. Pot-au-feu is a winter dish. It was winter. *Voilà*.

The morning of the dinner with Nadine, I returned to the duck farm where I'd bought those first, ill-fated magrets. Ferme Tomasella sat at the end of an unpaved, tree-canopied road outside a neighboring village called Aignan. It was a typical Gascon farmstead: a cluster of prim, tile-roofed buildings gathered around a gravel courtyard. Some moulards were waddling about a grassy enclosure behind the main house. Next to the house was a tiny shop selling canned duck confit, jars of foie gras, and, in a cold case by the door, freshly butchered duck parts. As I'd done the first time, I rang a bell, and just as before, the woman in the blood-smeared smock emerged from behind the farmhouse to ring up my order. When I realized my wallet was empty—I'd forgotten to stop by the bank—she just made a note on a chit, handed it to me, and said I could pay on my next visit.

WE'D SAID SEVEN O'CLOCK; NADINE arrived at a quarter to eight, not an excessive degree of tardiness for an evening engagement in Gascony. Nadine was unchanged since the last time I'd seen her: petite and broad-beamed, with a dimpled smile and sparkling eyes. She had the typical short, Gascon-lady hairdo, but her glasses were more old-fashioned than mod, with a cat-eye shape.

In keeping with what I would soon discover to be standard Gascon practice, Nadine had brought gifts. Lots of them. So many, in fact, that I had to help retrieve them from her car and then enlist Michele to create a sort of bucket brigade in the foyer, with Nadine handing a gift to me and me handing it to Michele to set down somewhere: a very tall potted orchid, a bottle of *vin de liqueur*, custom-made T-shirts emblazoned with the number 32, which is the postal code prefix for the Gers. For Charlotte she'd brought a French activity book, a bracelet-making kit, and a towering Styrofoam-core gumdrop tree wrapped in cellophane and tied at the top with a pink ribbon.

"You really shouldn't have," I said.

Nadine flashed me the same bewildered look she'd given me the first time I'd told her that.

We went out on the balcony. I opened the vin de liqueur. As we sipped our *apéro*, Nadine talked at length about an old widow in Viella whom she'd been taking care of.

"She lived all alone, *la pauvre*," said Nadine. "Her children were just waiting for her to die so they could sell the house. It's been quite an ordeal."

"That's awful," Michele said.

"*Bof*," said Nadine with a flip of her hand. "Things are back to normal now." She cleared her throat. "Well, not for her, *certainement*. She's dead."

I excused myself to start cooking the duck breasts, leaving Michele to manage as best she could with Nadine, who didn't speak a word of English. Charlotte was busy inside making rubber bracelets.

The salads were already made, and they were a handsome sight: On each plate, I'd fanned out six fat-rimmed slices of cured duck breast on a bed of lettuce garnished with a quartered hard-boiled farm egg and tomato wedges. Then I'd scattered nubbins of foie gras on top and added pieces of duck gizzard, which I'd cut up and sautéed until they were crisp on the outside and chewy in the middle. Duck gizzards, by the way, are a wonderful food, justly prized by the Gascons. The lobed gastric muscle is typically confited, often in the same kettle or crock as the other duck parts; confit duck gizzards are dense and smooth-textured, with a deep iron-oxide color and an even deeper, meaty flavor. One might characterize them as a sort of entry-level organ meat for novitiates.

I'd also prepped the magrets ahead of time, scoring the skin—

crucial for hastening the fat-rendering—and seasoning the breasts with salt and pepper. Now I put them in a cold skillet, skin side down, and brought up the heat. Clear liquid fat began to accumulate around the breasts as they started to pop and sizzle. The fat began to rise up the sides of the pan. My God, there was so *much* of it. Not that I should have been surprised, but still, it was impressive. I flipped the breasts to cook the flesh side. Then I transferred the breasts to a cutting board, covered them, poured off the fat from the skillet, and made the sauce, which entailed reducing the port to a glaze, adding the juice of an orange, some stock, then some cream, and cooking it all down to a nice sheen—a by-the-book French pan reduction.

I let the duck rest some more while we ate our salads. Then I returned to the kitchen, sliced the magrets, and lay the slices on a platter. The flesh was reddish-pink and juicy-looking. The skin was golden. I strained the lustrous sauce over the duck and brought the platter to the table.

Nadine clasped her hands together and said, "*Que c'est beau!*" I took a bite. The flesh was succulent, with a deep, beef-like flavor. The sauce was rich, concentrated, and tart-sweet, the way a duck-accompanying sauce should be. But the skin was a disappointment. It was thick and slightly rubbery instead of thin, crisp, and melting, an overcoat when a light jacket was called for. Michele and Charlotte were peeling it off and pushing it to the side of their plates. Though I'd followed the recipe to the letter, perhaps I had heated the pan too quickly, causing the skin to brown too fast, which in turn must have prompted me to flip the breast before enough of that abundant fat had liquefied. This, alas, was exactly the kind of mistake I was prone to making in the kitchen. I was impatient. I favored speed and high heat over gentle tending. I hadn't managed the fat.

If Nadine was bothered by the chewy skin, she didn't let on. She devoured her magret, fat and all, and served herself a second helping.

While Michele read Charlotte bedtime stories upstairs, Nadine told me about her late husband, a winegrower. I remembered seeing the vine rows behind Nadine's house and, in her living room, a photo of a beaming man whom I presumed to be Monsieur Cauzette.

"During the *vendanges*," she said, wiping some crumbs from the table into the palm of her hand, "I cooked for him and all his workers, lunch and dinner, every day, until the last grape was picked. *Mon dieu*, how those men could eat!"

She laughed, but she had tears in her eyes. This struck me as a peculiarly Gascon disposition: bemusement mingling comfortably with sadness.

"It was his work that killed him. In those days, they sprayed the vines with *n'importe quoi*. He came home every evening smelling of chemicals."

She dusted the crumbs off her palm into her napkin. "But enough about all that."

I asked if she lived alone.

"Hardly," she said, her voice chirpy again. "My daughter and grandchildren are right next door, and I have a—well, a boarder, you could say. Jenny was in the state home where I used to work—with *les handicapés mentaux*—but I took her in. She helps me with the house and the cooking. She's part of the family now."

I poured us each a little more wine.

Nadine smiled and raised her glass.

I told Nadine how fondly I remembered the meal she'd cooked. Then I confessed to her my frustration with magret, explaining how I'd stuck to the recipe and still ended up with too much fatty skin. Nadine reached over and touched my hand—the best home cooking, she insisted, is not learned from a book.

6

À Votre Santé

The year 2007 was a good one for winemakers in the Southwest of France—not because of a memorable harvest or exceptional weather, but because *The Red Wine Diet* was published that year. In that book, the British scientist Roger Corder, building on what was already a pretty wide global consensus that consuming a little red wine every day was good for you, singled out the Gers and its cherished Madiran for special mention. I can picture the berets of the local *vignerons* flying into the air when they got to page 79. There, the following summation appears:

> So what is special about living in the Gers? Is this the home of the real French Paradox? Foods high in saturated fats such as foie gras, cassoulet, saucisson, and cheese are regularly eaten here, so what is the protective factor? Could it be the wine?

Is this the French "Red Zone" (the zone of exceptional reds)? Well, after analysis of some wines in my lab the answer seemed to be definitely yes. If there is anywhere where red wine can explain a local improvement in wellbeing, it is here.

You can't buy publicity like that. Corder goes on to identify tannat, the main grape used for Madiran wines, as having especially high levels of procyanidins, a variety of plant chemical that promotes vascular health, and he points out that the traditional, slow-and-steady vinification methods favored by winemakers in the Southwest conserve a maximum of those health-giving compounds.

The directors of the local winemakers' cooperative, which goes by the name of Plaimont, were so happy that they held a ceremony later that year at a wine-country château in order to bestow upon Dr. Corder an honorary membership in the Royal Order of Madiran. Also invited, and receiving the same honor, was Serge Renaud, the pioneering French medical researcher known as the "father of the French Paradox." Pictures of the event suggest that both men had a good time and made no small contribution to their own vascular health.

Another observation about Madiran that Dr. Corder makes in *The Red Wine Diet*, and one that probably gets cited less frequently by locals, is this: "The wines can be astringent, almost brutally tannic, and not at all suitable for casual quaffing."

The notorious harshness of southwestern France's tannat is an old challenge for the vignerons of Madiran, an appellation that extends across a tiny swath of hill country at the junction of the Gers, the Hautes-Pyrénées, and the Pyrénées-Atlantiques. (You can drive across the viticultural zone in about fifteen minutes, on curvy roads at that.) In recent decades, a handful of winemakers in the Madiranais, as the area is sometimes called, have been able to make softer, more elegant red wines and sell them at higher prices. The most famous is Alain Brumont, a local winemaker's son who hit it big with a prestige wine called Château Montus. He is sometimes called "the King of Madiran." I met Brumont on my first reporting trip to Gascony. He was a hot-tempered man with a penchant for lecturing. After he drove me around in his Mercedes SUV to admire his many vineyard plots, after visiting Montus's immense, immaculate cellar, accessed via a gleaming elevator, and after a lengthy tutorial, delivered in his office and augmented by a speaker-phone call with a chemist in Montpellier concerning the naturally occurring compounds Brumont coaxes from the grapes to create a signature aroma of truffles in one of his wines, we sat down to lunch. The meal was served in a private dining room at Brumont's other Madiran estate, Bouscassé. A young chef brought out plates of roasted squab. We tasted many wines, maybe fifteen in all. They were very good. Throughout the meal, Brumont complained bitterly about the paysans, who, he said, begrudged him his success and were mired in superstitions. I was glad to get back in my rental car at the end of the day.

For the most part, though, Madiran's winemakers toil in relative obscurity, at least compared to the exalted regions of Bordeaux and Burgundy and the massively productive zones of the Loire, the Rhône Valley, and the Languedoc. About half of Madiran growers belong to the Plaimont co-op, which vinifies their fruit at one of three collective *caves* and helps them improve their methods for growing and harvesting.

The person who founded Plaimont in the late 1970s was André Dubosc, the same vigneron who had invited me to Nadine Cauzette's house a couple of years back. Like Brumont, Dubosc was born into a winemaking family. Their fathers knew each other well. If Brumont was the king in these parts, then Dubosc was the *éminence grise*—a man who, by many accounts, singlehandedly rescued winemaking in the Gers and in the Madiranais, not by creating trophy wines but by teaching paysans to be better farmers.

Dubosc was unlike Alain Brumont in every way except one: He liked to talk. At the memorable dinner at Nadine's, he'd held forth almost without pause, from the first glass of Pacherenc to the last sip of brandy—not just on the subject of wine but on local geography, history, mythology, cuisine, botany, you name it. He was a walking Gascon encyclopedia with a pencil mustache and a black beret. His tone was soft and euphonious, not sharp like Brumont's. He spoke with a professorial lilt, pausing from time to time to smile or chuckle at something he'd just recounted, evincing a genuine fascination with whatever topic he happened to be expounding upon.

When I called Dubosc after our arrival in Plaisance, he offered to take me out to lunch. I met Monsieur le Directeur in the parking lot of Plaimont's retail stand outside of town.

We got into his car, and he asked if I'd like to take a tour of the *vignobles* of Madiran and Pacherenc before lunch. I said I'd be happy to, if it wasn't an imposition.

He leaned toward me and put a hand gently on my arm. "Not to worry. I've been promoted to director emeritus. They've kicked me upstairs."

He grinned. "I'm a freshly minted retiree."

Dubosc, I realized, reminded me a little of a provincial French politician, someone whose job it was to please everyone. Except, with Dubosc, there was a hint of Gascon roguishness percolating under the surface. As we pulled out of the parking lot, I noticed a sticker on his dashboard, a cartoon drawing of a mischievous-looking, beret-wearing devil, complete with pointy beard and barbed tail, pilfering grapes from a vine.

"Ah!" said Dubosc, "my grandkids put that there. They say it reminded them of me."

We drove west from Plaisance, crossed the Adour River, and zipped south for a couple of miles along the western bank of the river on the busy trunk road to Tarbes. Then we turned right onto a route that climbed sinuously through a patch of forest and into the dense range of hills on the far side of the Val d'Adour. We'd left the Gers and entered the slim northern panhandle of the Hautes-Pyrénées. The road brought us out of the trees and delivered us into a lush landscape similar to the one I was familiar with around Plaisance. But this terrain was defined by more-dramatic uplifts and declivities. And with the exception of a few grazing pastures here and there, the land was covered in vines. We were in the Madiranais.

Retirement had made Dubosc even more loquacious. Incapable of keeping both hands on the wheel for more than a few seconds at a time, he accompanied his flux of words with graceful hand gestures that reminded me of an orchestra conductor's.

"*Là bas*," he said, gesturing at a vine-covered hillside, "is some of the best soil for tannat grapes in the world. Those are Brumont's slopes."

We overtook an ancient Renault piloted by a wizened farmer. "And over here," Dubosc said, leaning forward and pointing past me out the passenger window, "is all *petit manseng*, for one of our late harvest Pacherencs. Unfortunately, the monsieur who tends that parcel is not very hard-working—look at all that grass sprouting between the vine trunks."

I peered out the window, but all I could see was a blur of green leaves.

As we sped into another valley, Dubosc spoke about rainfall, microclimates, and the various *cépages* of the region—not just tannat and petit and gros manseng, the workhorse grapes of the Madiranais, but cultivars I'd only vaguely heard of, if at all: *arrufiac, fer servadou, petit courbu, béquignol, Mauzac, Saint-Macaire, valdiguié*. Dubosc characterized southwestern France as a wine geek's dream, the cradle of dozens of indigenous grape varietals that taxonomists were still figuring out how to classify and name. "I've got one named after me," he said.

The road flattened out for a stretch, and we whizzed by a ramshackle farmhouse on our left, causing Dubosc to change the subject. "The old man who lives in that house?" he said, craning his neck to get a better look as the car drifted across the centerline. "He has no electricity or TV. The floor of the kitchen is packed dirt."

"A Parisian château owner," Dubosc continued, "tried to buy the old man out, hoping to tear the place down—it was sullying his view. Pulled out a checkbook and said, 'Name your price.'"

"What did the old man say?"

Dubosc broke into another impish grin. "'*Je vous emmerde*.'"

Screw you.

"The hills around here used to be filled with tough paysans like him." Dubosc sighed. "But they're dying out."

We turned onto a road that climbed a ridge with vine rows spilling down on either side into the hazy distance.

Dubosc said that when he founded the co-op, most of the vignerons in the Southwest were farmers like that stubborn old man, making *vin à faire pisser*—lousy wine.

"It was all about yield, yield, yield," Dubosc said. "We spent many years trying to put an end to that."

He laughed. "Do you know how hard it is to convince a Gascon farmer to let some of his grapes drop to the ground so that the best fruit thrives?"

He rapped a knuckle against his head. "They are hardheaded, those Gascons."

"You're a Gascon, no?" I said.

"Ah!" Dubosc held up a finger. "I was born in the Béarn!"

I said I'd read that the Béarn was part of Gascony.

"Historically, perhaps, but don't say that to a Béarnais—or to a Gascon, for that matter."

We'd pulled up in front of a peach-colored building that looked as if it might have once been a farmhouse. Cars were parked haphazardly around it, some overflowing into a dirt clearing across the road. A sign above the front door read LE RELAIS D'AYDIE—HOTEL-BAR-TABAC-RESTAURANT.

Inside, a hostess greeted Dubosc by name. She led us across a packed dining room to a linen-covered table by a window with frilly curtains. Dubosc conferred with her quietly about the wine, laying his fingers gently on the woman's forearm as he spoke, just as he'd done with me earlier. Moments later she returned with a chilled Pacherenc that was honeyed and viscous, but with a stiff acidity.

Dubosc tapped the rim of his glass. "The grapes stayed on the vine until December. *Tu imagines?* Not an easy feat."

He put his napkin in his lap and cocked his head slightly in the direction of the other patrons, mostly men. "Everyone in here is a vigneron," he said. "Times have changed. When I was young, the growers and the field hands never ate at a restaurant. They had lunch with the winemaker's family. Twenty people *à table* every day."

I mentioned that Nadine had just been telling me the same thing.

Dubosc smiled. "How do you think she got to be such a good cook?"

Soon, the plates starting coming: a bright-red piperade in a cazuela, a wild-mushroom omelet the size of a small throw pillow, a confit-packed garbure, and, for my main course, an *axoa de veau*, the pepper-studded Basque stew that calls for chopping an entire veal shoulder into pea-size nubbins entirely by hand. (I knew this because the wrist-numbing task had fallen to me at one of the Co-scuella classes, and I'd vowed never to make axoa again, though I was quite content to eat it.)

The Madiran that arrived with our main courses was gentler than the tannic beasts I'd been consuming in Plaisance—it wasn't quite a Montus, but it more than met the definition of quaffable. I said so to Dubosc, who wiped his mouth, laid his napkin gently on the table, and raised his point-making finger.

"It took great effort for our winemakers to achieve a Madiran like this," he said. "Tannat is the hardest of grapes to tame. It is *dur, dur, dur*"—"tough, tough, tough."

For the better part of the next hour, as we emptied the bottle and worked our way through cheese and dessert, Dubosc spoke reverentially of his *sacré* tannat. For a while, he strayed deep into technical matters. He talked about how, in 1991, the first experiments in micro-oxygenation—a technique intended to soften and stabilize very tannic wines during fermentation—were conducted in Madiran, with excellent results. The practice soon caught on around the world. Then he started describing soil types. After that, he turned to maceration times. Next, he moved on to procyanidins and other polyphenols.

Eventually, somewhat to my relief, Dubosc drifted into more nostalgic terrain. He talked, and not without fondness, about his vexation with the Gascons, about how they were hardworking farmers but terrible businessmen. He recalled how André Daguin had dared to put a Madiran on the Hôtel de France's wine list in the 1950s, defying convention in an era when only Bordeaux and Burgundies were deemed fit for fancy dining. He reminisced about Alain Brumont, who had been considered a playboy in his youth and, according to Dubosc, had a chip on his shoulder to this day. And Dubosc spoke of his own father, also a champion of tannat, a man who carried jugs of wine, not water, into the vine rows to slake his thirst during the harvest.

The check had arrived.

"Forgive me," Dubosc said. "I've been going on much too long."

I told him I had nowhere to be, which wasn't exactly true—I'd promised Michele I'd run errands and make dinner.

"Ah!" said Dubosc. "Then we can make a stop or two on the way back."

"By all means."

Despite the one-sidedness of our conversation, I found Dubosc to be extremely pleasant company.

We drove to Madiran, the wine's namesake village, to see the site of a thousand-year-old abbey where monks had made wine from native grapes. After that, Dusbosc said he wanted to show me a small château nearby called Mascaraàs. We took a wrong turn on the way there, and Dubosc pulled over to ask directions from a woman who happened to be walking on the side of the road. She recognized Dubosc, as had every person we'd encountered that day, and the two chatted for some time about a mutual acquaintance's cataract surgery.

At the château, a moldering stone-walled edifice about the size of an average American suburban mansion, we were shown around by the owner, a retired college lecturer. He'd come into possession of the place a few years back and had been persuaded by Dubosc to let the co-op grow grapes on the property and sell the wine under the château's name.

"Having a château on the label can be quite good for sales," Dubosc said to me with another gentle arm-touch as we stepped inside. The professor, whose name was Derluyn, walked with a cane and, though the weather was warm, wore a tattered tweed blazer. He gave off a strong, well-marinated scent. Derluyn didn't say much as he showed us around the château's musty rooms, which contained an extraordinary accretion of relics, engravings, woodcuts, etchings, antique furniture, yellowed manuscripts, and other *objets*. When we stepped into one of the bedrooms, a startled bird flew out from under the canopy of a four-poster bed and exited through an open window.

In a cluttered library surveilled by a painted-marble statue of Saint Denis holding his severed head, I noticed a book propped up on a stand. It appeared to be a very old edition of Gatien de Courtilz de Sandras's *Mémoires de M. d'Artagnan*, the first, semi-fictionalized account of the life of Gascony's legendary musketeer, written twenty-seven years after D'Artagnan's death. In the absence of any actual memoir by D'Artagnan—the Gascon soldier apparently never picked up a quill—this was the book that Alexandre Dumas had culled from while writing *The Three Musketeers* and the two D'Artagnan romances that followed.

Derluyn noticed me inspecting the tome. "Ah, yes, our own Charles de Batz-Castlemore," he said. "A local brat from a moderately well-to-do family who didn't have anything better to do with his life than join the military." It was the most Derluyn had said since we'd arrived, and also the first time I'd heard anyone in Gascony cast D'Artagnan in anything less than a heroic light.

I shared this observation with Dubosc as we walked back to the car.

"I wouldn't take his comment to heart," he said. "Derluyn is Flemish."

The day was growing late, but Dubosc wanted to make one final stop before pointing the car back toward the Val d'Adour. We drove in the direction of Viella, turned onto a narrow, shady road that edged a steep incline, and pulled into a gravel drive that led to a modest tile-roofed house.

"This is where I grew up," said Dubosc.

He pointed to a small brick outbuilding. "You see that shed there? That's where I had my first drink of wine. I was ten. My father was working in the fields. I found one of his jugs and drank what was left in it. I was sick for a day."

Dubosc put the car back in gear. "*Tu sais?* That was the first and last time I ever got drunk."

Dubosc invited me on many other excursions after that. We paid visits to winegrowers, strolled through a plot of vines that had survived the phylloxera epidemic, toured the co-op's *caves*, explored cemeteries and churches, snuck onto the grounds of private châteaux that Dubosc hoped the co-op would one day acquire. Each of these jaunts was as amply narrated as the first. Each included an unhurried meal and a meandering Duboscian foray into the past.

Over one of our long lunches, I asked Dubosc how much stock he placed in all that business about procyanidins, vascular health, and Dr. Corder's various studies.

Dubosc narrowed his eyes and grinned, taking on a more than passing resemblance to the devil on his dashboard sticker. "We are winemakers, not chemists," he said.

Then he raised his glass, offered a "*santé*," and left it at that.

7
La fête

Much of present-day Gascony was part of the Basque Kingdom of Navarre until 1589, when Navarre's Béarn-born king, Henri III, united the northern part of the kingdom with France (in the process becoming Henri IV). The Iberian dominion receded back across the Pyrenees, but an affinity for Spain lingers among the Gascons, most famously in their enduring and occasionally fanatical love of bullfighting. In much of the Gers and parts of the neighboring Landes and Lot-et-Garonne, almost every village of a reasonable size has its own bullring. Plaisance's, a squat concrete structure built in the 1930s to replace an older wooden arena, stands on the banks of the Arros, just across the river from where we lived.

In Gascony, the season for *le corrida* is summer, which is also the period of the annual village *fêtes*, which, in turn, offer an occasion for much outdoor feasting, often to the accompaniment of

Spanish-style brass bands or flamenco dancing. Gascons take fêtes very seriously. A summer visitor to Gascony will be quick to notice the abundance of cheaply printed fliers plastered onto kiosks and shop windows announcing an extraordinary plenitude of cookouts, bandas concerts, and *soirées musicales*, and won't have to travel far before stumbling on a hamlet turned out for its yearly party. Grilled foods are the star attraction at such events. The offerings, consumed at long communal tables, usually include one or more of the following (in descending order of prestige): magret, beefsteak, sausages, and, a perennial favorite, duck hearts, which are springy and meaty and have the distinction of tasting remarkably like magret and costing roughly a quarter as much.

Michele, Charlotte, and I attended our fair share of village fêtes. They were a mixed bag. At an outdoor lunch organized by a local chapter of the Young Farmers Association, rain kept putting out the grill fire that was supposed to cook the many pounds of chipolata sausages that had been procured for the occasion, and so we waited for an hour under a tent with a hundred or so stoic Gascons, watching an unflappable amateur dance troupe perform flamenco moves on a waterlogged stage, their high heels splashing in the puddles. The weather proved more cooperative when we attended a *grillade* in the tiny village of Préchac, just next door to Plaisance. There, we struck up a conversation with a plucky ninety-year-old named Jacqueline Sanvert, who upon learning that we were American, spent the entirety of the cheese and dessert course expressing her contempt for the English, speaking of them as if the Hundred Years' War were still raging. When she found out we lived in Plaisance's old mill, she said, "We are neighbors! You must come for apéro." Then she looked at Charlotte with a wolfish, lip-smacking relish. "And of course you shall bring that *petite créature délicieuse*."

In some Gascon villages the annual fête and the much-anticipated bullfights are bundled into a single Bacchanalian weekend. On these occasions, Gascons enter a kind of altered state, requiring little sleep and abandoning the propriety that governs their usual, workday feasting. If a typical Gascon meal requires stamina of the uninitiated visitor, then the *fête-corrida* combo requires an almost superhuman fortitude.

The most famous bullfights and the most unbridled partying take place on Pentecost weekend in the town of Vic-Fézensac, about twenty-five minutes from Plaisance. I attended the Saturday-night *corrida* there and decided it wasn't for me. A few weeks earlier, in Plaisance's arena, I'd seen the local non-lethal (for the animal) style of bullfighting known as a *course landaise* and had found it to be quite sporting: It required the bullfighter merely to dodge the beast or, occasionally, leap over it rather than kill it. The corrida in Vic was a gorier affair. As the torero withdrew his sword from between the bull's blood-soaked shoulders, the animal looked in my direction with wet, imploring eyes before crumpling to its knees, keeling over, and being unceremoniously dragged out of the ring by a couple of horses, quite possibly to be butchered and made into a long-simmered *daube de taureau*, which, I must confess, is a most delicious dish.

I found the spectacle outside Vic's bullring to be kind of unsavory, too. The streets of the normally sleepy village heaved with drunk teenagers in white T-shirts and red kerchiefs, peeing in alleys and stalking the main avenue with arms draped over one another while singing at the top of their lungs. Before that, I'd never seen a Gascon get drunk, at least not in public. A few days later, when I mentioned my surprise to Henri, who of all people could reliably be expected to heap opprobrium upon such behavior, he simply shrugged his shoulders and said, "*C'est la fête.*"

Plaisance's annual festival fell on the long Bastille Day weekend and attracted its own fair share of drunk, flip-flop–wearing teen-agers, most of them rugby players. Carnival rides and beer tents had been set up in the parking lot of the bullring. So had a flimsy-looking stage fitted with towering loudspeakers, multicolored spot-lights, and a marquee that read DISCOTHÈQUE MOBILE.

On the first night of the fête, Michele and I were kept awake until four in the morning by the DJ's thumping beats, which would stop tantalizingly for a few seconds, filling us with hope that our misery was at an end, only to start again with a thunderous drop. Posters I'd seen around the village had advertised this nocturnal component of the weekend's festivities quaintly as a *bal dansant*.

"We should lodge a complaint," Michele said from under her pillow.

I told her that probably wasn't an option in Plaisance.

"There's got to be *something* we can do."

I shut the windows, got back into bed, and pulled the sheet over my head. *"C'est la fête."*

ANOTHER FESTIVE PHENOMENON THAT HAS seeped across the Pyrenees is that of the fraternal cooking club, a tradition widely agreed to be of Basque origin.

Plaisance had its very own such club. It was called Les Esbouhats, which means "The Winded Ones" in the old Gascon dialect. It con-sisted of a few dozen rugby players, ex-rugby players, and bullfight-ing enthusiasts who organized inter-village rugby tournaments and, more to the point, got together for epic Friday-night dinners at their clubhouse, which was referred to, in the Spanish style, as the *bodega*.

I attended my first Esbouhats gathering at the invitation of Al-phonse, my friend from the cooking classes. I had run into him on the second day of Plaisance's fête. He looked relaxed and rested, leading me to believe he lived well out of earshot of the *discothèque mobile*.

When he suggested I join him that night at the bodega, I demurred.

"I should probably tell you," I said, "that I've never played rugby in my life, and I'm not the world's biggest fan of le corrida."

Alphonse gave this a few seconds of consideration and then slapped me on the shoulder. "*Ça ne fait rien*," he said. "Just come with an appetite."

I'd never been a member of a social club or, come to think of it, even a guest of a member of a social club. The only image I was readily able to conjure was that of pot-bellied men sitting at card tables, smoking cigars, reading the Racing Form, and eating meatball sandwiches.

The Esbouhats was a different thing altogether.

That evening, I made my way to the address Alphonse had given me. It corresponded to a plain wood door in a narrow alley behind a Groupama insurance office. I knocked, but no one answered. Hearing loud voices inside, I pushed the door open and peeked in. A dozen or so men were crowded around a bar along one end of a cozy, grotto-like room festooned with bullfighting and rugby ephemera—old team photos, a rugby shirt the size of a bedspread, a framed silhouette of a bull.

I stepped inside. Three long tables in the middle of the room had been covered with white paper and neatly set with plates, glasses, and bottles of wine. There was a small kitchen behind the bar. A guy with a sandpaper beard was busily slicing something. Another man was seasoning some kind of meat.

Alphonse saw me and leapt up from his barstool, his head knocking into a string of dried peppers hanging from the ceiling. "There you are!" he said, coming over. "Let's get you a drink."

Alphonse installed me at the bar and introduced me to a man on the other side of the counter who went by the name of Basso. He had Popeye forearms and a walrus mustache not unlike the ones I'd seen adorning the paysans in Henri's book of water mills.

"What's your pleasure?" Basso said.

I asked for a beer, and Basso jerked back from the bar in mock indignation. "Eh oh!" he yelled. "You can do better than that!"

I asked for a whiskey instead.

"That's more like it."

Basso had deep smile lines around his eyes, which gleamed mischievously.

Alphonse corralled a plate of chorizo and a dish of anchovies skewered with toothpicks. Basso slid a bowl of potato chips in front of me. They were Pringles, an American import that the Gascons—who typically disparage foods that are extruded, expeller-pressed, or otherwise denatured—have for some reason warmly embraced as an apéro snack.

"So that you don't feel homesick!" Basso said.

More men were coming in. A lot of them seemed to be Alphonse's age—which I guessed to be in the vicinity of sixty-five, though with Gascons it was hard to tell—but many were younger. One man had brought his son, who looked to be about twelve and was sporting a faux-hawk. The club members were dressed mostly in T-shirts and jeans, with a few exceptions, among them Alphonse, who had draped a lavender cotton sweater over a madras shirt in the enduring French shorthand for laid-back male elegance. I recognized a few faces: Bernd and Thierry from the Coscuella classes, and also the local mechanic who had, free of charge, replaced our car's antenna after it had mysteriously gone missing.

Basso peered at my drink and decided it needed freshening. Then he topped off Alphonse's.

I asked what was on the menu for tonight.

"Duck steaks à la plancha," Alphonse said, pointing toward the stove. I could see a flat-top griddle fitted over the burners. I thought of my incinerated magrets and realized that a plancha would have come in handy that night.

Alphonse showed me a duty roster tacked to the wall and explained that cooking detail fell to two different members every week.

"We eat like kings at the Esbouhats!" Basso interjected. He proceeded to reel off an eclectic list of recent dishes: lamb navarin, Moroccan-style couscous, choucroute garnie, tapas, tête de veau, goulash.

Bernd wandered over, trailing cigarillo smoke. Then Thierry joined us. Then the garagiste. I was interrogated at length about American sports and politics. Henri Michel, a retired train conductor with an equine face and thinning hair, engaged me in a protracted discussion about pigeon hunting. After that, I talked to a soft-spoken man named Doudou, a native of Madagascar who, it turned out, was the school cafeteria cook. I told him Charlotte had been regaling us with descriptions of her daily lunches (for which, incidentally, the school allotted a full two hours).

More drinks and conversation flowed. I began to wonder if we'd ever sit down to eat.

Finally, at around ten thirty, one of the guys who'd been working by the stove shouted, "À table!"

Basso hadn't lied. The Esbouhats did eat like kings . . . or at least country lords. We started with a coarse, peppery homemade pâté de campagne, studded with soft fat. After that came a cold lentil salad with gravlax and fresh dill, as refined as the pâté was rustic. There were pickled cherry peppers stuffed with brandade. There were chive-topped deviled eggs. And at last the duck steaks, seared on the griddle for no more than a minute a side, perfectly *saignant*. Each man held the serving platter for his neighbor so that he could spoon up some of the bloody juices.

The men ate fast and talked faster. I couldn't quite figure out how so much food could disappear so quickly while everybody's mouth was running. The men jawed animatedly at one another across the tables, their words issuing forth in gusty, boastful bursts. It was the very definition of a gasconade.

Basso, sitting next to me, was the most blustery of all. He was a relentless wisecracker. Even when he wasn't talking, a joke or a put-down seemed poised to escape from beneath his mustache. All of his salvos began with *Eh oh!* or *Putain!* or sometimes both. *Putain*, by the way, literally translates as "whore" but has evolved, particularly in Gascony, into a supremely versatile expletive that can range in meaning, depending on inflection and context, from a resigned "Aw, hell" to a skeptical "Oh, come on" to a mildly stunned "Holy crap" to an ejaculatory "Shit!" or even "Fuck!" Indeed, *putain* sees a lot more action—if you'll pardon the idiom—in these parts than *merde*, a word Gascons reserve for life's exasperating or downbeat moments, like getting a flat tire or receiving news that a friend's dog died.

Basso was on a roll. By the time the apricot tart and the Armagnac had come out, he seemed to be winding up to a finale. He poured himself some of the brandy, laid a hand on my shoulder, and shouted to a short, straitlaced guy seated at the next table, "Eh oh! Francis! Tell our American friend what happened at the fête in your wife's village!"

Francis groaned and swiped a hand across his face.

"*Putain*," Basso said, looking at me but playing to the room, "Francis got so drunk, he climbed into bed with his mother-in-law!"

"Knock it off," said Francis weakly. But it was too late; the sharks smelled blood.

"It's true!" said Basso, slapping a hand against the table for want of a rim shot. "He screwed her three times before he sobered up!"

The room erupted. Francis hurled a piece of baguette across the table. It ricocheted off the Armagnac bottle and landed in my lap.

A FIXTURE OF ANY RESPECTABLE festival weekend is the morning *casse-croûte*. Most often a paper-plate meal of bacon and eggs, a casse-croûte is not unlike a church pancake breakfast, except that the Gascon version includes plenty of wine, has been preceded by a late night of feasting and drinking, and will be followed by a lunchtime *grillade* and, a few hours after that, an evening of more drinks and more feasting, all of it wrapping up with a bloody corrida.

Plaisance's casse-croûte took place on the morning after the Esbouhats dinner—Bastille Day—and had been described by Alphonse as a beloved local tradition not to be missed. It was held under the main festival tent next to the bullring and started at nine o'clock, but Basso had advised me to get there early to beat the crowds.

By eight thirty, people were already lining up at a small ticket kiosk. I could see Basso and Alphonse inside the tent, both smartly groomed and looking impossibly well-slept. Alphonse and a couple of other Esbouhats were placing bottles of red wine on long folding tables. Basso was connecting a propane tank to a rickety portable gas range topped with a couple of beat-up skillets and a cast-iron plancha. He saw me and rushed over.

"Eh oh! We weren't sure you'd make it in time," he said, ushering me past the crowd. He pawed through a cardboard box. "You can cook eggs, right?"

"I've fried a few, why?"

Basso grinned and tossed me an apron. "An Esbouhat has to work for his breakfast!"

I tried to think of the French expression for "bait-and-switch," but it escaped me.

Basso lit the burners on the range and handed me a spatula. "Two eggs per customer," he said. "Alphonse will cook the bacon." He jabbed a thumb toward a towering stack of egg crates behind us. "We cook until we run out or everyone's fed, whichever comes first."

At nine o'clock, villagers started streaming into the tent and lining up in front of our cooking station, plastic plates in hand. They wore the grave expressions of Gascons not accustomed to waiting for their first meal of the day.

Basso, who inexplicably donned a cowboy hat, poured some oil into his skillet. I did the same, and then followed Basso's lead, cracking six eggs into my pan, giving them a dusting of salt and pepper, and serving them two by two, sunny-side up, onto the attendees' outthrust plates.

I quickly fell behind. My burner seemed to have only one setting—high—and soon droplets of sputtering, superheated oil were leaping about festively, dappling my forearms with a hundred bee stings. The uneven bottom of my dented skillet, which should have been retired from service many bacon-and-egg breakfasts ago, kept sliding partway off the burner, sloshing oil onto my shoes and, by exposing the naked flame, causing my recently regrown knuckle hairs to curl and blacken all over again. My glasses kept slipping down my sweat-slicked nose. I looked over at Alphonse, who was unhurriedly lifting tidy rounds of *ventrèche*—the cured, unsmoked pork belly that is a beloved Gascon breakfast meat—off the griddle and onto the plates, and wondered how he'd gotten the easy job.

The worst part was, I was breaking and overcooking the yolks, discovering in doing so that Gascons paying to attend a Bastille

Day casse-croûte had no compunction about refusing an egg they deemed less than flawlessly done. I was discarding almost as many eggs as I was dispensing.

My travails seemed to cause Basso immense delight.

"*Putain, Dah-veed!* I thought you said you'd cooked eggs before!"

"I have," I said, dumping another ruined specimen into the garbage can. "Just not this many!"

Basso was turning out one jiggling duo of perfect eggs after another and, as if to show me how effortless it was, kept up a stream of banter all the while. Each customer received a customized bon mot.

"*Alors*, Mademoiselle," he said to a girl Charlotte's age, "how do you like yours? Medium? Rare? *Bleu?*"

To the middle-aged man in line after her, Basso rattled off a joke about a cuckolded pharmacist.

The svelte woman who came next got a scolding for asking for just one egg. "How do you expect to get fat like me if you keep eating like that!"

As we were getting near the end of the eggs, Michele and Charlotte appeared in front of me, plates in hand. It took me a second to register who they were.

"What are you doing here?" Michele asked.

"Long story," I said. "What are *you* doing here?"

"We got hungry and followed the crowd."

I served Charlotte her eggs. She looked entertained by the whole scene. Then I served a couple of eggs to Michele.

"Not that one!" Michele said. "The yolk's broken."

Into the trash it went.

By the time the eggs were gone, I was a scalded, sweaty wreck. As I was untying my apron, Alphonse tapped my shoulder. He was holding one last plate of food.

He handed it to me. "Eat up, *mon brave*."

8

Beautiful People

Not all Gascons are of paysan stock, to be sure. The Gers may be France's most agricultural district—with a greater percentage of its land given over to farming than any other département—but it's populated by more than just farmers, winegrowers, and ex-rugby players. In the towns at least, one encounters the same predictable set of livelihoods as in the rest of provincial France: schoolteacher, shop owner, small-time entrepreneur, functionary in a backwater of the French bureaucracy, and so on. What struck me about the Gers was the curious preponderance of people who didn't fall into the usual categories, who occupied the interesting spaces in between the strata of rural French society, or hovered around its edges.

One summer morning, a stranger appeared at our door. Stick-thin and in his late fifties or early sixties, he looked decidedly not like a Gascon, and indeed he wasn't one.

In a thick Australian accent and a shy voice, he introduced himself as Alan. He said he and his wife, a native Gersoise named Agnès, lived just across the esplanade and took their apéro outdoors every evening around seven, and we'd be most welcome to join them.

(This would be an appropriate moment to point out that those seeking anonymity or privacy would be well advised to settle somewhere other than a Gascon village. Laying to rest my early misgivings about being an outsider, the residents of Plaisance, having gotten wind of the American family living in the old mill, proved themselves to be enthusiastic practitioners of the pop-in.)

We arrived at Alan and Agnès's at the appointed time to find them sitting on garden chairs in front of their house.

"Ah, my dears, welcome!" Agnès said in British-accented English, setting down a glass of wine and extending her hand. She wore a broad-brimmed straw hat that forced her to tilt her head back to see her interlocutor. "I'm just having my nightly *vin mousseux*."

She reached over and touched Alan's hand. "Alain, *chéri*?" She pronounced her husband's name the French way. "Bring chairs for our new friends, *s'il te plaît*, and some of the good pâté."

Alan retrieved three more garden chairs from the house and invited us to sit. I'd brought a bottle of *floc*, an Armagnac-spiked aperitif I'd grown fond of; Agnès picked it up. "Ah! From my cousin's *domaine*. Alain, be a dear and fetch a corkscrew." Alan hopped up without a word and went back into the house.

After Alan had poured drinks, I fielded a series of questions from Agnès about how we'd ended up in Plaisance. She listened to my answers intently, peering at me from under her hat and sucking on a reed-thin cigarette.

At length, I turned to Alan and asked what he did for a living. He thought this over for some time, as if it were a question that had never before been put to him.

"I suppose you could say I'm a reader," he said at last.

"Alain *devours* books," said Agnès. Alan got up once again and returned with a well-thumbed hardback.

"I'm quite enjoying this one at the moment," he said. It was an old edition of a travelogue on Italy written in the nineteenth century.

"Alain is also a collector," said Agnès, holding her cigarette an inch or so from her lips. "*Chéri*, why don't you show them the house?"

With that, Alan invited us inside and led us around three floors of dusty, curio-filled rooms, each one accoutred with ashtrays containing the butts of Agnès's skinny cigarettes. Here and there, Alan paused the tour to tell us quietly about the provenance of a particular item—a working Victrola he'd bought in Melbourne, an antique mantelpiece clock from a *brocanteur* in the Gers—or to warn us about a loose floorboard.

When we got back outside, Agnès was refilling our glasses. She asked Alan to find a doll for Charlotte to play with, lit another cigarette, and looked over at me.

"Being a writer," she said, waving away some smoke, "you might be interested to know that I've written a small book myself. A memoir, you could call it. As yet unpublished."

For the next half hour or so, as Charlotte played with the doll and Michele strained to follow along, Agnès proceeded to tell us about her life.

The account, which was quite riveting, went something like this: Agnès was born Marie-Agnès Pinon, into a local aristocratic family, a daughter of the dwindling *petite noblesse* that had thrived in Gascony during the ancien régime, studding the countryside of the Gers with small but sturdy châteaux. The one Agnès had grown up in was a drafty old mansion called Château de Sabazan. Agnès described her youth there as harsh and lonely. Her mother, she said, was a cold patrician who never hugged her children and left parenting to a governess. Largely ignored at home, Agnès sought kindness among the paysans who populated the village outside the château's walls. As soon as she came of age, she spurned her roots in the nobility and, with the help of a modest inheritance, ran off to Australia. There, she married and had children with a man who turned out to be an alcoholic and also gay. She married again, this time to a Tanzanian, moved to Africa, and had more children, only to discover she was one of several wives, added to the harem because of her money. She returned to Australia, adrift, and became ill. By divine grace she met a shy antique collector named Alan; she married him. With her new husband in tow, she returned to the Gers, reestablished contact with her children, and reunited with her siblings, who had all but given her up for lost. Finally, she reconciled with her mother, who had been forced to sell the château and now resided in the retirement home in Plaisance.

"That's quite a story," I said when she'd finished.

Agnès sighed and stubbed out her cigarette. "I've had my trials, it's true," she said. "But that is all behind me now."

She smiled at Alan and took his narrow hand in hers. They gazed lovingly at each other.

We happened upon Agnès and Alan again a few nights later. They were in their usual spot, seated on garden chairs outside the house, wineglasses in hand. This time, though, they had company: an older, white-haired woman in oversize sunglasses, linen capri pants, and blue espadrilles. In one hand the woman clutched a glass of whiskey; in the other was a leash attached to a Westie terrier.

Agnès looked relieved to see us. "Ah, my dears," she said, arms outstretched, "how lovely you're here! And what fine timing. This is my mother, Irène Pinon."

I blinked, surprised to see the malevolent character from Agnès's story seated before me in the flesh.

The woman gave us the once-over from behind her enormous shades. "Ah, yes, the Americans I've been hearing about. *Dites-moi,* how are you getting on in Monsieur De Rességuier's old mill?"

Madame Pinon spoke in a clipped, rapid-fire cadence that I imagined to be a bygone affectation of the Gascon *haut monde.*

Michele, whose French was inching toward the conversational level, told her we were settling in fine.

"You likely already know that the De Rességuiers are a very old aristocratic family," she said. "Of course, they are *noblesse de robe,* not of blood. Monsieur De Rességuier's forebears acquired their title through the purchase of some land, if I'm not mistaken."

Henri was a member of the *noblesse*? Our retired schoolmaster with a flair for weed-wacking? This was news to me. I made a mental note to ask Henri about it. Or did one not inquire about such things?

Madame Pinon suggested briskly that Charlotte take her dog, named Petite Fleur, for a walk. I got the feeling that this was more to be rid of both the dog and the child than to please either of them. Then she began to gossip with Agnès and Alan about various doings in the village. After a few minutes, I spied a man I recognized as the father of one of Charlotte's schoolmates walking across the esplanade toward the bridge. Madame Pinon leaned in toward us, discreetly pointing a finger in his direction. "And *that one?*" she said under her breath. "His marriage is in shambles. Haven't you heard? The mother is threatening to run away with the children. *C'est affreux.*"

Agnès and Alan remained mostly quiet, and as Madame Pinon chattered on, I began to contemplate an exit plan. It was getting late.

Petite Fleur led Charlotte back to the table and was now begging for a cracker. Charlotte popped one into the dog's mouth, and Agnès's mother snapped at her. "*Ah, non, ça va pas!* You mustn't feed her!"

Charlotte looked like she'd just been slapped. I decided that was our cue. We said our good-byes and followed the Rue des Peupliers back home.

"That old lady was kind of mean," said Charlotte as we walked up to the house.

We saw Agnès and Alan only a few times after that—they decamped to Australia for half of each year, and we'd arrived in Plaisance toward the end of their stay. We had them over for drinks a few days before they left. As we were seeing them out, Agnès handed me a hand-stapled booklet the size of a Playbill. It had a grainy Xeroxed photo of a château on the cover.

"My humble autobiography," she said, smiling girlishly. "I'd be most eager to hear your thoughts one day."

I read the homespun memoir before bed that night. Written in the third person—on a typewriter, from what I could tell—it chronicled Agnès's travails and triumphs in soaring, dime store–romance style. The tale culminated in the heroine's return to "her old place, the Gers."

MANY FASCINATING LIVES AND STORIES, in fact, played out behind the façades of Plaisance's drab *centre ville*.

For example, our friend Patrick, who lived on the Rue de l'Adour above an old cinema. You could walk right by his place and not notice it, but inside was a creepily magnificent Art Deco treasure: a vast, tenebrous room littered with torn-out theater seats and dominated by an enormous stage flanked by blood-red curtains.

Like Alan, Patrick had simply appeared at our door unannounced one morning. I'd been out at the time, but I'd been alerted to the arrival of our unexpected visitor by a phone call from Michele.

"There's a very good-looking man at our house," she'd said, sounding as if she were muffling the phone. "He's invited us for dinner tonight."

By the time I got home, Michele was on the balcony, a glass of wine in her hand, laughing and chatting in English with a youngish fellow in jeans and Timberland boots. He was a head taller than me and had an urbane, simpatico air that seemed to have been cultivated a thousand miles from the Gers.

"I hope you don't mind me springing an invitation on you like this," he said, breaking into a luminous smile that was more eyes than teeth. "I figured you might like to meet some people your own age."

We were the first to arrive at Patrick's that night. He served us drinks at a long bar that ran along the edge of the high-ceilinged room, which was lit from above by red spotlights, giving the space a lurid, night-clubby feel.

Patrick noticed me gawking at the surroundings. "The place hasn't shown a movie in years," he said, sliding a pastis to me across the bar, "but I've thrown some great parties here."

I asked him about the photographs hanging on the walls: dozens of stark black-and-white nudes, both male and female, in various athletic poses.

"I took those," Patrick said. He poured himself a drink and then, with a disarming candor that I was beginning to think was a congenital Gascon trait, told us about himself. As he recounted it, his life was lighter on melodrama than Agnès's but, to me at least, no less interesting.

Patrick explained how his grandfather, who sounded like a paysan version of Agnès's icy mother, had, through much sweat and toil, lifted his family from peasant roots into Plaisance's petite bourgeoisie. Patrick's father became a prosperous entrepreneur, running a building-supply business. Like virtually every father in this part of Gascony, he expected his son to play rugby. Patrick didn't like rugby. He took up photography instead. He didn't fit in. He got picked on. In a gesture of adolescent indignation, he started calling himself Tripak, which is what a lot of friends call him still. When his schooling was done, he decided he wanted to see the world. He became a flight attendant for Air France. Soon he was traveling to New York, San Francisco, Tokyo, West Africa, South America, taking pictures everywhere he went. But Plaisance never stopped being home. He met a guy named Arnaud. Patrick, by way of coming out to his parents, brought Arnaud home for dinner one night.

Patrick took a gulp of his drink. "Instead of telling them, 'Hey, I'm gay!'" he said, "I told them, 'Hey, I'm in love!'"

Michele, who had been hanging on Patrick's every word, asked, "What did they say?"

"They were okay with that."

Patrick's friends showed up with dishes of food and bottles of wine and beer. They were an artsy, international, and good-looking bunch, and they all knew one another. I felt as if I'd tapped into an undiscovered vein of hipness buried deep beneath Gascony's hills and valleys.

A sudden shyness came over me, but it soon abated—everyone seemed genuinely happy to meet us.

Michele and I started chatting with a chic Englishwoman in red-and-white cowboy boots who restored antique furniture and sold it at her *brocante* shop in a nearby village. She introduced us to a skinny, shaggy-haired rocker named Tim—another Aussie, as it happened—who'd married a Gersoise, lived in a converted Armagnac distillery, and played in a band. Michele looked ecstatic to be conversing with a native English speaker about music, and before long she and Tim were talking about groups I'd never heard of. I migrated down the bar and found myself in conversation with a tall, garrulous Belgian in a bright yellow tie. His name was Fred. He said he and his wife, Lut, made meticulous reproductions of medieval and Renaissance leatherwork and sold their pieces to museums, château owners, "and occasionally to rich people with yachts." Fred seemed to take a twisted pleasure in warning me how cold we'd be in the old mill come winter. "I've seen that place. You will suffer, my friend," he said with a ghoulish shudder. "But don't worry, our house has central heat and satellite TV. You can take refuge there."

Glasses were filled, emptied, and filled again. Charlotte had made friends with Tim's daughter, a cute, gap-toothed girl named Charlie. The two of them retreated to a corner of the room with Charlotte's markers and drawing pad. Finally, sometime around nine thirty, we sat down to eat. Patrick had made, of all things, baby back ribs, which we ate with our fingers in the American fashion. This pleased Charlotte immensely. Other dishes got passed around: a saffron-tinged chicken tagine, a tortilla española, an herb-flecked tomato tart, a huge salad. More wine was opened. There was nothing particularly Gascon about the food, except that it was delicious, and offered in ridiculous abundance.

By the end of the meal, after the cheese and pastries had come and gone, the table was a cluttered mess of dishes and empty bottles. Charlotte and Charlie had joined a couple of other kids in a noisy game that involved jumping off the stage onto an old trampoline, which squeaked gratingly with each landing. Most everyone had broken off into pairs, each deep in conversation. A couple of joints were making their way around the table. Michele had her back to me and was speaking French—amazingly well, from what I could hear, considering the hour and all the wine we'd drunk—with Arnaud, Patrick's partner.

I ended up in a tête-à-tête with Tim's wife, Chloé.

"Dave," she said, taking a drag on a cigarette. "How in the world did you end up in the Gers?"

"I wanted to ask everyone else here the same question," I said.

Chloé smiled and gave this some thought. "I suppose some of us sort of crash-landed here," she said, "maybe hoping to find something, or maybe hoping to get away from something."

The trampoline springs squeaked loudly; Charlotte had just made another stage dive. I did my best to ignore the racket and started off on a tangent about my family genealogy. Chloé smoked and listened, smiling beatifically.

Eventually Charlotte and Charlie fell asleep on a threadbare couch at the far end of the room, in an alcove that had once housed the cinema's ticket kiosk. As the evening drew to a close, Patrick sat down between me and Michele and showed us one of his recent photographic projects: a beefcake calendar featuring players from Plaisance's rugby team. The team members were going to sell copies of the calendar around town to raise money. The photos looked pretty racy for a publication that would be sold to local grandmas and displayed in the window of the hair salon. May's page showed the backside of a naked rugby player diving into a lake. Mr. August was a naked rugby player on a Jet Ski, his private parts obscured by the handlebars. December was a group of naked rugby players in a hot tub popping champagne.

When I pointed out that Patrick had developed an interest in rugby after all, he practically fell over laughing.

We saw a lot of Patrick after that, and not just at his expat gatherings. It was unusual for me to go into town and not run into him.

More often than not, he was on a photographic mission of one kind or another: scouting locations for next year's rugby calendar, say, or taking aerial photos of the village using a drone (which eventually ended up in the river). Other villagers, young and old, would frequently stroll over to say hello to Plaisance's resident artiste and social impresario, inquiring about his latest travels.

9
Garbure

Writing in *Le Nouveau Cuisinier Gascon*, André Daguin had this to say on the subject of soup: "Soup is primordial cooking, born of ancient times. True soup is food for those of strong heart and good stomach, those with a clear conscience."

In *La Cuisine du Pays*, Simin Palay makes an equally sonorous if less koan-like pronouncement: "In our land," he intones, "there is no such thing as a good meal without a hearty soup."

Paula Wolfert, Northern Californian that she is, strikes a lighter tone: "If France is a country of soup-eaters," she writes, "the South-West is the land of soup-*lovers.*"

Indeed, the kinds of soup to be found in the greater Southwest are legion. Palay's book contains recipes for no fewer than three dozen: bean soups, *bouillons*, Basque saldas, cheese soup, pot-au-feu, plus many potages even most French people have never heard of—

panturoun (made with lamb), *jerbilhoû* (thickened with corn flour), *cousinette* (flavored with sorrel), and more.

In the very heart of Gascony, though, when one is offered soup, it is, almost without fail, a garbure. That beloved dish of simmered cabbage, beans, and salt pork (and usually many other things) is the soup that trumps all others. It is sustenance and comfort in equal measure. It is the ne plus ultra of Gascon peasant dishes. Often, it arrives at the table unbidden, as essential and commonplace as a basket of bread.

None of this is to say that garbure—a specialty generally thought to have originated in the Béarn but now firmly entrenched all over Gascony—does not have its myriad regional and even microregional variations.

In fact, so disparate were the recipes that I'd rounded up in preparation for cooking my first garbure that when I sat down to make my shopping list, I soon fell into a state of confused paralysis.

At one end of the spectrum lay Paula Wolfert's multipage epic, which called for two pounds of pork shoulder, one pound of unsmoked pork belly, one pound of garlic sausage, a ham hock, smoked bacon, six confit duck legs, one pound of white beans, five kinds of vegetables, and an aerobic-sounding workout of mincing, sweating, puréeing, straining, simmering, and skimming, as well as the dunking of whole confit duck legs into the broth, the transferring of the meats to warming plates, the rubbing of pieces of stale bread with garlic, and the placing of those pieces of bread in the bottom of the soup tureen before serving the soup and meats separately with various pickled and spicy condiments.

At the opposite extreme was a recipe that Nadine (who would have been disappointed by my continuing reliance on cookbooks) had given me:

Put six liters of water, a dozen cut-up potatoes, and a ham hock in a pot. Bring to a boil. Add two sliced turnips and a bunch of blanched and sliced kale, plus whatever bits of duck confit you have handy (wings, necks, etc.). Add eight cloves of minced garlic and simmer for an hour and a half. Season to taste.

Unlike Wolfert's mighty garbure, which was supposed to be so thick that a "wooden spoon stands up straight" in it, Nadine's was clearly a soup of the more watery kind. They were two entirely different dishes.

I was also in possession of a brown envelope that Henri had dropped off. It contained a dozen recipes that a friend of his, a local historian, had collected several years back from—according to a handwritten note—"elderly housewives of the Val d'Adour." Each recipe had a woman's name attached to it: *la Daube d'Odette, la Poule au Pot d'Adrienne, la Brandade de Marie-Amélie.* The one for garbure, from a lady named Suzanne, was slightly more involved than Nadine's, but still a masterpiece of brevity. The main difference was the suggestion, echoed by Wolfert, to lay pieces of stale bread in the bottom of the tureen.

As for Simin Palay's book, the Béarnais poet proposed three garbure recipes. One suggested adding grilled chestnuts. Another called for spooning a layer of goose fat over the thick soup, flambéing the fat, and then covering the pot lid with hot coals to create a kind of gratin.

This wasn't really clearing up my confusion.

Palay did, however, make one enlightening point. He said there was a long-accepted distinction between what he dubbed "classic" garbures, extravagantly meaty affairs typically eaten in the evening as a full meal—dishes like the one in Wolfert's book—and simpler "everyday" garbures like Nadine's, more often served as a starter or a light lunch.

In the end, ignoring the great chef Escoffier's advice to "*faites simple*," I decided on the former.

I WAS NOT THE TYPE of cook who makes a joyous mess in the kitchen. Before diving into a new recipe, I liked to have my chopping and mincing done ahead of time, my *mise en place* bowls at the ready, my counter freed of clutter, my utensils close at hand. I washed my dirty cookware as I went along. I set timers. I took a certain Midwestern pride in efficiency and order. In domestic matters in general I was a speedy multitasker. On a typical weeknight, in the time it took Michele to give Charlotte a bath and brush her hair, I could prepare a simple supper, take out the recycling, sort the mail, and empty the dishwasher. Then, after I'd rinsed the last pot and wiped down the countertops, I would pour myself a drink and power down. In fact, if I stopped to think about it, I really had only two operational gears, high and neutral, and two modes of waking activity: work and reward. This was perhaps not the healthiest way to live, but there you go.

Making a "classic" garbure required a certain retooling of my modus operandi.

The procuring of the ingredients stretched over several days. The undertaking began with a visit to Plaisance's weekly market, for the various root vegetables and herbs. For the duck confit, I drove to Ferme Tomasella. Obtaining the pickled condiments and the dried white Tarbes beans, which had to be soaked overnight, necessitated a trip to a supermarket in another town.

On the morning of garbure day, after deciding that only the finest-quality pork products would do, I made the forty-five-minute drive to Éauze, a village that boasted what Henri had described to me as the best butcher shop in the Gers. Boucherie Cugini faced a busy ring road encircling the medieval *centre ville*. I entered the crowded shop, took a number, and waited my turn behind a scrum of middle-aged women engaged in lengthy negotiations with the apron-clad countermen. I ordered the items I needed, with the exception of the garlic sausages, which they were out of. I figured I could get by.

Henri had warned me that Cugini was *très cher*, but I hadn't lent much credence to his remark, since a warning about high prices was a standard local refrain, Gascons being a frugal bunch. In any event, Henri had been right. Now, driving home in possession of a small fortune in meat, I felt added pressure not to mess things up.

Never had the kitchen of the old mill felt smaller than it did that day. With the ingredients for my garbure spread out over every square inch of free counter space, I set to work. I pulled out our pear-shaped (and barely bigger than pear-size) cutting board and began trimming the turnips and cutting up the potatoes. I drained the white beans. I blanched the cabbage. I tied the bouquet garni. I sliced the leeks and sweated them in duck fat. I removed the skin from the confit duck legs and chopped it up to make cracklings. I pierced an onion with cloves and finely sliced another. Charlotte came into the kitchen to ask me something. I brusquely shooed her away. I plugged in our Moulinex food processor and puréed the parsley, garlic, and bacon for the *hachis* that would augment the stock, making a greasy mess of the superannuated appliance. Finally, I started simmering the beans, the ham hock, the pork belly, and the pork shoulder, realizing as I did so that I should have started that step before everything else.

Feeling spent—though I was far from finished—I rinsed my hands and looked at the counter. It was littered with onion skins, turnip tops, flecks of parsley and thyme, globules of duck fat, and lengths of wet butcher's twine. I picked up a dishcloth, then put it back down. *No.* Instead of cleaning up, I sloshed a little wine into a glass and stared out the kitchen window for a while, observing the comings and goings on the bridge.

The water in the pot had grown cloudy, and the air in the kitchen was thick with the scent of boiling pork. Foam rose to the water's surface. I skimmed it off. I added some of the hachis. More foam rose up. I skimmed it off. I added the bouquet garni. More foam. More skimming. This went on for some time. Now the kitchen was starting to smell good; the herbs and aromatics were doing their thing. I felt relaxed, and not particularly needful of distraction beyond the foam-skimming, bridge-gazing, and wine-sipping.

After a while it occurred to me to check the time. It was close to six. Henri and Monique, whom we'd invited for dinner, would be arriving in a couple of hours. I'd planned to devote part of the afternoon to washing the car and doing some spider-web removal in the living room, among other things, but the day was all but gone. There were no shortcuts with a classic garbure. Once you were in it, you were in it. I made peace with this circumstance, reconciling myself to the fact that today was no longer about doing lots of things, or even several things. It was about doing one thing: making garbure.

Before cleaning up, I performed one of the final steps: adding the duck legs. After that, I gave the pot a stir and let go of the wooden spoon. It stayed upright. Charlotte walked halfway down the stairs and peeked at me through the railing. I waved for her to come down. I handed her a jar of dried espelette pepper, lifted her up, and told her to give a few good shakes over the soup pot. Then I told her to add a few pinches of salt. At last, I stirred in a spoonful of duck fat, as one of Simin Palay's recipes had advised, "for a touch of finesse."

I took a taste.

"Is it good?" Charlotte asked.

The garbure had an oniony bite that an overnight rest in the fridge probably would have cured, but it was full of profound, meaty flavors.

"I'd say it's just about right."

WHILE HENRI AND MONIQUE WERE having apéro on the balcony with Michele and Charlotte, I followed Wolfert's suggestion to remove the meats to a warmed platter so that they could be sliced and eaten with cornichons and pickled peppers. But the great hunks of pork and confit fell apart at the first touch of the knife. So at the last minute, I separated out the duck bones and slid the meats back into the pot. My garbure looked more like a deconstructed cassoulet than a soup.

This fact did not stop our guests from oohing and aahing when I brought the tureen to the table.

Henri took a bite. "Now *this* is a garbure," he said.

Monique had a taste, and let her spoon hover respectfully over the bowl. *"Formidable."*

"Not too heavy?" I asked.

"Not at all," Henri replied.

"You're spoiling us," said Monique.

Michele leaned toward me and said sotto voce, "My God, it's like eating with your parents."

Henri, who had taken a keen interest in our daughter's acquisition of French, asked Charlotte what she was planning to do over the weekend. Charlotte offered a short but, to my great pleasure, grammatically correct reply, and I noticed for the first time that she pronounced *samedi*—Saturday—"sa-muh-dee," in the local way. Some Gascon-ness had rubbed off on one of us, at least.

We had leftover garbure for dinner the next night, and the night after that. Each time, I stretched out the soup with a little water and added some salt and pepper. And each time, it tasted better than the time before: mellower, softer, with deeper bass notes and more harmonious flavors. Thus concluded my first object lesson in the making of Gascon soups, stews, and braises: If made right, they improve with age.

10

Dinner at Henri's

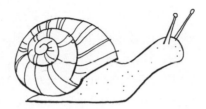

In Gascony, the past feels close and incandescent. Visible traces of it are everywhere: the churches and graveyards, the ancient place names, the châteaux and crumbling *maisons féodales*. When you ask locals of a certain age where they're from, they're as likely to answer with the name of a bygone *comté* or barony—Bigorre, Lomagne, Astarac—as they are to name a modern administrative district.

Some Gascons, it's true, feel a deeper connection to the past than others.

Henri, for one, was besotted.

Certainly, living in his old moulin had given us some indication of Henri's predilections, but it wasn't until we attended a fancy meal at his house that I understood the full scope of his fixation.

The De Rességuiers lived just up the road, in a sleepy bastide village called Marciac. It was known for its summer jazz festival, which had revived the town's fortunes in recent years, turning the arcaded central square into a more spruced-up version of Plaisance's main bastide.

Michele and I arrived at eight fifteen and loitered hesitantly for a few moments in front of Henri's three-story town house.

"Is there a doorbell?" Michele asked, scanning the plain façade.

"Literally," I said. I tugged on a wood-handled chain hanging from a small hole in the wall, and a bell tinkled faintly somewhere inside the house. A half minute later, one of the enormous wood double doors yawned open, and there was Henri, beaming. He greeted us warmly, first cheek-pecking Michele and then grasping my hand with both of his. There was an extra touch of graciousness in his bearing, an extra flourish of gallantry. Tonight, we were his guests, his peers. *"Entre, entre, je t'en prie,"* he said to me, using the informal *tu* with us for the first time.

Henri led us down a dark, narrow front hall, the walls of which were decorated with framed botanical drawings and what appeared to be antique gardening implements. We passed a library whose towering shelves were crammed with clothbound books; more dusty-looking tomes were piled precariously atop a handsome old wood secretary.

"They're calling for rain," Henri said over his shoulder as he glided ahead of us toward a wide staircase at the end of the hall, "so we're having drinks upstairs in the *salon*."

The wooden steps of the staircase sagged in the middle and were worn shiny-smooth by many years of footfalls. Lining the stairs were dozens of wicker baskets like the one Monique was usually carrying when she popped by our house to give us a jar of jam or some picture books for Charlotte.

Turning left at the top of the stairs, we entered a room the likes of which I'd never seen outside of a museum. Henri's salon could have passed for the stage set of a Molière comedy. Lit by antique wall sconces and furnished with needlepoint-upholstered fauteuils, marble-topped side tables, and gilt-edged mirrors, the salon was a period-perfect seventeenth-century drawing room, free of any signs of modernity. An oil painting of a stormy seascape hung above the fireplace mantle, on which sat a polished-stone fleur-de-lis.

A dozen guests were chatting politely, most of them clustered around a table set with silver platters of canapés and bowls of olives. Monique's singsong voice could be heard above the others. She was talking to a gruff-looking, hirsute man about her new pastime, sport shooting.

Henri handed us flutes of champagne and started introducing us around the room. We met a deeply tanned widower who had been married to a department-store clothes model (he showed us her picture on his phone); a couple who owned a riding club nearby; and a shiny-headed veterinarian named Jacques, who had published an illustrated history of Marciac and was raising money now to open an "alimentary-themed" amusement park outside the village.

Henri introduced me to a genial fellow in a rumpled blazer. This was Alain Lagors, the historian who'd collected the housewives' recipes. Monsieur Lagors worked as a professor at the local junior high school and, Henri added, was a member of the Société Archéologique et Historique du Gers.

Lagors shook my hand and hung on to it as he spoke. "As a recent transplant to Plaisance, you might be interested to read my monograph on the history of the village."

He edged closer as if about to reveal a secret. "Did you know, *Dah-veed*, that Plaisance is one of only a handful of villages in France with two bastides?"

Jacques, the Marciac chronicler, had drifted over, and now chimed in. "One should point out," he said, "that only one of them is a real medieval bastide. The other was—"

"A bastide is a bastide," interrupted Lagors. "*C'est une question d'architecture.*"

At nine or so, Henri stepped to the doorway, clasped his hands in front of him, and announced, "Dinner, everyone! Bring your glasses if you like."

Downstairs, he directed guests to their seats at an elaborately set table with a huge flower arrangement in the middle. As he did so, he consulted a slip of paper he'd pulled from his pocket.

Michele looked at me. "Is that a—?"

"My God, it is," I whispered.

It was a seating chart.

I was placed between Henri and Monsieur Lagors. Michele was exiled to the far end, between the dark-haired man Monique had been talking to and the woman who ran the riding club. Neither of them appeared to speak English.

Michele's questionable seat assignment aside, the meal that followed was one of the more impressive feats of social and culinary engineering I'd ever witnessed. For two hours, we were ushered seamlessly from one gustatory moment to another, without the least appearance of exertion on the part of our hosts. It was the kind of meticulously choreographed dinner party that I assumed had gone the way of silver-domed serving platters and butler's pantries.

The proceedings began with glasses of very cold Sauternes, poured by Henri with practiced grace, and neat rectangles of foie gras rimmed with yellow fat. Each square was served on a fine-china plate adorned with a single parsley sprig. Monique, whose role appeared to be that of conversation facilitator, revealed that the foie gras had been made by Henri's mother. After the first course was cleared away, six plump escargots *en persillade* appeared before me and my wineglass was refilled, this time with a bone-dry Jurançon Sec.

"The snails are from our garden," Monique announced. I thought that was pretty cool, though none of the others seemed particularly stirred.

Next came a plate containing a trio of delicious small things: marinated sardine fillets, slices of cold stuffed baby artichoke hearts, and a scoopful of zucchini *tian*.

From where I was sitting, I could see into the kitchen. It was a cramped room, typical of old Gascon maisons bourgeoises, with a smoke-stained stone hearth, an enameled sink, and a well-used gas range. I was amazed by what Henri had been able to accomplish in such modest confines, and even more so by his nimble maneuverings in the dining room. Plates arrived and were whisked away with astonishing stealth. Before I'd even noticed his absence, Henri was back in his seat, chatting away, with nary a bead of sweat on his face—much less the armpit stains, knife cuts, and cheese-grater abrasions that often accompanied my own dinner-party hosting back home.

As we finished the second course, Monsieur Lagors topped off my glass. "The De Rességuiers have apprised you of the history of their moulin, I trust?"

I told him that Monique had filled me in on the basic details.

"Then perhaps you already know that upon the death of Dominiquette de Saint Pierre Lesperet in 1894 the mill was sold to a Monsieur Rosapelly and refitted with a Gramme magneto—a brand-new invention at the time, I might add—in order to supply the town with power."

"You don't say."

"*En effet*, the village was one of the first in France with electric streetlights."

The professor seemed pleased to have an ear to bend, and as we were about to start in on the main course—*paupiettes de veau* in an herbed chanterelle sauce—he took possession of a bottle of Saint-

Emilion for the two of us and embarked on a (slightly) condensed oral history of Plaisance in the years leading up to the Third Republic.

"Plaisance," Lagors began, "was a great crossroads at the time. It sat astride one of the main routes to the Pyrenees, right at the junction of the Béarn, the Bigorre, Bas Armagnac, and the Pays Landais—a meeting point for the old, feudal *contrées* of Gascony. This drew in people not only from the hills of the Gers, but also from the Madiranais, the Vic-Bilh, and beyond."

The profusion of place names pleasantly lulled me. Content, I chewed and listened as Lagors described a nineteenth-century village bursting at the seams with commerce and industry. "Every trade thrived in Plaisance," he said. "Carpenters, blacksmiths, leathersmiths, coopers, wagoners, wheelwrights. People had to stand outside during Sunday Mass at the old church. All the pews were filled." Lagors went on to say that money flowed into the town coffers in those days. Improvements were made in sanitation. Streets were paved. Work began on the new bastide. It was the most ambitious rebuilding effort ever undertaken in any bastide town across all of Gascony, carried out in the forward-looking, urbanist spirit of the times.

Hearing about my adoptive village in its glory days, I felt a sudden, proprietary nostalgia.

Lagors took a piece of bread and mopped up the last of the sauce from his plate. For a moment, he seemed to be lost in thought. Finally, he wiped his mouth and said, "Those were heady times," sounding as if he'd lived through them himself.

Now Henri was leaning between us to lower an enormous wooden cheese board onto the table. I served myself pieces of everything on it. Freed momentarily from conversation, as Lagors had been buttonholed by Monique, I paused to eavesdrop. The tan widower was talking to Henri about, if I understood correctly, lingerie. Monique was describing to Lagors an angry letter she'd written to Marciac's mayor about a lack of parking during the jazz festival. Jacques was staring morosely at his plate. The riding-club wife was making energetic hand motions at a weary-looking Michele—something about dressage, or maybe ballet, I wasn't quite sure. The woman's husband was embroiled in a testy debate with the dark-haired guest, whose hairy arms were crossed tightly over his chest. I couldn't quite get the gist of their argument, but it concluded with the dark-haired fellow waving his hand disdainfully and saying something loudly about "lazy foreigners."

Monique frowned. "*Ça suffit.*"

Henri folded his napkin and stood up. "No politics at the table," he said sternly, then went into the kitchen to fetch dessert. Henri told me later that the prickly guest was a family friend visiting from Provence—"not a Gascon, *bien sûr.*"

Henri brought out a homemade *gâteau Basque*, as well as a bowl of kumquats, a plate piled with squares of dark chocolate, and four bottles of Armagnac, two of which were older than me. Monique came around carrying a cut-crystal bowl of *crème anglaise* for the cakes. When she got to me, she pointed at the handle of the ladle sticking out of the bowl.

"The De Rességuier coat of arms," she said.

Just as I was trying to imagine what would motivate a person to engrave a coat of arms on a soup ladle, it occurred to me that this might be an appropriate moment to ask Henri about his family's aristocratic pedigree. When he'd finished pouring a round of Armagnac, I decided to broach the subject by complimenting him on his taste in art and antiques.

Henri leaned back in his chair, a glass of the caramel-colored brandy in his hand. "Ah, yes," he said, "collecting is my *maladie.*"

"It seems like a fitting pastime for a member of the nobility," I replied, then worried I'd been too forward. But Henri laughed.

"I'm a skilled bargain-hunter, not a nobleman," he said. "As for my family's background, yes, we inherited a title but—"

He rubbed his thumb and forefinger together and uttered the only English I would ever hear him speak.

"—no money."

Monique and Henri sent us on our way at the end of the night with a bag of kumquats and a children's book for Charlotte called *Pouf et son cousin*. It had a picture of two kittens in roller skates on the cover.

Michele and I stepped onto the cobblestones outside Henri's house. The street was utterly still, soundless, washed in the yellow glow of a sodium lamp.

11

Into the Mountains

The most famous cheese in all of Southwest France is Roquefort. But most Gascons, while they wouldn't turn up their noses at the stuff, would not consider Roquefort local. That creamy, blue-veined cheese comes from Roquefort-sur-Soulzon, in the Aveyron département, more than 100 miles east of Toulouse. That's practically a foreign land. To a Gascon, a local cheese is, by and large, one that arrives from the opposite direction, namely the Pyrenees: usually either as rounds of pale-yellow cow's milk or sheep's milk cheese—known as Tomme des Pyrénées—or cylinders and pucks of chèvre.

The deep grooves of those ancient mountains—the Ossau Valley being the most famous, cheese making–wise—are populated by thousands of dairy farmers, sheep farmers, and goatherds. Some work on spreads with big milking sheds and shiny equipment. Others toil in cottage operations: a few goats or ewes in a pen out back, a cheese-making room off the kitchen, maybe a handmade-woolens business on the side. A few hardened traditionalists, especially in the Basque region—generally an excellent place to find hardened traditionalists—pasture their herds high in the mountains during the summer and bring them down to lower elevations for the colder months, in an age-old practice that goes by a mystical-sounding name: transhumance.

Of the various Pyrenees cheeses sold by Amandine, I had developed a fairly stubborn addiction to two: the downy-white fresh chèvre and a long-aged ewe's milk cheese. This *fromage de brébis*—a *brébis* being a "ewe"—was a magnificent ogre, with a thick, discolored rind and a crumbly interior so sharp from fermentation that it burned the tongue. In the comparatively tame world of Tomme des Pyrénées, it was an outlier.

The problem with this cheese was that all too frequently Amandine was out of it. This was not the fault of Amandine but of the cheese maker, a solitary shepherd who, according to Amandine, seldom picked up his phone, often failed to show up at their meeting spot in a market town south of Pau to deliver his rounds of tomme, and, to hear Amandine tell it, was a generally unreliable character. His name was Marcel, she said, although she referred to him more often as "the crazy fucking Basque."

I couldn't help but notice that Amandine used saltier language when talking to me than she did when conversing with the older market-goers, whom she never failed to favor with a dazzling smile and the *politesse* typical of rural French merchants. As I slowly got to know her, I took this as a sign either that she had grown especially comfortable with me or, perhaps, that she considered me a transient foreigner on whom such niceties would be wasted. Whatever the case, it seemed to me that Amandine didn't fit the Gascon mold. She was reticent, guarded, a little caustic, and so I felt a certain satisfaction that she'd warmed to me enough that I could sustain a Gascon-length market-day chat with her. I had an ulterior motive, too, for getting to know her: I was hoping that she might invite me to ride along on one of her day-trips to the mountains so that I could meet her cheese makers.

As it happened, Amandine did me one better.

After a particularly long period of deprivation, I made my weekly trip to the market one crisp morning and discovered, to my delight, that Amandine was carrying Marcel's cheese again. A gnarly wheel of it was sitting in her case, guarded by sheep figurines.

Amandine said Marcel's longer-than-usual disappearance owed to the fact that he'd been busy getting ready to herd his animals down to the lowlands for the season. He spent his summers, she said, at a high mountain refuge, in intimate communion with a thousand sheep.

I asked Amandine if she'd ever visited him *en haut.*

"It's 8,000 feet up," she said. "No road. No way for me to get the goods back down the mountain."

"How does Marcel do it?"

"Donkey," Amandine replied. "Or so he says."

She stepped on the cigarette she'd been smoking. "The crazy fucking Basque."

Transhumance was something I'd always wanted to witness. The very word seemed to connote a peaceful communion of mankind with nature. Deciding to push my luck, I asked Amandine if there was any chance she might be willing to take me to meet Marcel.

Amandine rested a hand on her hip and squinted at me in a way that seemed to say either *you're an idiot* or *that's not a bad idea.*

She pulled an old flip-phone out of her pocket. She let it ring for an incredibly long time, then walked over by her van and talked animatedly for several minutes before snapping the phone shut.

"It's your lucky day," Amandine said. "Marcel is bringing the flock down next week. He says we can come up and help."

I offered to pay for gas and food.

Amandine looked down at my sneakers.

"You might want to get some hiking shoes."

BEFORE THE TRIP, I DECIDED to brush up on the Basques. From what I could glean, they and the Gascons were once essentially the same people. The words *Gascogne* and *Basque* are both believed to be corruptions of *Vasconie*, the name of a vaguely bordered trans-Pyrenean duchy that in the early Middle Ages split apart to become Basque Country and Gascony. The two peoples' shared ancestors, the Vascons, spoke a strange language that predated the arrival of Indo-European tongues. Eventually the Vascons on the north side of the Pyrenees, tired of fighting off the Franks, began to hew to what would become France, content to allow their language to be Romanized into a local dialect of Occitan. Meanwhile, their beleaguered Vascon brethren closer to the mountains, beset by the Visigoths and then the Muslims and then the warring kingdoms of Spain, retreated ever further into their enclaves with their curious language and folkways, forming a sort of Vascon rump state and becoming the Basques, emerging into the world in modern times to display a penchant for *pelota*, nationalism, and experimental cuisine.

I'd heard Gascons refer to Basques variously as *têtu* (stubborn), *fou* (crazy), and *fêtard* (hard-partying), which sounded to me like Gascons on steroids. My few previous experiences with Basques, at least on the French side of the border, had borne this out. On an earlier trip to the Pyrenees, Michele and I had found ourselves in a remote village in the Pays Basque called Saint-Étienne-de-Baïgorry. When we asked some locals to direct us to the nearest restaurant, they invited us to a communal lunch in the *salle des fêtes* instead. The meal lasted five hours and included six courses, many bottles of Irouléguy wine, and shots of a sloe-infused liqueur that tasted like a cinnamon stick wrapped in a licorice whip. Children ran around the table, poking the grown-ups in the back with wooden spoons. A young Basque with a scraggly beard and a Thin Lizzy T-shirt insisted we stay the night with him and his wife. We said that we'd already paid for a hotel room nearby. At this, his friend—a chain-smoking playwright who'd told us that a Basque theater troupe had just performed one of his plays in Chino, California—waved a bunch of euros in the air. "How much?" he bellowed. "I'll pay the cost of the hotel! How much?" We straggled out of there well after dark. Michele and I still get e-mails from the Thin Lizzy guy: "When are you coming back?"

According to Amandine, Marcel was a more complex character—*têtu*, yes, and a little crazy, too, but also somber and moody. She was telling me this as we rattled out of Plaisance in the direction of Pau in her cheese van, an aptly named Citroën Jumpy. After Pau, we were going to bear southwest, making for a wrinkle in the mountains called the Vallée d'Aspe. Somewhere deep in that valley, close to the border, was a village called Lescun. Once there, according to the instructions that had been conveyed to Amandine, all we had to do was ask the first stranger we saw how to find Marcel Etcheberry, and we would be pointed to the trailhead.

A word about direction-giving: It's not that the people of rural southwestern France have an aversion to GPS, but if you live on an unnamed farm road with no numbered address—or, as the case may be, in a mountain hut—Google Maps won't do visitors much good. This circumstance has resulted in an anachronistic flair for dispensing directions that can stray into the realm of the poetic. Here's part of an e-mail sent to me by a Gascon winemaker I wanted to visit: "Upon leaving the route of Madiran, at the end of the great, descending way, you will find a lane on your left, opposite a small barn. Take it, and soon you will see our home: a square house of an orangish color. Next to the house will be a paddock and, in it, a donkey who answers to the name of Pencil."

Sliding around in the back of Amandine's van were our two backpacks, each containing a change of clothes, a sleeping bag, and provisions. Amandine had insisted on taking care of the victuals, as she knew a farmer outside Plaisance who gave her a *commerçant* discount on ham and pâté. I'd been taken aback by how much food she had purchased for an overnight excursion: two baguettes, two cans of pâté, another of boudin, two *aller-retours* of dry-cured sausage, and a small ham, plus a bottle of Armagnac and three liters of water.

"We're never going to get through all this," I'd said as she stuffed half of the supplies into my pack.

"You get hungry in the mountains" was her response.

As we made our way along the Tarbes trunk road, I tried to get Amandine to tell me a little about herself. She said she worked at several outdoor markets around the Val d'Adour, getting up at four o'clock in the morning to load her cheese cart and its wares into her van, which she'd bought from the old man who'd sold her his vendor's license. On non-market days, Amandine drove into the Pyrenees to buy fresh product. About her family and her childhood, I was able to extract only the following information: She was born twenty-three years ago outside of Maubourguet, not far from Plaisance, and had a Spanish father, last name Belmonte. When I tried to inquire further, she changed the subject.

After twenty miles or so, we made a stop in a run-down village called Lahitte-Toupière.

"This'll just take a minute," said Amandine as we pulled up in front of a squat, flat-roofed dwelling protected by a chain-link fence. "You can stay in the van."

A middle-aged woman came to the door. A large dog was straining to get outside; the woman held it by the collar. Amandine walked
up and gave the dog a kiss. Then she cheek-pecked the woman,
handed her what looked like a wad of cash, and came back to the van.

"My mom," said Amandine before I could even ask the question.
"She's been a basket case ever since my dad left."

"When was that?"

"When I was twelve." She wriggled a Marlboro out of a pack on
the dashboard.

An awkward silence ensued as we drove on toward Pau. We
skirted the city via a seemingly endless series of roundabouts and got
on the route toward Oloron-Sainte-Marie. The Pyrenees heaved up
on our left, now starkly close, ranks of gunmetal peaks melting into
lush green foothills peppered with farms and settlements.

Amandine popped a Bob Marley CD into the player.

I groaned.

She looked at me sideways through aviator sunglasses. "What."

"Why does every French person under thirty think Bob Marley
is *le top*?"

Amandine gave a slightly sinister smile. "It's going to be a long
drive for you, my friend."

IT WAS MID-AFTERNOON WHEN WE got to Lescun, an end-of-the-road
hamlet of shingle-roofed houses clinging to the wall of a green
valley just inside the French border. I got out and did as we'd been
instructed, asking the first person I saw—an old lady sweeping
the steps of a *chambre d'hôte*—if she knew where we might find
Monsieur Etcheberry, the cheese maker. Without hesitation, she
raised a bony arm and pointed at a quartet of needle-like peaks.
"Up there."

I pressed further, eliciting a series of hand gestures and instructions for getting to the trailhead. It took us a half hour to find it. Amandine locked the van, and we hoisted our packs and started up a muddy switchback that climbed through a forest. With twenty pounds of preserved meats on our backs, the going was slow. I hadn't heeded Amandine's advice about footwear, and soon mud had worked its way over the edges of my shoes.

Amandine stopped to lean against a tree, panting, probably regretting the cigarettes she'd smoked in the van.

After a while, the trees parted and the trail crossed a natural amphitheater, vast and grassy, lorded over by granite summits. We put our packs down and gazed around us, too winded to speak, though in the face of such an awesome panorama I don't think I could have found words. I was a native of the flatlands, and being near mountains never failed to destroy utterly and exhilaratingly my sense of scale. Being *in* the mountains, as we now were, made me feel as if I'd left my home planet altogether.

An hour and a half later, as the sun was sinking into a saddle of gray rock above us, we emerged, bedraggled, in a boulder-strewn clearing. Before us, the terrain swooped up toward the four barren spires the old lady had pointed to earlier. Hundreds of sheep were spread out across a near-vertical slope some indiscernible distance beyond, looking like flecks of dandruff. Cottony bits of cloud drifted below the summits. Behind us, a *V* of two mountain walls parted to reveal ranks of smaller peaks below.

At the center of the clearing stood a steep-roofed cabin with mortared-stone walls, two tiny windows, and two wood doors. It was the most forlorn dwelling I'd ever seen. We set our packs on a table next to a stone cistern that stuck out from the cabin.

"Is this the place?" I asked.

"Has to be," said Amandine.

Marcel was nowhere to be seen. He had told Amandine that a couple of other acquaintances of his were coming up to help herd the flock, too, but there was no sign of them, either.

I tried one of the doors. It opened to reveal a pristine cheese-making kitchen with a stainless-steel basin for curdling the milk, and a long stainless-steel table covered with circular plastic molds. Everything had been battened down for the season.

I opened the second door. The room behind it was of a different type altogether. It called to mind a frontier homestead with a touch of Unabomber thrown in. A sawhorse table was cluttered with empty wine bottles and tins of various foodstuffs. Rusted tools and cans of solvent and paint thinner blocked the steps of a wood-plank ladder leading to a pitch-dark attic. More boxes of food lined sagging shelves in a kitchenette lit by a fluorescent ring.

Back outside, I took a seat at the table across from Amandine. The sun had disappeared behind the ridge, causing the temperature to fall so fast that it felt as if the warmth were being vacuumed right out of the air. I dug around in my pack for my sweatshirt and jacket, wondering where we were going to sleep.

Presently a sound made itself heard from the trail below. It started as a distant mewl, then rose to a whine, and now became a roar. An olive-drab 4x4 burst from the trees into the clearing, kicking mud from beneath its tires and bouncing over boulders like some kind of adrenalized moon rover.

Amandine stood up. "This'll be Marcel."

"I guess he traded in his donkey," I said.

The vehicle lurched to a stop next to us. Three lean dogs bounded from the flatbed. A man unfolded himself from the driver's seat. His face was a map of creased, wind-toughened leather, with a horse-shoe mustache affixed to the front and muttonchops on the sides. A mane of thick pewter-and-black hair peeked from beneath a beret.

The man's body, or at least what was discernible of it underneath the dirty beige parka he was wearing, seemed to consist entirely of sinew.

Marcel nodded a perfunctory hello to Amandine and looked at me, his eyes dark pinpricks.

"Your American made it up the mountain in one piece," he said to Amandine.

"He did all right for a city guy," said Amandine.

I pointed to the 4x4. "It would have been easier with one of those."

Marcel smoothed his mustache and turned to regard the machine as if for the first time. "*Eh bien,* four wheels are faster than four hooves," he said.

"Where are the others?" Amandine asked.

"They'll be up tomorrow," said Marcel.

He whistled to his dogs. "Let's take a ride."

Before I could politely decline, we were crammed elbow to elbow in Marcel's vehicle, tearing along a—it couldn't be called a road, or even a path. It was more of a vague horizontal tendency scratched into the wall of the mountain. Marcel's dogs were sprinting in front of us, their tails inches from the front tires. The noise of the engine and of rocks slamming against the undercarriage made it impossible to talk. I gripped the roll bar and braced my knee against the inside of the wheel well in order to keep from being thrown into the void. Marcel didn't seem to have a specific destination in mind, and, to my relief, before long we were approaching the cabin again, but from the opposite direction. In the time we'd been gone, hundreds of shaggy-haired ewes—presumably the ones I'd seen on the distant slope earlier—had descended into the clearing. They scattered before us as we pulled up to the cabin. Marcel killed the engine. Suddenly there was nothing to be heard but the dull clanking of sheep's bells and an eerie, toneless chorus of *maaa*'s.

"Again!" Amandine said as we got out. Thankfully, it was getting dark.

We took a seat at the outdoor table and drank Ricard from chipped glasses that Marcel had rinsed in the cistern. I knocked my drink back quickly, hoping to fend off the chill and unknot my muscles. Marcel rolled a cigarette and talked with Amandine for a while about the cheese business—government regulations, supply and demand, elderly ladies who liked to taste but not buy. Amandine matched the Basque's droopy-eyed world-weariness shrug for shrug, drag for drag. Then, Marcel's appetite for conversation apparently sated, we sat wordlessly as the sheep, one by one, lay down for the night. I was shivering now, and increasingly haunted by the feeling that we were at the end of the earth, or the top of it, irreversibly cut off from humanity.

Finally, Marcel invited us inside. He built a fire and flipped on a clock radio, filling the room with staticky pop music. Amandine got out the food we'd brought and started carving thick slabs of ham with a fearsome Walther hunting knife she'd pulled from her pack. I was asked to open a can of pâté with my Swiss Army knife. Marcel laid the ham slices into a skillet and started frying them. Then he cracked a half dozen eggs over the ham, let them cook for a few minutes, and brought the skillet to the table along with a wedge of his *brébis*. We ate ravenously, arms darting across the table to tear off hunks of bread.

When we were finished, Marcel opened the bottle of Armagnac we'd brought and poured a round. We sat hunched over our glasses, bathed in firelight as darkness engulfed the mountain.

Marcel asked me if there was good cheese in America. I told him there was.

"I want to see the Rockies," said Amandine, gazing into her glass, "and Nevada. Buy an old RV and drive around for a year."

A log threw an ember onto the floor; it skittered over by an open can of mineral spirits. Marcel and Amandine took no notice.

I asked Marcel where he grew up. He thrust his chin in a north-westerly direction. "In the foothills. My older brother got the farm, and I went to the mountains. That's how it is in Basque families."

He poured another round of Armagnac and got up to stoke the fire.

Amandine took a sip and pushed her glass away.

"I think I want to get out of the cheese business," she said after a while. "Sell the van and just move around with the seasons, picking crops."

Apropos of nothing, Marcel told us he had a daughter.

"Oh, really?" I said.

"She'll be twenty this year."

"Does she ever visit you up here?"

Marcel scratched at some candle wax on the table with the tip of a switchblade.

"Haven't seen her since she was thirteen."

"*Ah merde*," said Amandine softly.

Marcel flipped the knife closed and sat back in his chair. "What can you do?"

With that, he got up and said he was turning in.

"You two can sleep upstairs," he said, pointing at the black maw in the ceiling. Then he disappeared behind a door on the far side of the room.

Amandine and I cleared away some of the junk from the ladder steps, and up we went. The frigid garret contained a bare lightbulb hanging from the center beam and two rusty metal bed frames, one next to the other. Pock-marked foam pads had been laid over the springs. We unrolled our sleeping bags and got into them wearing our clothes. I sat up and pulled the light chain. We were enveloped in blackness.

I burrowed into my cocoon and tried to fall sleep. I could hear Marcel snoring downstairs, the sound wafting up through the floor-boards.

LET'S PUT TO REST ANY misperceptions: The seasonal culmination of transhumance isn't peaceful. It's a dirty, smelly, exhausting business. This stands to reason, if you think about what it takes to escort a thousand less-than-intelligent grazing-and-pooping machines down a steep, narrow forest trail, across a vast upland meadow and several rushing streams, and into a fenced enclosure at the bottom of a mountain.

Actually, though, the whole thing kicked off in a pretty civilized way. Marcel's friends showed up as promised the next morning, having started up the trail at dawn, and they'd brought with them the makings of a fine picnic lunch—boiled chestnuts, hard-cooked eggs, fresh cherries, a bottle of Bourgueuil—to which Amandine and I contributed the rest of our pâté and ham. A family of three, the newcomers weren't the types I expected to see fraternizing with a temperamental and reclusive Basque shepherd. It turned out that the wife, as cheerful as Marcel was cantankerous, was herself a former shepherd who'd moved to the town of Orthez to assume the life of a *bourgeoise*.

We ate at around eleven thirty, just as the sun got high enough to surmount the spires and bathe the clearing in glorious warmth. At one o'clock, after a ceremonial round of Armagnac-spiked coffees, Marcel finished locking down the cabin, everyone shouldered their packs, and the procession got under way.

At first the sheep seemed to herd themselves. The dogs had rounded them up into a big circle, and the clanking and *maaaing* beasts moved as a single, fluid mass across the clearing and right into the mouth of the trail.

Marcel, I'd noticed with a twinge of uneasiness, had sped off ahead in the 4x4.

As we fell in behind the flock, I asked the ex-shepherd woman where Marcel was going.

"To the bottom, to set up the fence," she said.

"Shouldn't he be back up here with the sheep?"

"I think we can handle it."

She seemed to know what she was doing, so Amandine and I followed her suggestion to bring up the rear while she and the others worked the middle of the column and the dogs kept things orderly near the front.

Amandine and I followed the hoofed, woolly river into the forest. At first we tried to avoid stepping in the droppings the animals were leaving behind in terrific abundance, but eventually we gave up. Soon, the ex-shepherd's family and the dogs were far ahead of us.

"I take it you've never done this before either?" I asked Amandine as my shoe sank into a fresh *crotte*.

"I'm more of a horse person," she said, wiping her brow with a shirtsleeve.

It had gotten warm, and Amandine had taken off her army jacket and was carrying it under her arm. Just as I was about to offer to help secure it to her pack, I noticed something: The sheep river was developing tributaries. The more independent-minded members of the flock were straying into the woods, lured by the sight of a green shoot or tuft. Amandine and I started bushwhacking through the foliage to outflank the animals, whooping and waving our arms in order to get them back on the trail. Every time I got one errant sheep back in line, though, another two would saunter back up the mountain. I was finding out the hard way the most basic principle of shepherding: A flock can be pursued but not led—get out in front of some sheep, and they will turn and start ambling in the opposite direction. Amandine appeared to be learning the same lesson with some rogue ewes of her own on the other side of the trail. Before long, both of us were darting back and forth through the woods as if possessed by some Wiccan spirit.

Eventually, somehow, we reached the great pasture we had gawked at the day before. The sheep in the rear of the column now joined the rest of the flock, which had already spread out across the clearing to feast on the grassy banquet. We all rested for a while, and then the dogs rounded up the flock again and the sheep surged en masse toward the trail, just as they'd done before.

After that, the going got easier, as the path was flanked by rocky embankments that offered fewer tasty distractions. We reached the trailhead in the late afternoon. Amandine and I sat in the shade, completely spent, and watched as Marcel and his friends goaded the flock into the temporary corral, where the sheep would spend the night before being transported to their winter quarters in the Gers.

Marcel invited everyone for beers at Lescun's lone café. He was in good spirits and insisted on paying for our drinks. The dark cloud that had been shadowing him the night before had lifted.

He gripped my hand as I was about to get into Amandine's van. "*Alors*," he said, "when are you coming back?"

AMANDINE AND I DIDN'T TALK much on the way home.

We listened to reggae as the mountains receded behind us. We skirted Pau again, passing an ugly strip of big-box stores— Bricomarché, Géant Casino, Leader Price—and got on the route toward Lembeye. Being back near sea level was filling me with a vague melancholy. Amandine was gnawing on a piece of saucisson and bobbing her head slightly to the music.

As we were crossing the Adour River, I decided to break the silence.

"That was fun," I said for lack of anything better.

"Yep," said Amandine.

"Quite a character, that Marcel."

"He's really got it made up there."

"You mean cut off from everything like that?"

"Sure," said Amandine. "*En haut*, you don't need anyone. Just your dogs."

It was well after dark when we finally pulled into Plaisance. Amandine stopped at the end of the moulin's gravel drive and got out to open the back so I could grab my pack.

"See you at the market probably," she said as she swung the door shut. We did the customary good-bye *bises*, but at the last second I went in for a bear hug.

"Sorry," I said, "but that's how we do it in Chicago."

Michele and Charlotte were asleep. I found a couple of green-gage plums and some skinny radishes in the fridge. There were eggs, too, so I made an omelet. I pulled out a wedge of Marcel's cheese, wrapped in Amandine's checkered waxed paper, and broke off a chunk from near the rind, where the cheese darkened and took on a near-ammoniac sharpness. I saved the rest—maybe the crazy fucking Basque would be more reliable now that he was back in the Gers, but I wasn't going to make any assumptions.

12

Poule au Pot

Despite everything that the forward-thinking Henri IV accomplished in his lifetime—uniting Navarre with France, enacting the Edict of Nantes, becoming the first French monarch from the House of Bourbon—a remark about chicken remains the most famous thing the Gasco-Béarnais king ever said. Speaking to either the Duke of Sully or the Duke of Savoy, depending on which history book you're reading, the monarch uttered some version of the following pronouncement: "As long as God keeps me, I shall make sure no laborer in my kingdom lacks the means to have a chicken in his pot." Thanks to his words, the enduring peasant dish known as *poule au pot* is now forever associated with le Roi Henri.

As a rule, Americans don't boil chicken. We prefer to fry it or grill it or sear it or roast it, occasionally with a beer can up its backside. We like our chickens young and white-fleshed. We like them mild-tasting and quick-cooking. Poule au pot is the opposite of all those things.

And it is so much better.

This truth was revealed to me when Nadine finally had us over for lunch.

We arrived at Nadine's early in the morning. I was feeling wobbly. I'd gone to the Esbouhats the previous evening, intending to stay for one drink, but ended up making a night of it after Basso had chided me in front of everyone.

"Eh oh, once you walk in, you're in till the end!" he'd shouted. To my protests that I'd already eaten, he countered, "A real Gascon eats two dinners!"

This was surely an exaggeration, but even so, some ninety minutes after the evening meal I'd shared with my family, I had a second one, working my way through a couple of roasted tomato halves, several thick slices of roast pork, a pile of egg noodles bathed in *jus*, a wedge of cheese, and a large piece of eau-de-vie–drenched tiramisu. I'd gone to sleep sitting up, hands on my belly, and awakened feeling less than sanguine about a garbure-esque session of toiling over a soup pot, followed by a big lunch. As we pulled up in front of Nadine's maize-colored farmhouse, I was more in the mood for dry toast than boiled bird.

Nadine's kitchen looked tinier than I remembered it. This may have been because of the staggering abundance of ingredients piled everywhere. The table was a Flemish Master still life: bunches of untrimmed turnips and carrots, a pile of fresh leeks, a riot of parsley and thyme and chervil, a whole cabbage, capers, shallots, heads of garlic, cooked and uncooked eggs, a bowl of uncooked sausage, a hunk of beef shank, four veal tails, and, at the center of it all, a very yellow plucked hen, its three-toed feet sticking into the air in a vaguely salacious way.

"Isn't she a beauty?" Nadine said after we'd had a coffee and put on our aprons. She plucked a stray quill from the carcass. "You can hardly find old birds like her anymore. One has to know the right farmer."

Nadine introduced us to Jenny, the live-in helper she'd told us about. Jenny looked away from us shyly when we said *bonjour*. She was asked to fetch something from the *arrière-cuisine*, and disappeared down a long, narrow hallway.

Nadine crossed her arms, exhaled with puffed cheeks, and took stock of the table.

"*Bon*, let's get started." She pulled out a chair for me. "*Dah-veed*, you can make the *sauce gribiche* for the chicken."

I sat down. Tentatively, I reached for the hard-boiled eggs. There were definitely eggs in a sauce gribiche. And capers—that I was sure of.

"You *do* know how to make a sauce gribiche, yes?" Nadine said.

"I used to," I said.

She refreshed me on the basics and plunked down the other ingredients—oil, vinegar, chervil, tarragon.

Now she gave Michele a roll of kitchen twine and asked her to make a few bouquets garnis for the broth.

Michele took a seat opposite me. Her hands hovered uncertainly over the piles of herbs.

I leaned across the table. "You *do* know how to make a bouquet garni, yes?"

Michele held my gaze coolly and extended her middle finger. She pulled out a few sprigs of each kind of herb and started tying them together.

"Oh, my," said Nadine, coming over. "That won't do at all."

She sat down next to Michele and took the twine from her. "*Regarde*."

Nadine grabbed three leeks, three stalks of celery, an entire bunch of parsley, a fistful of fresh thyme, and a dozen sprigs of rose-mary, and bound them all up like cordwood. She placed the enormous bundle in front of Michele. "Two more like this should do the trick."

Jenny had returned, and she and Nadine started making the forcemeat stuffing. This entailed mixing a few pounds of fresh sausage with the minced heart and liver of the hen, a minced onion, lots of parsley and thyme, a couple of raw eggs, and some bread that had been soaking in milk. *Cook that all up with some fried eggs,* I said to myself, *and you'd have dinner for six.* To all this Nadine made the superfluous addition of some rolled oats.

She winked at me. "They're good for the colon."

Now Jenny was holding the bird open by the legs while Nadine spooned in the stuffing. The two women worked together like well-meshed gears, exchanging barely a word. Nadine sewed the cavity shut using a long needle and some of the kitchen twine, and then used the excess twine to secure the legs snugly to the body. She brought the ends of the twine around the tail nubbin and snipped them. I'd never seen anyone truss a bird with more authority. It looked like a yellow football with limbs.

I was done with the sauce gribiche. Nadine looked in the bowl and frowned. She poked at the sauce. "*Oh la,* this should all be minced finer." She sucked her finger and then assumed a chipper tone. "*Pas grave.*"

A brown enameled cookpot filled with water had been heating on the stove since our arrival. It was a very big cookpot. You could have bathed a medium-size dog in it. Nadine carried the trussed bird over to the stove. She lowered the hen into the bubbling water and then added the hunk of beef shin, the veal tails, the three gargantuan bouquets garnis, two chicken necks, and four chicken feet.

"Wow." It was all I could think of to say.

Nadine flashed me one of her *Why so surprised?* looks. "I like a hearty broth."

She gave the pot a stir, put down the spoon, and started rummaging through one of the kitchen drawers. She pulled out a box of surgical gauze.

I asked her if she'd cut herself.

Appearing to have taken this as a joke, she laughed and walked back over to the table, where she scissored off four lengths of the gauze. Then she and Jenny used them to make skinless boudin-like sausages with the rest of the forcemeat stuffing. Nadine tied off the end of one of the zeppelin-shaped packets. "We'll drop these into the pot just before the bird is done," she said. "Surgical gauze," she added, "is a Gascon cook's best friend."

She took off her apron. "Now we let it simmer. Come, let's find something to put out for apéro."

While Jenny stayed behind to skim the broth, Michele and I followed Nadine down the hall and into a chilly, concrete-floored backroom. Cinder-block walls were lined with metal shelves stocked with hundreds of hand-labeled mason jars. On a long table covered in plastic were piles of canning equipment. This was Nadine's arrière-cuisine.

Perusing the shelves and studying the labels, I realized I'd stumbled into the Alexandria Library of canning cellars. The room was a shrine to every imaginable Gascon farmhouse recipe—civets of hare and wild boar, daubes of beef and cèpe mushrooms, *salmis* of wood pigeon and squab, conserves of haricots Tarbais and tomatoes and green beans. Three shelves were devoted to foie gras alone—plain foie gras, foie gras with apples, foie gras with raisins, foie gras with Armagnac. Duck confit got an entire shelving unit: duck legs, duck necks, duck gizzards, duck wings, duck breasts.

"It's a terrible mess in here," said Nadine, raising a pair of glasses to her nose to examine a jar. She put it back and pulled down a different one. "Ah, here we are. I think foie gras with figs would be nice for today, no?"

It didn't seem possible, but I was starting to feel a dull intimation of hunger.

There was plenty of sweet stuff on the shelves, too: grape jelly, red currant preserves, rhubarb preserves, strawberry, raspberry, mulberry, blackberry.

I picked up a jar labeled *"gratte-cul"*—literally, "ass-scratcher." Nadine told me it was the nickname for rose hip. "Because of what the bristles do when you're trying to pick it." She scratched her haunch.

Then she took the jar and put it in an empty apple crate. "You can take it home for Charlotte."

She started plucking more jars from the shelves and adding them to the crate—two, four, six, eight.

Now she was gazing with glistening eyes at a particularly tall one in her hand. "Goose neck stuffed with foie gras, my husband's favorite."

Into the crate it went.

"Nadine," I said, "you don't have to give us that."

"*Pff*, please. It's not like *he's* going to eat it."

Michele was inspecting a shelf of sauces and coulis. "Who *is* going to eat all this?"

Nadine shrugged. "Grandkids, friends. It was different when there were lots of hungry men around. I suppose I keep doing it out of habit."

By the time we returned to the kitchen, it had filled with a bewitching aroma—a deep and chicken-y scent, a scent thick with promise.

We still had time to kill while the bird finished cooking, so Nadine made more coffee. Preparing the poule au pot had put her in a sentimental mood, and she reminisced for a while about the dishes she'd eaten growing up. One was called *sanguette*, which she described as a duck's blood omelet. Another was *alicot*, a slow-simmered ragoût of unglamorous duck parts—giblets, necks, wings, feet. The name, she said, came from the Occitan *ale y cot*, for *aile et cou*, which means "wing and neck." She dwelled with particular relish on *graisserons*, a sort of scrapple made from the bits of meat and cartilage left over after making confit.

"You spread it on toast," she said. "*C'est magnifique.*"

NADINE HAD INVITED HER FRIEND Danielle to join us for lunch, and also André Dubosc, who lived just up the road. He walked in with a carton of wine and a toothy grin. When I introduced him to Michele, he practically genuflected.

"You're in for a rare treat," he said, clasping Michele's hands in his. "No one makes a finer poule au pot than Nadine."

Jenny had cleaned off the kitchen table, and we all sat down. Dubosc poured glasses of Pacherenc, and Nadine served the foie gras on slices of toasted black bread. The fullness I'd been weighed down with earlier was now a memory.

Dubosc told a story about how, many decades ago, the town of Viella had been gerrymandered out of the Madiran appellation because of a local feud.

"In those days," he said, "villagers seldom traveled outside their *commune*. People from Viella considered people from the other side of the Adour River outsiders. People from the Béarn considered the Gers a foreign country. This created misunderstandings."

Dubosc said his father persuaded the quarreling parties to put aside their differences, resolving the dispute and bringing prosperity to the village.

"He was a true gentleman, your father," Nadine said to him.

"So was your husband," said Dubosc. "*C'était un vrai monsieur.*"

They clinked glasses.

Nadine went into the kitchen, prodded the contents of the cookpot with a wooden spoon, and took a taste. She pronounced the poule au pot ready.

First came bowls of the bouillon by itself, strained and then thickened with a little tapioca powder. It was a broth of fathomless richness, chicken soup's platonic ideal.

Then, borne by Nadine on an enormous platter, came the main attraction. Dubosc closed his eyes and inhaled deeply as it passed in front of his face on its way to the center of the table. Danielle, seated across from him, did the same, causing her glasses to steam up.

Like a number of dishes beloved by Gascons, poule au pot is defiantly unphotogenic. There is no crisp, burnished skin, no oven-caramelized vegetables, just pieces of boiled chicken and mounds of khaki-colored stuffing on a bed of limp-looking turnips, leeks, potatoes, cabbage, and carrots. But it is a thing of beauty nonetheless. It is beautiful *because* it is delicious. A real poule au pot is the product not so much of cooking as of alchemy. In the crucible of the stewpot, the humblest ingredients are rendered sublime, infused with flavors of stupendous depth and intensity.

I took a bite of each thing on my plate. Each ingredient tasted a hundred times better than it ever could have if it had been cooked and seasoned on its own.

I told Nadine, without exaggerating, that it was the best chicken dish I'd ever had.

She gave an *oh you!* wave of the hand.

"Don't be silly," she said. "It's simple peasant food."

13

Hills and Valleys

The Gers has just one city: Auch, with 23,000 residents, a nice cathedral, one fancy-ish hotel, and a bunch of shops selling foie gras gift boxes. Beyond that, you'll find around a dozen gritty rural hubs known colloquially as *bourgs*, with populations in the vicinity of 5,000, and also a couple of dozen *bourgades*, which are villages like Plaisance: big enough to have, say, their own post office and at least a few of the standard-issue *commerces*—pharmacy, tobacconist, newsstand, butcher shop, bakery, and so on. Finally, scattered more or less evenly across the Gers like grains of rice are hundreds of somnolent hamlets possessed of a church and maybe a tiny *mairie*. With no big urban centers to connect to, the Gers has just a handful of rail lines and only a couple of stretches of four-lane highway. Both of those are on the route between Auch and Toulouse, and both are very short—no sooner have you set the cruise control than the highway peters out again, as if its builders had knocked off early for a round of floc and never bothered to finish the job.

The deeply rural character of the Gascon heartland owes in part to its distinctive terrain, which is, geologically speaking, runoff from the Pyrenees deposited over millennia in a fantail formation, creating a vast bed of fluvial sedimentary deposits known to geologists as *molasse*. The Gers is also one big collecting basin for the Garonne and Adour rivers, which enclose the département like a pair of cupped hands. The hundreds of rain-fed brooks, riffles, streams, and small rivers that empty into those two great waterways have, over a great deal of time, carved the molasse into a dense mosaic of arable hills and rich-soiled valleys ideal for sustaining small farms and villages but not particularly conducive to building cities.

The Gers is, more than anything else, a place where edible things grow. Plums, walnuts, hazelnuts, apples, tomatoes, pears, melons, berries, peaches, legumes, oil-seed plants, cereal grains: All are commercially farmed in the département. Quite a few of those things are raised by non-farmers, too. Gascons are consummate gardeners, and their *jardins potager* tend to be bigger and more professional-looking than the kitchen gardens to be found in American backyards— sprawling, neatly furrowed beds bursting forth riotously with fruits and vegetables in summer, often flanked by fruit trees, sometimes with a few rows of grapevines added to the mix, for the *vin maison*.

Ducks, of course, are raised in abundance—some 18,500 tons' worth per year, nearly half the production of the entire Midi-Pyrénées region—as are, to a lesser extent, geese. The Gers has its own heritage-breed cows, called *vaches mirandaises*, and heritage-breed chickens, called *poules Gasconnes*. There's also a local race of pig, the free-foraging *porc noir de Bigorre*, which, as its name suggests, is black, and has what must be one of the more eclectic porcine diets in all of France: It includes chestnuts, acorns, earthworms, snails, white truffles, apples, and wild grasses, among other delicacies. During our strolls in the hills outside Plaisance, it was not unusual for Michele and me to surprise a few *porcs noirs* nosing around the woods.

Intensive farming has made inroads in the Gers, in the form of monoculture crops like corn, soybeans, rapeseed, and sunflowers. The rapeseed and sunflowers turn whole swaths of the countryside bright yellow in summer. Big agricultural operations have altered the landscape here and there—trees cleared away, the land flattened or graded. But to a surprising extent, old-fashioned polyculture still thrives: small farms raising a few different kinds of crops and live-stock, often of the web-footed variety. This has gone a long way toward preserving the variegated, patchwork feel of the Gascon countryside.

The particular brand of beauty proffered by the Gers is neither grandiose nor stark. The Gers lacks cliffs, waterfalls, deserts, canyons, dramatic rock formations, and most other kinds of natural assets that attract photographers and generate coffee table books. The fertile core of Gascony is inviting but unimposing: a hodgepodge of oddly shaped farm plots, forest remnants, vineyards, oak and hawthorne groves, shrubby hedgerows, irrigation ponds, orchards, grazing pas-tures, and miles and miles of paved and unpaved farm roads—some 7,000 kilometers of them in all—extending across the Gers like fine capillaries, plus many more miles of foot paths, including a segment of the Chemin de Saint Jacques pilgrimage route.

And yet, the undulant landscape has a way of getting under your skin. In *Les Paysages du Gers*— by far the most informative book I've found on the département, and one of the most lavishly detailed vol-umes I've read on any subregion of France—the French geographer Bruno Sirven allows that the Gers often inspires its chroniclers to rhetorical excess (a tendency to which he himself falls prey):

Many an author has praised the qualities exuded by the countryside of this beguiling and convivial province, whose aesthetic raptures are numerous . . . and where the sensuality of the land's contours inflames erotic metaphors, attributing to this carnal terrain an unconditionally feminine soul: rumps, buttocks, breasts, friendly hillocks, intimate valleys.

Such associations are strictly in the eye of the beholder, but I'd agree that there is something decidedly sensual about the topography of the Gers. It's the kind of landscape you want to wrap your arms around.

The heart of Gascony is one of the finest places I know of for a long walk, especially if you're of the ilk who enjoy hot running water and a bed after a day of lugging a pack across hill and dale. The Gers may not be very populous, but its villages are spaced close together, and strolling from one to another along the region's backroads and hiking trails doesn't require traversing busy highways or ugly exurbs, as the département is largely devoid of both.

A couple of millennia of continuous human habitation have seeded the countryside with all manner of interesting man-made things that a car traveler might easily miss: crumbling stone windmills with trees growing out of their foundations; dovecotes that once belonged to grand feudal estates; Roman-era footbridges; moss-covered mission crosses and Virgin Mary shrines, which are remnants of the various religious revivals that came on the heels of the Revolution; grass-covered earthen mounds, called *mottes castrales*, that served as village fortifications at the dawn of modern times; medieval wash basins; abandoned railroad tracks; wells; hunting blinds; cemeteries—the eye seldom wants for something to gaze at.

Modernity hasn't completely passed over the rural reaches of the Gers, but a traveler who happens onto even a substantial village or bourg is likely to encounter a quaint datedness. In the hotels and restaurants catering to the Gers's seasonal influx of mostly domestic— and occasionally English and Dutch—tourists, you might find a few Spanish dishes, but generally the specialties are Gascon, served in an ambiance that ranges from frumpy to fussy.

Because of—and, on occasion, in spite of—that, hiking through the Gers can be a very enjoyable kind of time-travel.

IT HAD BEEN QUITE A WHILE—twenty years, at least—since I'd backpacked the rural byways of France on my own. As I embarked on a two-day walk from Auch to Condom—a span of thirty-odd miles extending north from the geographical center of Gascony—I fell briefly under the spell of nostalgia. Images from my youthful travels spooled forth like flickering home movies: empty train platforms, cheap hotels, hitched rides, seedy roadside cafés, cigarettes and cheap wine, sore feet and damp clothes.

At first these recollections were like gauze draped over my eyes, filtering everything through the distorting welter of memory. After a while, though, I started to find my rhythm and tune in to my sur- roundings. I began to undergo the rejuvenating mental cleansing that comes from putting one foot in front of the other thousands of times. Also, I got reacquainted with the pleasures of solitude—I wouldn't cross another person on the trail for the entirety of my walk.

Michele had dropped me off in Castin, a village just outside of Auch, and I had set off in a northerly direction, following the direc- tions in my TopoGuide, which had surely been written by a Gascon: "Follow the lanes that snake. . . . Skew to the right and take the em-pebbled path that traverses a wooded zone. . . . At the place of the lone oak, cleave leftward to a grove of trees and a patch of fallow land."

It was fall, and the bright hues of summer had given way to gradations of ocher, beige, and brown, colors rendered more subdued by the weather, which was drizzly. The vistas that unfolded around me were stygian and lovely. Sunflowers that had been flanking the trail—which at present overlapped with a stretch of dirt road—had been recently harvested, leaving behind a strange, stippled landscape. Near the top of a gentle rise, a rain-streaked water tower, probably from the 1950s, came into view, a dour concrete monolith set against bruised clouds. It had four buttresses at the top that looked like fins on the upturned tail of a rocket. A little ways beyond, half-hidden in a grove of trees, sat the rusted hulk of a Peugeot 405. I passed the remains of what might have been a stone farm building, or maybe an old *cabane de vigneron*. For a stretch, the path descended into a tunnel of dripping bramble, then emerged into a field of tall grass, which was quite pleasurable to walk through, since someone had mowed a wide corridor so that hikers wouldn't lose their way.

The village of Lavardens, which rose from a spur of bedrock and boasted what passed in the Gers for a very large château, had been shifting, mirage-like, on the horizon for some time. And now suddenly I was upon it. At the foot of the promontory, I passed an ancient stone lavoir, where, I imagined, peasant women had once washed doublets and pantaloons.

I ate a picnic lunch in Lavardens, on a bench next to the town hall, and resumed my walk. I needed to get to Castéra-Verduzan, the nearest village down-trail with lodging, before dark. About halfway there, I veered off the path to inspect a crude stone chapel that I'd seen rising from a crinkle in the hillside. It was nothing more than four stone walls and a *clocher-mur*—the humblest kind of belfry there is, a chevron-shaped extension of the façade with an aperture punched through it, for the church bell. There was no village around the chapel, and, in fact, no other work of man at all, just trees. According to Bruno Sirven—he of the friendly hillocks and intimate valleys—at least 700 isolated *chapelles Gasconnes* are thought to still exist in the Gers. Many of them were built on the site of an even older place of worship from early-Christian times or before, often where an underground spring—apparently a sign of divine intent—bubbled forth. A soggy laminated printout tacked to the church door by the *Fondation du Patrimoine* said the edifice had been built in the twelfth century and had doubled as a defensive outpost during times of siege.

I took off my pack and sat on it, resting my feet for a spell and soaking up the quiet.

The rain had stopped. I followed a gravel road—no wider than a car's axle—over a ridge. The ceiling of clouds had risen enough to bring the farther-flung reaches of the landscape into relief. From this vantage, I could see what Sirven had described as the Gers's "sea of hills," extending into the beyond.

THE HÔTEL DES THERMES, THE only of Castéra-Verduzan's meager lodging options that appeared to be open, was, like a lot of two-star establishments in the Gers, prim and clean but showing its age. It sat at the southern end of the village's main street, next to a natural-hot-springs spa, for which the town was locally famed. The hotel's décor was a palimpsest of styles that seemed to start in the 1890s and end in the 1980s. The reception desk was fronted with wainscoted wood panels that had flowers painted on them. The adjacent restaurant was adorned with neon-hued, Leroy Neiman–type prints depicting bullfighters in balletic poses. A Victorian birdcage stood at the dining room's entrance, two lovebirds flitting about inside. And across from a small bar—which lacked stools, in the eternally vexing French tradition—a lounge area had been furnished with colorful upholstered cubes that were presumably meant to be sat on. When I checked in, tired and sore from the hike, the disheveled proprietor—perhaps because I was an American and would thus know a little something about the invisible hand of the market—complained at great length and with no prompting about the pay-to-play business of getting listed in France's major travel and dining guides. He applauded my savvy decision to stay in a place, like his, that *wasn't* listed in those publications.

After getting settled, I walked across the street to the spa. I paid a small fee to a white-clad receptionist in return for a locker key and a very small bathing suit, then spent forty minutes beneath a sparkling glass-topped rotunda in a warm soaking pool, my feet positioned in front of soothing water jets. After that, I returned to the hotel, put on fresh clothes, and proceeded to the lounge. The entirety of my evening plan consisted of a drink followed by dinner at Castéra's only other notable attraction: Le Florida, the venerated restaurant of Bernard Ramounéda, one of the Ronde des Mousquetaires chefs. I'd read that Ramounéda was rarely at the stoves anymore and that his son, Baptiste, was doing most of the day-to-day running of the place, which Bernard's grandmother, Angèle, had founded after the war, but I was still curious to try it.

Presenting myself at the Hôtel des Thermes's bar, and feeling I had earned something stronger than a watered-down pastis, I ordered a martini. It's a drink that's well known in most parts of France, if not well loved—the French generally preferring their strong spirits in the form of a *digestif.*

My request caused confusion.

Receiving silence and a furrowed brow from the shy young woman behind the bar, I described the making of the cocktail, pointing to the gin and dry vermouth that were plainly displayed on a shelf just over her left shoulder.

She chewed her lip.

I told her she could make it on the rocks and simply charge me for a double gin.

She went over to consult with a colleague who was exiting the dining room. I overheard her say, "Go find Marc." The second woman sped off.

A minute later, a pale, thin man in a black vest and bow tie strode into the room and took the girl's place behind the bar. He tamed a rogue lock of his comb-over and asked, in the most deferential possible tone, what I was having.

I explained my order again.

Marc blinked rapidly a few times and sucked his teeth. Then he tapped both hands on the bar in a decisive gesture. He put a few cubes of ice in a tall glass and added a slice of lemon. On top of that he poured just enough gin to wet the ice. I made a twirly "keep going" gesture with my forefinger. He did so, then stopped again. I twirled my finger some more. He poured some more. Now I pointed to the bottle of vermouth and held my thumb and forefinger a hair apart. He followed my instructions and slid the drink over. I took a sip and nodded.

Marc looked immensely pleased. Tapping the bar again as if he'd just made another bold decision, he pulled down a second glass and made himself a martini, too.

He produced a bowl of snack crackers and rested an elbow on the bar. "We don't get too many Americans," he said. "Mostly Dutch and English, here to take the waters."

I told him I'd just enjoyed a *détente thermale* at the spa.

"And don't you feel renewed? Rejuvenated?"

I did, as a matter of fact.

"They are quite miraculous, the waters," he said. "Famous since Roman times."

I ate a cracker.

"I do hope you'll spread the word," said Marc.

"Of course."

He topped off the snack bowl. "Will you be dining with us this evening?" he asked.

I told him that I was thinking of trying Le Florida.

His face darkened.

"It's not good?" I asked.

"You'll eat quite well there," Marc said. "But . . . " He slid the bowl aside so he could lean across the bar unimpeded. "Monsieur Ramounéda isn't well-liked around here."

I reached around him for another cracker.

"He's an excellent chef," Marc continued, "but he cut the grass from under our feet."

I said I didn't quite get his meaning.

Marc elaborated. "He started letting rooms above his restaurant to tourists, stealing our clientele. It was a dishonorable thing to do. We'd had an arrangement for many years."

I reflected on this for a moment, then asked whether Ramounéda minded that the Hôtel des Thermes had a restaurant that might attract *his* clientele.

Nettled, Marc stood up straight. "It's not the same! He's a well-known *chef gastronomique*. He already has all the customers he needs."

I gazed over at the hotel's still-empty dining room and decided to stick with my original plan. I thanked Marc for the martini.

"*Avec plaisir*," he said with what I think would qualify as a bow.

Le Florida, though it was only slightly more crowded than the hotel's restaurant, was a pleasant surprise. The typical *restaurant gastronomique* in rural southwestern France is a fusty sanctum with starchy napkins that match the drapes, the kind of place where you can inevitably hear other patrons' chewing. Le Florida was quiet, certainly, and the napkins were a little scratchy, but the dining room was inviting, with thick roof beams, exposed stone, plenty of windows, and mirrors framed in blond wood. (Michele would have approved.) Jazz emanated from a pair of tiny speakers suspended discreetly from the ceiling.

I was comfortably ensconced at a corner table, a basket of bread and a half bottle of wine in front of me, and had a nice view of the room. Two Dutch couples occupied a nearby table. I pegged them as international spa-hoppers. Across from them were, to judge from the accent, a man and a woman of more-local provenance, both middle-aged, out for a nice dinner. I could hear no one's chewing but my own.

As for the food, it achieved the rare feat, at least for a restaurant in the Gers, of treading the line between stuffy and rusticated. The demitasse of cold white bean purée, which, in an admittedly silly flourish, arrived on a slab of rough-hewn slate, was a kind of homage to the garbure, and was appropriately rich and fortifying, even though there wasn't much of it. The cumin-spiced octopus salad with pearls of couscous was urbane, but also pleasingly simple. So was the roasted guinea fowl with lacquered skin and wild rice. So was the miniature croustade, a perfectly shrink-rayed version of the ubiquitous Gascon apple tart. Overall, I realized with some amazement, it was a meal one might have been served in a bistro in a hip neighborhood in Paris, except it was much cheaper.

When I returned to the Hôtel des Thermes, the lobby was dark and empty, save for a spectral-looking Marc, who was placing a cover over the birdcage for the night. I offered a *bonsoir*, and he responded unsmilingly with another deep nod of the head.

I was the only guest at breakfast the next morning. My muscles were stiff and my shoulders felt raw where the pack's straps had rubbed at them, but I was eager to get back on the trail. I brushed crumbs from my TopoGuide and traced the day's route with my finger. More strange place names: Jamon, Bidet, Bomit, l'Inquiétude—ancient *lieu-dits* for even more-ancient settlements—and, at journey's end, Condom!

When I got outside, the streetlamps were still on. A soupy fog had descended overnight. After twenty minutes of walking, Castéra and its outskirts had completely disappeared behind me. I was alone again, on a ribbon of pebbly asphalt curving through a mist-shrouded tableau of oak groves and more stubbly fields. My muscles started to loosen up. The trail dipped between hedgerows of broom and honeysuckle. I noticed a perfectly symmetrical spiderweb stretched between two stalks of a thistle-like plant, each strand of silk glistening with dewdrops.

Soon the path diverged from the road and edged a vast vineyard. I'd entered an Armagnac-making zone known as the Ténarèze. Beyond the vineyard, arching prettily over a low hilltop, was a plum orchard—the fruit destined to become prunes, which Gascons like to soak in Armagnac mixed with sugar syrup and vanilla. Beyond that, more sunflowers, these ones still on the stalk, their heads black and drooping morosely, their seeds waiting to be hulled and pressed. A farmstead came into view on my left. In a garden some distance from the house stood dozens of staked tomato vines, all of them taller than me.

I was nearing Valence-sur-Baïse, a village that had once been protected by thick stone ramparts. Small sections of the fortifications remained. I realized I'd driven through Valence on an earlier visit to the Gers, on my way to somewhere else, but the village looked completely different to me now as I approached it on foot. I entered the medieval *centre ville* via a narrow lane that passed underneath a lancet-arched portal known, according to a plaque nearby, as the Hedgehog Gate. The plaque didn't say why it was called that.

I had a bite to eat and rejoined the trail. The sun had come out, and soon I was sweating through my shirt. As I pushed on toward Condom, I stopped to snap a photo here and there—a lichen-covered postbox in a deserted hamlet, another chapel with a clocher-mur, a quartet of enormous and very old cypress trees that had outgrown a tiny, walled cemetery. Not far outside Condom, the path took me past a grass airstrip—just a meadow, a wind sock, a mothballed two-seater, and a small building that had been locked up for the season. I peeked inside and could see a couple of café tables and a short counter with a coffee machine and a few bottles on it. Nearby, where the trail crossed a road, a weather-beaten sign was being swallowed by greenery. It had been lovingly hand-lettered—and, to judge from the outdated phone number, not recently:

AÉRODROME
tél: 28–09–06
ÉCOLE DE **PILOTAGE**
il est formellement *Interdit de Pénétrer sur* La **PISTE**
pour les **VOLS** et *visites des* **AVIONS**
Ser au **BAR**

I was mesmerized by this for some reason. I loved the sign's calligraphic panache, its quirky lettering and abbreviations, its arbitrary italicization and capitalization, its obliviousness to France's mania for standardized signage. I loved the way its huffy warning—"it is Strictly Prohibited to Set Foot on the RUNWAY"—gave way in the next breath to an invitation: Inquire about flights at the bar.

CONDOM, A BOURG OF 7,000 souls, is an unlovely place at first glance, long on auto body shops and cheap eateries and short on cozy medieval charm. Its limited offerings to the leisure traveler include a some-what high-end restaurant (which accounts for one of the Gers's three Michelin stars), the vestiges of an old bishopric, a larger-than-life bronze statue of Dumas's musketeers touching sword tips, and a mid-size cathedral, which has the not-inconsiderable distinction of serving as the venue for the most, and to my knowledge the only, glamorous social event of the year in the Gers: an annual black-tie gala called—yes—the Dîner des Mousquetaires. (It bears mention-ing that this gala is thrown by a Gascon fraternal organization whose *capitaine* is the Duc Aymeri de Montesquiou; readers may recognize the last name as that of D'Artagnan's mother, whom the duke has claimed, not without controversy, as an ancestor. I had occasion to meet this dignitary at one of the galas; he was very tan and wore a blue sash affixed to his tuxedo with a pin in the shape of a muske-teer's sword.)

If people outside of Gascony know the humble *sous-préfecture* of Condom at all, it's probably because they've seen *Le Bonheur est Dans le Pré*, a hit movie from the '90s about a middle-aged Parisian who leaves his wife for a beautiful goose farmer from the town. (The erstwhile soccer star Eric Cantona played the girl's brother, his native Marseille accent passing for a Gascon one.)

Wander around Condom for a few hours, though, with no par-ticular destination in mind, and a curious kind of beauty reveals itself. It's not the beauty of very old things restored to grandeur, like that of France's celebrated churches and châteaux. It is the beauty of moderately old things unaltered from how they've always been.

After arriving in Condom in the middle of the afternoon and checking into a cheap hotel, I explored the streets for a while, filled with a pleasant wistfulness. Here was the very kind of faded pro-vincial bourg I used to stumble on in rural France back in the day. Here was the grubby bar with its foosball table and brown-tobacco smells, the rusty security gate being noisily cranked down for the night, the narrow commercial streets with their slightly gone-to-seed '70s vibe and plastic shingle signs advertising mundane services and amenities: COIFFURE MESSIEURS, PHILDAR LAINES ET TEXTILES, CHAMBRES TOUT CONFORT.

I strolled by the locks of the canal at the edge of town, past an abattoir and a lumberyard, then circled back to the center and ascended the Rue Gambetta. Down a side street, in the window of the local chamber of commerce, someone had installed a display of black-and-white photos of a Dîner des Mousquetaires gala from the 1960s: men with shellacked hair and skinny ties squeezed in at banquet tables crowded with bottles and ashtrays. The last names of certain of the *grands hommes* in attendance had been written in grease pencil next to their likenesses—"Lapeyre," "Abeillé," "Serres," "Gerbaud," and, near the image of a young, be-sashed man, "de Montesquiou."

Michele picked me up the next morning. I had considered asking her for another day, so I could hang around Condom some more and explore its environs. But when I phoned, she sounded eager for me to come home; there was a mouse problem that needed to be dealt with, and Charlotte had caught a cold.

Being in a car again felt strange. The countryside hurtling by outside the window was like a sped-up movie of my two-day walk: hill-valley-hill-valley-hill-valley. I could see bits of old-looking structures peeking up from indentations in the landscape, and longed to know what those structures were. But they went by too fast. Before I knew it, we were back in Plaisance.

In a little over an hour, we'd crossed half the Gers.

14

Dessert

Sweets in Gascony tend to be of two varieties: the kind the average home cook might make on a whim on a Tuesday night, and the kind the average home cook would never attempt in a million years.

In the former camp dwell a multitude of simple, rustic cakes, tarts, and sweets. Take the *gâteau millasson*, for example: A flan of humble origins, it's made with nothing more than corn flour, sugar, eggs, milk, and, sometimes, orange-flower water. Or consider the *gâteau de noix*, a similarly round, low-slung confection, this one made with ground walnuts. Then there's the gâteau Basque, only slightly more complex, made with almond flour and containing a middle layer of pastry cream.

Even the gâteau Basque is so easy, in fact, that when I complimented the version Henri had served at his dinner, he insisted on coming to our house a few days later to show us how to make one. He arrived carrying all the ingredients in one of his many wicker baskets. After fifteen minutes of sifting and stirring, he popped the cake into the oven, told us to take it out in twenty-five minutes, gathered his belongings, and bid us au revoir.

Some time after that, Henri gave us another lesson, appearing at our door, again with his wicker basket, to demonstrate the making of an even simpler treat: *sucettes au caramel*. His basket contained the following items: an apple, some wood skewers, a box of sugar cubes, and a roll of aluminum foil. While Charlotte looked on, transfixed, Henri liquefied twenty-five sugar cubes in a saucepan until the syrup turned golden. Next he spread out a length of aluminum foil, halved the apple he'd brought, and placed each half, cut side down, on opposite ends of the foil to hold it in place. He dipped the ends of the wood skewers into the syrup, then laid each skewer onto the foil to let the caramel harden a bit. When he'd dipped ten skewers, he started over again with the first one, dipping it back into the caramel so that the deposit would build. After repeating this routine four or five times, he had ten half-dollar-size lollipops of translucent, sparkling amber. He stuck the suckers into the two apple halves, making a smart little candy-shop display.

Gascons have a deep fondness for easy-to-make sweets like Henri's sucettes, and so it is all the more baffling to outsiders that the most beloved of all Gascon desserts—the strudel-pastry-topped tart known as a croustade—is not remotely easy to make. In fact, during our time in Gascony I was unable to find a single home cook who was willing to show me how to prepare one. When I asked Nadine, she said, "*Ouf,* I've only made two in my life, and that's enough."

The croustade—sometimes, confusingly, called a *pastis*—was once the bailiwick of grandmothers, but even in a land that resists change as fiercely as Gascony, times have done just that. Today the making of croustades is mostly left to *pâtisseries* or, often, small-time artisans. The best croustades where we lived, it was widely agreed, came from a lady in the nearby village of Goux; she worked out of her home and, with the help of her daughter, produced six croustades per day. She occasionally did croustade-making demos at village fêtes, and, having seen one such exhibition, I can say that six croustades per day is a heroic output.

The vexing challenges of making a proper croustade lie, in roughly equal measure, in the correct fabrication of the building material—that is, the strudel-pastry dough—and in the construction of the tart itself. The most famously tricky part is the rolling out of the dough: A grapefruit-size ball of it must be transformed into a translucently thin sheet that's large enough to cover a large card table—a process that demands constant but gentle tugging around the edges until the dough sheet is hanging slightly off all four sides of the table, upon which it is carefully trimmed. For the dough to withstand such extreme stretching, it has to be made with a special kind of unbleached flour, and it must be worked over like a punching bag. All the while, accommodations must be made for fluctuations in humidity, temperature, and, when working in certain environments, breezes.

Assuming one succeeds in stretching the dough, having taken care to avoid creating holes or other irregularities, the building of the tart itself can begin. This task requires of the baker an origami artist's precision. The dough sheet must be cut into strips and very quickly—time being of the essence, on account of how quickly a see-through dough sheet dries out—brushed with clarified butter and laid into the bottom of a greased tart pan in an overlapping radial pattern. This done, the tart can be filled, usually with a mixture of cooked apples, sugar, and sometimes Armagnac-prune syrup (which must be made no fewer than two weeks in advance, to allow the prunes and sugar to properly meld). Now the baker may begin pulling the overhanging ends of the dough strips up over the filling, twisting each strip's end in such a way as to create a shape reminiscent of a rose. Once this step has been repeated with all the dough strips, the croustade gets dusted with confectioners' sugar (and, if desired, spritzed with Armagnac) and baked until its coiffure of strudel flower petals is crisp and golden.

If it all comes off, the result, it has to be said, is sublime. A true Gascon croustade is a textural masterpiece: The crackly outer layers of the petals shatter at the touch of the fork, which then travels through the strudel's slightly softer, more caramelized precincts, into the just-barely-firm filling, and finally through the crunchy-chewy crust. An optional dollop of sweetened crème fraîche or a scoop of ice cream will introduce an unctuous medium in which the sugar-crusted pastry shards can swim and mingle. That is a beautiful sight indeed.

There is, as far as I know, only one country-style dessert known to the denizens of Southwest France that requires more patience in the making—if slightly less fine-motor dexterity—than the croustade. The tall, conical, hearth-baked confection known as *gâteau à la broche*, "cake on a spit," resided at one time, like the croustade, in the culinary repertoire of many a Gascon grandmother. Believed by most locals to have originated somewhere deep in the Pyrenees—though versions of the cake show up in other parts of Europe where there are mountains—the gâteau à la broche is a relic of the open-hearth-cooking epoch. But these days, owing to a decline in old women willing to spend an entire afternoon drizzling cake batter onto a hand-turned spit in front of a very hot fire, the fabrication of this dessert has fallen almost entirely to professional bakers, who generally rely on electric or gas rotisserie ovens to do the job. Even so, store-bought cakes are very expensive, as each one requires un-

interrupted tending over several hours and, thus, a generous alloca-
tion of paid labor.

All that being said, a few tradition-bound holdouts making
gâteau à la broche in front of *la cheminée* can still be found.

HERE ARE THE INGREDIENTS FOR Marinette Lagors's gâteau à la broche:
thirty-six eggs, three pounds of butter, three pounds of flour, three
pounds of sugar, ten packets of vanilla-sugar, one cup of dark rum,
one handful of pulverized roasted hazelnuts (preferably from your
own hazelnut tree), a generous pinch of salt (preferably from an ancient tin salt cellar nailed to the kitchen wall), and six egg whites for
the icing. All these supplies had been laid out on Madame Lagors's
kitchen table, suggesting a baking project of industrial proportions.

Marinette Lagors—no relation to Alain, the local historian—
was the stepmother of Alphonse, my pal from the Esbouhats. She
was ninety-four years old and lived with Alphonse's stepbrother in
Vic-en-Bigorre, a town on the main route between Plaisance and
the mountains. Alphonse referred to her simply as Mamie. At one of
the Esbouhats dinners, Alphonse had shown me cell-phone photos of
Mamie's homemade gâteau and had promised that he would take me
to see her one day so that we could make one. What I didn't realize
until that day came was that Mamie no longer did the baking. Too
frail to crack an egg, she had passed the torch to her son and stepson.

This gâteau à la broche—in a departure from centuries of
tradition—would be an all-male undertaking.

When Alphonse and I arrived at Mamie's house, his stepbrother,
whose name was Michel, was out back splitting wood. He sunk the
ax into a stump and came over to shake my hand. Bald and stocky,
with two-day stubble and hands like catcher's mitts, Michel was
Alphonse's coarser alter ego.

Alphonse looked at the pile of split logs and told Michel that we'd need a lot more. The two men argued about this for several minutes. Then Alphonse took me inside to meet Mamie.

He led me into a chintz-wallpapered living room. Mamie was asleep in an enormous recliner in front of the fireplace, her lap covered by an afghan, her toes by crocheted foot-warmers. She looked elfin and tiny.

Before waking her, Alphonse warned me that her hearing was poor, as was her eyesight, and that one had to shout to be heard.

Alphonse squeezed Mamie's arm and shook it gently. A pair of bright, bead-like eyes blinked open. He leaned in close and announced that she had a guest.

Mamie smiled at me and reached for my hand.

"What a handsome young man," she whispered.

I took the compliment for what it was worth.

Alphonse's wife, Lorette, had just arrived and was in the kitchen, unpacking an enormous picnic basket containing the makings of lunch. The amount of food she was taking out augured well for the meal.

Michel came in, and we got started on the cake batter. It was a relatively simple one, notable mainly for how much of it there was.

Michel and I started cracking the eggs into an immense earthenware bowl. This took quite some time. Alphonse melted the bricks of butter in a pan and then set the pan in a cold-water bath to cool. Alphonse and Michel bickered ceaselessly—about just how cool the butter had to be before being added to the bowl, about how much sugar they had or hadn't already used, about whether to pour in the rum before or after the hazelnuts, and, most histrionically, about how fast to add the flour. The flour-sifting, I surmised, was a long-standing source of friction between the stepbrothers. Michel, who was stirring the batter with a long wooden spoon in the same way one might tend to a bubbling cauldron, was urging Alphonse to dispense with the sifting altogether and just pour in the flour.

"Hurry up, *bordel*!" he snapped.

Alphonse ignored him and continued his sifting, the flour swirling into the thickening mixture in a cyclone pattern.

Bad enough to see two grown men argue over cake batter, but when it came time to prepare the cake mold—a conical length of blackened pear wood with an iron handle inserted in the blunt end—they literally came to blows, whacking each other's hands away as they secured parchment paper around the mold with kitchen twine.

"*Putain*," I heard Alphonse say, "you have to tie it like a roast, not a Christmas present!"

Now Michel started hauling in firewood. I have to say, it was some of the most expertly split wood I'd ever seen: dozens and dozens of near-identical pieces, each no wider than a baseball bat. Meanwhile, I helped Alphonse set up the spit assembly—two iron posts with cradles like upside-down coat hooks, for resting the cake mold in—over by the fireplace.

Lorette announced it was time to eat. The spread she had put out—in the same room where Mamie was sleeping—was a fine one indeed: sausage-and-puff-pastry canapés (which, I explained, to everyone's amusement, were known in America as pigs in a blanket), slices of ham that Alphonse had cured himself, blinis topped with crème fraîche and smoked salmon, steamed potatoes, and *rouleaux* of beef tripe in tomato sauce.

The prospect of lunch seemed to cool the internecine flames. Michel and Alphonse went over to Mamie and gently woke her up. Alphonse pressed a button at the base of the recliner, and its back rose with an electric whir. Then he and Michel slid Mamie to the head of the table. Dwarfed by her enormous chair, she took on a strangely imperial air.

Alphonse served apéros: a finger of Long John whiskey for the men, a glass of white wine for Lorette, and, for Mamie, a healthy dose of Suze with crème de cassis, served in a cordial glass. Then some wine was opened, and we started in on lunch.

At the risk of overstating the matter, I would like to pause for a moment to marvel, once again, at the Gascon appetite. It is one thing to witness thick-necked rugby men devour great amounts of food in a short amount of time. It is quite another to see a ninety-four-year-old woman do so. The quick work Mamie made of her lunch—two helpings of everything, each portion as big as my own, though consumed in smaller pieces—constituted one of the most amazing food-vanishing acts I'd ever seen. This feat, though, was merely an example of a broader phenomenon, which is this: When it comes to eating, Gascon women are no less valiant than the men. In my experience, they do not ever order appetizers as a main course or consider a salad—even a salade Gersoise—a full dinner. They eat with the same delight and stealthy alacrity as their husbands, brothers, fathers, and sons.

We spent a good hour and a half at the table that afternoon, though Mamie had to have a catnap before dessert and coffee. During the meal, I learned that Alphonse and Lorette had run a funeral parlor near Paris for many years before coming back to their native Gascony to retire. This revelation was unexpected for two reasons. First, Alphonse and Lorette were the least undertaker-like people I'd ever met. Second, it is unusual to hear a Gascon mention his work. What one does for a living is, at best, a fifth- or sixth-rung conversation topic, something to fall back on after the subjects of food, wine, rugby, bullfighting, and weather have been exhausted, and usually in that order. I was flattered that Alphonse had decided to share.

ALPHONSE DESCRIBED THE MAKING OF gâteau à la broche as a three-person job: one to turn the spit, one to drizzle the batter, one to feed the fire. Michel, he said, was going to be on fire detail. Alphonse would drizzle. I'd be the spit-turner.

Foretelling the nature of the toil that lay ahead, Alphonse had stripped to his undershirt. I did the same. Michel was adding more wood to the fire, banking the freshly split pieces against the back of the hearth to create a wall of heat. Mamie was snoring away, having been returned to her usual spot. A nap sounded extremely appealing.

Alphonse told me to set the parchment-covered mold into its cradle to let it heat up. After a minute or two, greasy splotches spread across the paper. Alphonse explained that this was melted butterfat from gâteaux of yore, seeping out from deep within the wood's grain. The mold, he said, was more than one hundred years old.

Michel set two chairs in front of the fireplace, one for me and one for Alphonse. The hearth was small, maybe two feet wide at its opening, but Michel had turned it into a furnace. Within seconds of sitting down, I felt as if my face and kneecaps were being scorched.

Lorette brought Alphonse and me each a bottle of water and urged me to keep drinking while we worked.

I asked Alphonse how long the process would take, but he didn't seem to hear me. He was already in the zone, carefully placing a metal drip tray underneath the mold and then situating the bowl of batter between his feet. The batter was the color and consistency of puréed bananas.

Alphonse turned to me now. In his right hand, scepterlike, was a spoon affixed to a long wooden dowel. "Do an eighth of a turn at a time," he said. "And very slowly. Once we start, we have to keep going. If we stop, the batter will burn or fall off the mold."

And so our work began.

Alphonse dipped the spoon into the batter and started depositing a thick layer of it across the top of the mold. I gave the spit an eighth of a turn. Alphonse added more batter. By the time the spit had made a full rotation, the first layer had turned golden, a little like a waffle, and the points where the batter had started to drip off the mold had become firm, like stalactites. Alphonse referred to these drippy protrusions as *pics*.

"Beautiful pics," he said, "are the sign of a real gâteau à la broche."

We worked without a break, pausing only long enough for Michel to lay more wood on the fire. Slowly, as more layers of batter were applied, the cake got thicker. I finished my water in short order. Lorette brought me and Alphonse small bottles of beer. I don't recall what kind it was, but it was the most refreshing beer I've ever had.

After a while, I asked Alphonse if we could switch roles. Turning the spit was getting boring, and Mamie's snoring had me on the verge of dozing off. I'd been studying Alphonse's technique and had determined that the proper application of the batter required jiggling the spoon almost imperceptibly while tilting it toward the vertical in the tiniest increments as it moved from left to right along the length of the mold.

Alphonse handed me the spoon. "*Vas-y.*"

I dipped the spoon in the batter and tipped it ever so gently over the top of the mold. The entire gooey mass fell off in an ugly glop. The batter was like liquid concrete.

Alphonse motioned for me to hand back the spoon. "It takes practice," he said.

This cake was too far along to risk letting an amateur screw it up.

Alphonse grew reflective after a while. "In Mamie's day," he said, tipping the spoon over the cake for the umpteenth time, "the women would spend a whole Sunday afternoon working like this in front of the fire while the men played cards. I can still remember that."

I suggested that the men had it pretty good.

"Not even grandmas have time to make gâteau à la broche anymore," he said. Then he gave a mirthless laugh. "Just retirees."

It was nearly five o'clock by the time the batter was gone. We'd been working in front of the fireplace for two and a half hours. I touched my eyebrows to make sure they were still there. The cake had grown to the size of a small Christmas tree. Alphonse wrapped his hands in dish towels and lifted the mold off its supports. He removed the handle from the base, and set the mold upright in the middle of the dining table. It was a thing to see: a three-foot-tall vertical cake, bristling with pics that had turned deep golden at the tip.

Alphonse and I stood there for a few moments, admiring our creation, then he yelled into the kitchen for Lorette to bring out the egg whites, which she'd whipped until they were very fluffy.

While Michel held up a bed sheet to protect Mamie, who hadn't stirred since lunchtime, Alphonse and I whipped handfuls of the egg whites at the cake. They landed with a splat and, as the cake was still hot, cooked on contact, creating lacy patterns that looked like hoarfrost, enhancing the Christmas-tree effect.

Getting the gâteau home was a delicate operation. The cake couldn't be covered or wrapped, as the airy pics broke off very easily. We carried the confection, naked to the elements, to Alphonse's car, and I held it carefully between my knees in the passenger seat, the base of the mold planted on the floor, the tip gripped in my hands. It was the most nervous car ride I'd had since driving Charlotte home from the hospital after she was born.

A proper gâteau à la broche has to set for at least a couple of days before being removed from the mold. So Alphonse and I decided to unveil our dessert two days later, at the Esbouhats' Friday night dinner. At the end of the meal, I helped him lift the cake gently from the mold and peel the parchment paper from the cavity. We sliced the cake crosswise into rings, which we doled out on paper plates. Every cross-section of cake revealed a fine pattern of concentric inner rings, each one representing a single full turn of the spit. The pieces looked a little like a finely marbled pound cake.

How did it taste? Improvidently rich, which is an attribute one might reasonably expect in a dessert made with thirty-six eggs and three pounds of butter. But the cake had a surprisingly light, melt-away quality, too, and it was only mildly sweet. In fact, it could have used a dusting of confectioners' sugar or a drizzle of honey. But I didn't mention it.

The gâteau was a crowd-pleaser. Alphonse and I got quite a few compliments. At one point Basso, crumbs in his mustache, shouted to me across the table, "Eh oh! You and your boyfriend should open a bakery!"

15

A Day in the Vines

Like a lot of outsiders stunned by the richness of the food in South-west France, I initially dismissed as apocryphal the claim that Gascons live considerably longer than their countrymen. But when I did the research, the numbers held up. According to the Institut National de la Statistique et des Études Économiques—a.k.a. Insée, France's all-seeing census bureau—the residents of Midi-Pyrénées, which encompasses most of Gascony, enjoy the longest lifespan of all of France's regional populations, living a full ten years more, on average, than the natives of France's choucroute-loving Northeast. If you drill down on the numbers a little further, the Gers in particular starts to look like an anomaly within that happy anomaly. According to Roger Corder, the British researcher and red wine enthusiast, when you control for regional migration men in the Gers have the highest relative longevity of any département in France.

It's also worth noting that the Southwest is where the French scientist Serge Renaud decided to focus his field work for his 1992 study on French cardiovascular health. Renaud had become globally famous the year before, after appearing in the TV series *60 Minutes* to discuss his earlier research on what had come to be called the French Paradox. (The segment, which included a sociable interview by Morley Safer over what by all appearances was a magnificent French lunch, became a minor television event that sent thousands of Americans rushing out to buy cases of red wine and wheels of Brie.) What Renaud discovered in his follow-up study was, effectively, that the Southwest is the statistical epicenter of the French Paradox, with the lowest incidence of heart attacks in the country, and one of the lowest in the Western world—on the whole, residents of Midi-Pyrénées had four times fewer heart attacks than their counterparts in the United States and Britain, despite a diet rich in fats. Suddenly a lot of attention was being paid to the life habits of Gascons, particularly what they ate and drank. Was it the polyphenols in tannat wine grapes? Was it the lipid profile of duck fat, which is high in good HDL cholesterol? Was it the iron content of foie gras? The winegrowers favored one argument, the duck farmers another. Meanwhile, the Gascons kept on eating and drinking as they always had.

The hype about longevity and health in the Southwest has died down since then, though local newspapers still run an obligatory article on the subject when the Insée numbers come out every few years, confirming anew the Midi-Pyrénées' hold on the longevity title.

I hadn't come to Gascony to conduct a study, but I did have quite a bit of time to collect anecdotal evidence, and the more I got to know the Gascons, the more I came to believe that, as is the case with so many things in life, their secret lies not in any single choice or habit but in a whole bunch of converging factors. Certainly, inhabiting a rural place, with much fresh air and little urban stress, has something to do with Gascons' well-being. As does, without a doubt, having lots of family and friends close by. And diet can't be discounted—though, to my mind, what Gascons eat and drink counts for less than *how* they eat and drink. Gascons aren't excessive imbibers, village fêtes notwithstanding, and they seldom drink or snack between meals. When they do sit down for lunch or supper, they tend to eat what they like, and as much as they like, and they don't hurry things.

And yet, over time, I couldn't help but think there was something intrinsically different about the Gascons, something in their physical and emotional makeup that set them apart from their compatriots. I could see it in their even-tempered demeanor, in their generosity, in their work ethic, in their attitude toward life—especially the equable way they dealt with its vexations and hardships, whether a broken sewer pump or the death of a spouse. As different as they were from one another, the Gascons I knew—Henri, Nadine, Patrick, Dubosc, Alphonse, and the rest—all seemed equally comfortable in their skin.

ERIC FITAN, A VIGNERON INTRODUCED to me by André Dubosc, did not at first glance appear to possess a Gascon's robust constitution. He was quiet and self-effacing, verging on obsequious. At Dubosc's suggestion, Eric had invited me to take part in the wine harvest, a rite of passage I'd somehow missed out on in my younger expat days. Dubosc had described Eric in heroic terms. "He is one of our best, a true *passioné*," he told me. "The Gers needs more men like him."

When I arrived at Eric's vineyard, a few pickers, stirring amid the greenery, were already at work. I approached one of them, a heavyset Gascon in a stained T-shirt, and asked where I could find Eric Fitan. He pointed down a vine row to a tall, ungainly figure dumping a bucket of grapes into a steel hopper attached to a tractor.

Dubosc had mentioned that Eric had been a doctoral student in engineering at a prestigious university in Toulouse but had returned to the Gers to take over his family's farm and vineyard. And indeed the young winegrower, who wore wire-rim glasses and had school-boy bangs, looked the part of a nerd more than that of a paysan. When I introduced myself, he shook my hand in a gentle and seemingly un-Gascon way.

Handing me a pair of pruning shears and a bucket, Eric informed me, with a slightly pained expression, that by law he wasn't allowed to pay me for my work but that I was cordially invited to have lunch with him and his parents at the family homestead. I considered this more than fair remuneration.

Eric led me into the vines and showed me how to snip the grape clusters at the base of the stem, where it joined the vine branch, explaining that I had to take care not to damage the fruit.

"Otherwise it will begin macerating too soon," he said, and then laughed nervously. "And we don't want that."

Picking grapes, though it has inspired much romantic imagery in movies and wine-marketing campaigns, is devilishly hard work. To reach the fruit, one has the choice of either squatting or bending over. For a while I squatted, but my knees did not take well to that at all. So I switched to bending, which, after a vine row's worth of toil, caused my lower back to twitch painfully. I observed the other pickers, most of whom, to my surprise, were a good deal older and, I dare say, less fit-looking than me. Some were squatting, others were bending. None of them looked remotely uncomfortable.

On the contrary, they were quite spry. Every minute or so, one of them would shout *seau!*—which means "bucket"—and Eric would jog over to replace the full receptacle with an empty one. The frequency with which that word was being shouted was astonishing. Each of the other pickers was filling three or four buckets for every one of mine. What's more, in true Gascon fashion, they talked nonstop while they worked, tossing free-form *aperçus* across the vines in buoyant patois.

"Word is, the Chinese are making wine in Mongolia . . ."

"They say the wood pigeons are passing late this year . . ."

"Our grandkids can kiss social security good-bye . . ."

"Used to see more kinds of insects in the vines . . ."

"Global warming . . ."

"Yep."

Before long, my neck and forehead were sticky with sweat, and my hands were black with dried grape juice—snipping the fruit without breaking the skins was harder than it looked, as the grapes were ripe to bursting.

"*Pas très beau ça,*" remarked one of the pickers on seeing the mushy mess in my bucket. Not a pretty sight.

At one point late in the morning, Eric came rushing over to me. "Ah *non!*" he said as I was about to snip off a cluster of grapes. "Not those, not those!"

He plucked a leaf from the vine in front of me and tried to show me how it was subtly different from the five-lobed leaves of the vine next to it, but I was having trouble seeing the distinction.

"You have to watch out for ones like this," Eric said. "It's not tannat."

"What is it?"

"Who knows. This plot was planted eighty-five years ago."

Eric explained that old indigenous grape varietals were still insinuated amid the tannat vines, a harkening back to the bad old days when paysans got paid by the hectoliter, no matter what went into the press.

"Back then," Eric said, "they just wanted to *faire pisser les vignes*."

That literally meant "make the vines piss," which called to mind the expression Dubosc had used for bad wine: vin à faire pisser.

None of it sounded very thirst-quenching.

At twelve o'clock sharp, we broke for lunch. While the other workers unpacked picnics, Eric and I drove the mile or so to his parents' house on his tractor, with me hanging off the side, feet planted on the running board.

A PROPER VIGNERON LUNCH IS a wonderful thing, especially during the *vendanges*, and especially in Gascony. The homemade confit comes out, the vin maison is opened, and the feasting is set to. The Fitan family's meal was true to this tradition, and extra-special in my opinion because the confit in question wasn't duck but goose: two enormous magrets—each nearly twice the size of a duck breast— sliced into thick slabs that looked like corned beef but tasted much better. At that moment it struck me as sad that the raising of geese, once the preeminent waterfowl in southwestern France, has been relegated to something of a niche pursuit, the realm of nostalgists and stubborn holdouts, since geese are harder to breed and require much more time and finesse to fatten than the modern moulard crossbreed.

In Gascony, at any given domestic meal, it is common to be in the presence of several generations of family, including, not infrequently, great-grandparents. The Fitans' particular contribution to the Gers's longevity ranking was Eric's *papi*, a diminutive nonagenarian in bedroom slippers and a buttoned-to-the-top plaid shirt.

When Eric mentioned that I was American, his grandfather laid a hand on my forearm and squeezed.

"We have much to thank you for," he said, looking at me with an earnestness that set me back on my heels.

"Papi was in the Résistance," Eric said.

"You Americans saved our hides," said Papi. "Was your grandfather in the war?"

I said he wasn't.

Papi gave a blasé chin-thrust and reached for his glass.

Eric's father, a lean, cowboy-like fellow in jeans and work boots who looked not all that much older than Eric, had poured a ceremonial round of juice from the previous day's harvest. After a morning in the sun-broiled vines, it tasted like the most sublime nectar.

Now a tureen of garbure was being passed around. This was followed by a piperade, then a sculptural salad worthy of a '50s-era *Better Homes* cookbook, consisting of an elongated mound of tuna covered in homemade mayonnaise and garnished around the edges with crumbled hard-boiled eggs. It looked questionable but tasted very good. And, finally, the goose confit.

I ate and drank, then ate and drank some more, pausing occasionally to observe the customary, quietly awesome display of Gascon voracity, Eric's granddad showing himself to be the most dedicated *gourmand* of the family.

Lunch concluded with rice pudding and glasses of cold Pacherenc, and straightaway I found myself in the familiar post–Gasconlunch dilemma of wanting very badly to go to sleep just as everyone else was preparing to get back to work. I have yet to figure out what metabolic quirk allows Gascons to avoid this problem.

Making my pace look even more glacial than before, Eric and his field hands fell to their afternoon tasks with renewed verve, mowing through the vine rows even faster than they had in the morning, the effervescence of their banter undiminished.

Eric had mentioned that six o'clock was quitting time, and as the hour approached, the pickers' pace—though I didn't think this was possible—accelerated further. It seemed we were getting close to finishing the entire vineyard parcel, and esprit de corps dictated that we buckle down.

And so it was that we finished picking the last row of vines at the stroke of six. Afterward, the whole crew repaired to Eric's parents' house for a round of floc. I was crushingly tired. If any of the others were too, none showed it. Everyone was talking with great enthusiasm about what they were going to have for dinner.

Before I went home, Eric showed me around the half-finished house he was building for his family just a few hundred yards from the one he grew up in. We walked through empty rooms coated in plaster dust and smelling of caulk.

Eric showed me the kitchen cupboards he'd installed the night before, and then pointed to some Sheetrock he was going to hang tonight.

I asked if he'd be back in the vines tomorrow.

"As soon as it's light."

There were two more plots to be picked, he said, and the harvest had to be completed by week's end, as rain was forecast for the weekend.

I asked, not the least bit sarcastically, when he found time to sleep.

Eric smiled, looking unsure of what to say, as if I'd posed a trick question.

As we walked back to my car, a couple of Eric's dogs at our heels, Eric casually related to me how, in addition to working full-time as a vigneron, he raised corn and livestock, served as the president of a local growers' association, and led a bandas orchestra called Les Dandys d'Armagnac.

Eric shook my hand and promised to send me a bottle of the

year's *milléssime* as soon as it was ready. (I have since had a chance to taste the wine made from the grapes we harvested on the Fitan property, and though there is a petty side of me that would rather not say so, given everything else Eric has clearly got going for him, it was excellent.)

That night, after putting Charlotte to bed, I recounted my experience to Michele, emphasizing, with only slight exaggeration, that Eric Fitan probably got more done in a day than I did in a week. I also confessed to her that Gascons, as much as I loved them, sometimes had a way of making me feel like a wimp and, on occasion, a less than fully actualized paterfamilias.

Michele, who didn't typically indulge self-pity, generously offered that, grape-picking aside, she thought I'd been doing a pretty good impression of a Gascon overall.

16

Slow and Low

At some point over the past century, Americans decided that, when it came to cooking meats, they were in a hurry. The result is that today, stewing, simmering, and braising have taken a backseat to searing, roasting, and grilling. Beef stew, pot roast, and other venerable dishes of the slow-cooked variety have come to be regarded as old-timey comfort foods, edged out by the more-fashionable steak, tenderloin, and fillet. This is probably because Americans in the postwar era suddenly had quite a bit more money and quite a bit less time than their forebears and thus developed a taste for costlier, more tender cuts of meat, the kind that taste good after just a brief encounter with a hot oven, grill top, or skillet.

Gascons have never fully made that shift. Though they'll toss meat on the grill in the summertime, and roast a chicken at almost any time of year, in a Gascon kitchen no implement is more cherished than the cast-iron Dutch oven, known in France as a *cocotte*—that magical, heat-trapping vessel in which even the most sinewy cuts can be gentled into tender submission over time, their well-worked muscle fibers softening, the collagen in their connective tissue breaking down to thicken the cooking liquid, which, in Gascony, is usually wine.

Gascons are some of the world's most committed practitioners of slow-and-low cooking, with an emphasis on slow. I've come across recipes that call for two-, three-, even four-day regimens of simmering, skimming, cooling, and reheating. Gascons favor different kinds of braises for different kinds of foods. For game birds, there's the salmis, which calls for oven-browning the birds and then napping them in a wickedly dark red-wine sauce fortified with the animal's giblets. For game of the mammalian variety—namely hare and wild boar—there is the civet, a stew traditionally thickened with the animal's blood. For beef (and more specifically, during the season of le corrida, bull meat) there is the daube, which in my book is the mother of all stews: a red-wine braise, popular across much of France's southern tier, that's rich enough to conquer the most wretchedly raw winter nights.

Most people tend to associate hearty braises with a particular kind of weather, but it must be noted that in Gascony the weather is, to use a phrase favored by a friend of mine in Auch, *pas certain*. By which he means, you can't count on it. In general it is cool and wet in spring, except when it's not. Summers are hot and dry— usually—with the rains typically ending no later than July 1, though sometimes it can be as late as August 1 or, as was the case during our stay, September 1. Fall will often start off with several weeks of California-like sunshine—a localized Indian summer known in some years as *l'été Gascon*—but by November, or sometimes as early as October, the warm weather gives way to low skies and daylong drizzles. December is extremely cloudy and dark, though when we were there, I recall walking in shirtsleeves under a sparkling sky on the solstice. January and February are, as a rule, the rainiest months; this is when many rivers in the Gers, including the Arros, routinely overflow their banks. (Henri showed me a photo, taken the previous year, of our beloved moulin inundated up to the windowsills.) Very rarely, it snows.

This is all to say, Gascons make stews and braises in virtually any kind of weather, even during the sultry days of summer, when daube de taureau is a menu-du-jour staple. For my part, I could not bring myself to inaugurate our Le Creuset cocotte until it got properly cold out—which it ultimately did, and quite suddenly, too, at which point our friend Fred's dark prophecy about how chilly we'd be in the moulin quickly proved true.

During our first cold week—which began with a delivery of fresh firewood from Henri, who'd arrived in our driveway in the company of a farmer towing a trailer-load of knotty logs behind a De Gaulle–era tractor—I decided to embark on the making of wine-braised duck legs. I'd come across a recipe that suggested an interesting twist to the browning of the meat, which is the first step in almost any braise. For this version, the browning process began with a flourish: I was to flambé the duck legs in Armagnac.

Somehow, in all my years of cooking, I had never flambéed anything before. With the first batch of duck legs, I was too timid with the brandy, calling forth only the most ephemeral flicker of orange along the edge of the pan. With the second batch, though, I achieved a spectacular column of flames. Charlotte, viewing the spectacle from her usual perch behind the staircase railing, clapped.

As with many Gascon soups and stews, the flavor base for this dish was a fine hash of aromatics and fatty pork—in this case shallots, garlic, and fatback. To make the hachis I again conscripted our

Moulinex, which, despite its being exceedingly difficult to clean, had earned my respect; the appliance was small, but its tiny and stubbornly stuck blade delivered incredibly uniform results. Like the duck legs themselves, the hachis had to be browned in a pan—those caramelized flavors created by direct-heat cooking being essential to the character of the braise. Then I added a little flour and began to pour in the red wine ever so slowly, stirring all the while. At length the sauce became smooth, shiny, and as thick as porridge. I put the browned duck legs into the cocotte along with a bundle of herbs and some salt and pepper, and poured the sauce over the top. Then I set the covered cocotte over low heat to cook for an hour, just until the sauce started to percolate. Finally, I took the cocotte off the heat, let it cool down, and slid it into the fridge.

Two more days of mothering lay ahead.

The benefits of a multiday braise are simple enough: The overnight chilling allows the fat to rise and congeal so that it can be popped off the surface of the cooking liquid effortlessly, like a layer of candle wax, making for a more refined sauce, while the gentle and repeated reheating of the tightly covered cocotte at a relatively low temperature causes the meat's muscle fibers to relax and soften to an exceptional sumptuousness—that is, provided the simmer is never allowed to accelerate to a boil, at which point those muscle fibers may shrink and tighten like banjo strings, making for much desultory chewing at the dinner table. Meanwhile, during all that simmering, the moisture and mild acidity from the cooking liquid—in this case the wine—causes the collagen in the meat to turn into gelatin, which is what thickens the braise and gives the sauce its luscious, enrobing qualities.

To rush any part of this process—by heating or chilling too quickly, by applying too much heat, by shortening the cooking time—is to risk ending up with a pot full of stringy meat and hot wine.

So, bear all that in mind when I say this about my wine-braised duck legs: I tried. I really did. Overcoming my hard-wired predilection for rushing things, for blasting the heat to finish the job in time for dinner, for boiling when simmering would do, I followed the slow-and-low precepts as faithfully as I could for two days. But on the third day, with the dinner hour upon us, I found myself caught short—I'd forgotten to take the duck out of the fridge earlier in the afternoon to let it warm up gently before reheating, and so I cheated on the final step, placing the still-cold duck into the oven and bumping up the heat to compensate, not wanting to delay the meal.

We had Patrick and Arnaud over that night. Like Henri and Monique, they heaped praise upon my creation. But though the braise was full of flavor, I couldn't help but think the whole dish felt more like duck pieces with a tasty sauce around them rather than a truly harmonious union. Also, the duck was still a little tough. It should have fallen apart at the sight of a knife, but instead I had to saw at it a bit. This didn't seem possible after three days of cooking, but such is the nature of muscular moulard duck legs.

The next morning I put the leftovers into a low oven and warmed them for an hour and a half so that we could have them for lunch. And wouldn't you know it: On the fourth day, the duck was perfect.

MICHELE AND I DECIDED TO throw a party for Charlotte's seventh birthday. To date, our entertaining at the moulin had consisted of having couples over for quiet meals or drinks. It was time to break out the champagne flutes and invite a crowd—a small one, at least.

For dinner, it was decided: I would make a beef daube. In light of the shortcomings of my earlier braise, I considered my methodology carefully, studying at great length the recipes for *daube de boeuf à la*

Gasconne and *daube de boeuf à la Béarnaise*—both versions of roughly the same dish—that I had on hand.

The longest one, no surprise, appeared in Wolfert's book. She attributed her daube recipe to none other than Plaisance's own Maurice Coscuella, who in his early days had apparently built much of Le Ripa Alta's reputation on the strength of this dish. The recipe was baroque in its complexity. It called for three days of marinating and four kinds of beef—short rib, bottom round, chuck, and a piece of shin with its marrow—plus a pig's foot, which had to be cooked on its own, deboned, and diced. It also suggested lining the cast-iron cocotte with pork rind; separating out the marinating liquid and reducing it; sprinkling the meat and vegetables with Armagnac halfway through cooking; sealing the lid of the cocotte with a paste of flour, water, and oil; puréeing a third of the cooked vegetables and a third of the cooked meat with the beef marrow; and straining the marrow mixture over the remaining, unpuréed meat and vegetables. This was an ostentatiously chef-y daube.

By contrast, "La Daube d'Odette"—one of the recipes that Alain Lagors had collected from Gascon housewives—instructed the cook to do nothing more than brown chunks of brisket and some carrots in duck fat and simmer it all in red wine for an afternoon, with no marinating or reducing or puréeing. Falling somewhere in between those two was Simin Palay, who suggested, curiously, adding lemon juice and veal cheeks, and also lining the pot with greased butcher paper and nestling the vessel in a bed of hot coals. Always with the hot coals, this guy.

To muddle things further, I happened to run into Coscuella in town later that day. I made a quip about curling up next to the fire to read his epic daube recipe. The joke fell flat.

"You're going to make a daube?" he asked.

I told him I was.

The chef leaned toward me in that I'm-about-to-lay-some-wisdom-on-you Gascon way. "There's nothing to it," he said. "You cut up some carrots and leeks"—he made chopping motions with a stubby hand—"and throw them in the cocotte with the chunks of beef. Then you cover it all with red wine and cook it over low heat for a few hours."

"That's it?"

"You can throw in a veal knuckle if you want."

I asked him about the puréeing and the reducing and the pig's foot.

"No need for it."

Somehow, with the passage of years, Coscuella's recipe had shrunk from three pages to three sentences.

After thinking it over for a while, I decided to follow a middle road. I took the simplest recipe—La Daube d'Odette—and then appended to it those ingredients and techniques that I deemed worthy of cherry-picking from the others. Did I really need four kinds of beef? Having admired the gorgeous, fat-streaked slabs of *poitrine de boeuf* behind the glass case at Boucherie Cugini, I figured that in my case brisket alone would probably do just fine. And was it really necessary to marinate the meat and vegetables for three whole days? I decided that with good-quality brisket twenty-four hours would suffice. On the other hand, did I really want to skip browning the meat, as Coscuella had so breezily suggested? That seemed like one shortcut too many. Finally, I figured that if I cooked the wine-marinated meat a day ahead, gave it an overnight rest in the fridge, skimmed the fat, and reacquainted it with heat in the slowest and gentlest possible manner over the course of a second afternoon, I would get more than satisfactory results.

And so I arrived at a happy medium. Nadine would have been proud: I hadn't dispensed with cookbooks altogether, but for all intents and purposes I was cooking—to borrow a favorite expression of hers—*au bout du nez*: "From the tip of the nose," which is to say (to give a more idiomatic translation) "from the gut."

Two days before the party I drove to Boucherie Cugini to buy the meat. The same young guy who had served me before took my order and cleavered a fine piece of brisket into handsome, uniform chunks.

I took the meat home, seasoned it, and put it into the cocotte. Then I chopped some leeks and garlic and threw those in, along with a few sprigs of thyme and parsley and a bay leaf.

Charlotte got home from school in time for the fun part. I opened a bottle of Madiran and told her to pour it in.

"The whole bottle?" she asked.

"The whole bottle."

"Don't you want to drink any?"

I took a ceremonial sip and handed the bottle back to her. She emptied it into the cocotte.

Charlotte stared for a moment at the hunks of meat swimming in wine. "Do all kids here have this for their birthday dinner?"

I told her no, but that she was probably not the first.

I BELIEVE THAT LIFE OFFERS a person only so many chances to whisk a hot piece of enameled cast iron to the table and remove the lid with a flourish. So when it came time to serve dinner on the night of the party, that's what I did. Michele rolled her eyes, but in my defense, the beef daube was good. I'd even say it was great. The meat was tender but not mushy, bathed in a glistening sauce that had darkened to a color somewhere between burgundy and obsidian. I was happy with my middle road.

We were about a dozen at the table: Patrick and Arnaud; Tim,

Chloé, and their daughter, Charlie; Fred and his wife, Lut; and our friends Nico and Diane, who lived up the road in Pouydraguin and had brought their eight-year-old son, Adam; plus me, Michele, and the birthday girl.

The daube did not outlast the first bottle of wine. Fortunately I had put out lots of steamed potatoes, a huge salad, and plenty of bread—a prime pleasure of any braise being the sopping of the sauce. When all the beef was gone and everyone had mopped their own plates clean, hands clutching bread began to reach for the cocotte in order to soak up whatever sauce remained inside it. This left a dozen drip trails between pot and plate. Henri, that paragon of dinner-party decorum, would have cringed.

I'd purchased a croustade from the lady in Goux. In short order, the only evidence of its existence was an empty pie plate surrounded by a blast zone of pastry shards. For the kids, Michele had made, of all things, Rice Krispies Treats, which is what Charlotte had requested as her birthday dessert, apparently in a moment of homesickness. We'd been able to locate the necessary ingredients at a nearby super-market. So, I screwed seven candles into the confection, and we sang "Happy Birthday" in French. Charlotte seemed satisfied.

I've always thought that a reliable measure of a dinner party's success is how long people stay on, drinking and talking, after the last plate has been cleared away. If people linger, it's a sign that the meal and the company made them happy and that they don't want the fun to end. Of course, old-school Gascons like Henri hedge their bets by keeping guests at the table so long that they simply don't have the strength to do anything but go home after the last *mignardise* has been served. My daube dinner, by contrast, had been dispatched rather quickly, so I was happy when, after I'd brought out the Armagnac and Michele had turned up the music, everyone hung around in droves.

Before long, a half-dozen conversations were going on at once around the room. It was a scene reminiscent of Patrick's soirée many months before, except now none of these people were strangers. I will say with a certain pride that while it is always gratifying to throw a winning dinner party, to do so in a far-flung place where you have moved with your family at considerable effort and expense, and with more than a little uncertainty as to how the whole thing is going to turn out, feels especially good.

17

To Bag a Bird

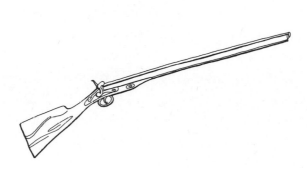

Omnivores that they are, Gascons at one time hunted virtually every kind of winged vertebrate that happened into their general vicinity: wood grouse, hazel grouse, woodcock, partridge, thrush, quail, pheasant, you name it. Most local game-bird populations have dwindled over the years, but one kind—the wood pigeon, a.k.a *la palombe*—still pays an annual visit to the Southwest of France in numbers sufficient to deprive many Gascon families of their adult males during the three-week hunting season.

There are two favored methods for killing the European migratory *Columba palombus*, a bird closely related to and, by my reckoning, almost indistinguishable from the feral rock dove, which is the kind of pigeon one sees in great profusion in New York City, pecking at trashed Chinese food and cigarette butts. One way is to hunker down on a low mountain ridge and try to shoot the birds as they fly overhead. This method is all about location, location, location, as there are only a few mountain passes the wood pigeons will use to cross the Pyrenees on their way from their Nordic nesting territories to their wintering grounds on the Iberian peninsula. The second method calls for building a camouflaged blind—known as a *palombière*—in the woods and connecting that blind to a Rube Goldberg system of wires, pulleys, and metal platforms extending hundreds of yards into the trees. Tethered to the metal platforms are domesticated lure pigeons, called *appeaux*. By tugging on wires connected to those platforms, hunters can induce the appeaux to flap their wings enticingly, so that their naturally sociable brethren might be attracted to earth, upon which the prey is either netted or shot. Hunters using nets tend to build their blinds on the forest floor. Hunters using guns tend to build their blinds in trees. To stumble on either kind of encampment while hiking through the woods can be unsettling, as if one has stepped into an elaborate snare set for a giant.

My personal interest in the hunt, truth be told, did not extend beyond wanting to learn how to make a wood pigeon salmis. I'd found a doable-looking recipe in Simin Palay's book, and figured that it wouldn't be hard to find a hunter willing to sell me a couple of palombes.

The Esbouhats had more ambitious plans for me.

A day after I'd casually mentioned my interest in wood pigeons to Basso, he phoned to inform me that he would be taking me hunting the following day. He'd gotten the okay from Francis, his preferred roastee at the Friday-night dinners and, as it happened, the Esbouhats' preeminent pigeon hunter. Basso emphasized that Francis was a *fanatique* who had built his elaborate hunting blind by hand and set aside all his paid vacation days each year for the hunt.

I couldn't resist asking what Francis's wife got up to during all that time. Basso, who seemed to know no greater pleasure than getting on Francis's nerves, had a good laugh at this.

We'd be accompanied on the hunt by Henri Michel, the retired train conductor, and by Francis's son, Maxime. Basso asked me if I knew how to handle a firearm. I told him that my dad had taken me pheasant hunting a few times when I was in high school, but that I would prefer to come along strictly as an observer.

"*Comme tu veux*," said Basso. "Get your beauty sleep. I'll pick you up at five thirty."

FRANCIS'S PALOMBIÈRE WAS OF THE tree house variety. It could more aptly be described as a man-cave in the sky—crude but surprisingly accommodating for a slapdash assemblage of cast-off lumber, chipboard, corrugated plastic, and cedar boughs nestled in the crown of a forty-foot oak tree. Accessed via a rickety ladder, it was furnished with a two-ring gas burner, some pots and pans, a ten-liter water jug, shelves crowded with foodstuffs and coffee tins, a plywood folding table, a wooden gun rack, and a few cheap upholstered barstools hemorrhaging stuffing. Extending from one wall, beneath a well-camouflaged roof hatch, was a shoulder-high platform with a swivel stool bolted to it. This was where the spotter sat, surveying the skies for passing prey. The palombière had flip-up windows on all sides that offered a spectacular view—coming into relief now as the first rays of sunlight prepared to laser over the horizon—of the forest canopy and the ridgelines of the Madiranais beyond.

At least I thought we were in the Madiranais. I didn't fully have my bearings. Basso and I had arrived at the wooded compound in total darkness, having followed unfamiliar back roads out of Plaisance and then a rutted dirt track that cut across a field and plunged into the trees. The track ended at a makeshift plywood carport covered in a green tarp and tree branches. Francis's son, Maxime, a bearded guy in camo pants with a shotgun slung over his shoulder, emerged into the beam of Basso's headlights, pulled back the tarp, and motioned for us to advance. The whole thing had a clandestine feel, as if we were being ushered into a forest hideout of the Maquis.

Basso, who was on cooking detail, had brought a cooler of food and wine, and also an oven. It was a grease-stained gas range that he'd gotten for free from an old lady he did odd jobs for. With lots of grunting and straining, and a crushing fear that I was going to reinjure the inguinal hernia I'd had repaired some years earlier, I helped Basso carry the appliance from his car, down a narrow footpath, and into a small shed near the foot of the big oak tree. All of this was done in the dark, save for the headlamps strapped to our skulls. As Basso hooked the range up to a propane tank, he echoed the claim he'd made the first time I met him: "We're going to eat like kings!"

Meantime, Francis, Henri Michel, and Maxime had set the appeaux, affixing them to metal perches and then, using a pulley system, raising the perches into the treetops surrounding the blind. As the sky got lighter, I could just make out the vast network of wires and rigging all around us. There were about twenty lure pigeons in all. Francis and Maxime had force-fed each of them a slurry of grain and water from a plastic syringe—so that they wouldn't need to be fed again all day—and fitted each with a hood that had realistic-looking eyes painted on it and resembled in miniature an old-time leather football helmet. Eight lure pigeons in a wire cage were brought directly into the blind and placed, untethered and unhooded, onto two wood poles that jutted into the void. These birds were the *volants*, domesticated pigeons that had been trained to fly around freely on command, as an added temptation to their migratory friends.

Now Basso, after hauling a few breakfast provisions up the ladder, picked up a broomstick with a shredded plastic shopping bag tied to its business end. He shook it, making a shushing, pompon noise. "If the spotter says *volants!*, then I shake this at the birds and they fly off."

He picked up a rusty soup can filled with nails. "And this is how you call them back." He rattled the can loudly. "That can be your job!"

Henri Michel brewed some coffee in a metal *cafetière* and distributed it in plastic cups. I handed a cup to Maxime, who was perched on the spotter's stool, testing the appeaux. This entailed pulling on a series of rope-handled wires dangling over the edge of the roof hatch. I asked Francis, who was placing shotgun shells into slots sewn into his expensive-looking hunting jacket, if I could climb up to see how the appeaux worked.

I hoisted myself onto the spotter's platform. Maxime pointed to the top branches of a scraggly ash tree thirty yards away. "You see it?" It took me a few seconds, but then I did: a lure pigeon, half hidden by foliage, perched on one of the raised platforms.

Maxime tapped one of the ropes and told me to pull it. I did, and the distant platform jerked, causing the pigeon to flap its wings rapidly before regaining its balance.

Maxime pointed to another pigeon a little farther away and then told me to flip what looked like a light switch. When I did, the bird and its platform slid along a wire from one treetop to another, the bird's wings flapping all the while. Maxime said each appeau mimicked a different kind of pigeon behavior: hunting for acorns, preening for a mate, and so on.

It was the most fiendishly ingenious setup for killing your own dinner I'd ever seen.

At around seven thirty, as the sun popped up over the hills, we had breakfast—boudin, saucisson, ham, and red wine. The other men attacked the charcuterie with large Opinel switchblades. I pulled out my Swiss Army knife.

After breakfast, the morning proceeded something like this: Basso would crack jokes while Henri Michel sat and rolled cigarettes and Maxime and Francis scanned the sky from the spotter's perch. Suddenly, Francis would hiss at Basso to shut up, Henri Michel would yank the blind's window flaps shut, and guns would be taken in hand. Maxime would whisper a running commentary: "A good *paquet* of them coming from the east, just over the ridgeline."

"I see 'em! I see 'em!" Henri Michel would say, peering through peepholes cut into the window flaps.

"*Volants!*" Francis would command.

Basso would shake the pompon thing, and the eight birds would take to the air.

Then one of two things would happen: Either our prey would change course and continue their Spain-ward journey unmolested, in which case the smoking and joke-cracking would resume, or else a few palombes would come into range and Maxime or Francis would start working the appeaux, hands flying like a busy switchboard operator's, causing the others to dart around the blind frantically, peering through the peepholes to see where the birds were going to land. Then two of the men would poke their gun barrels through the holes, a third would count to three, and both guns would discharge deafeningly at once, filling the blind with the smell of cordite. After that, Henri Michel would climb down and retrieve the dead game from the forest floor.

Since only two men could fire at a time—one person being needed as a spotter, another having to do the count, and me, the unarmed can-rattler, not really figuring into the equation at all—the guys took turns. Henri Michel and Maxime were the best shots, bagging two birds each by late morning. Francis was having poorer luck; he missed twice.

As for Basso, the morning didn't go well. On his second turn, he shot one of the appeaux.

"*Oh putain*," he said, setting his gun down. "*Putain, putain, putain.*"

Francis shook his head and bit his lip. Henri Michel turned his attention to his rolling papers. Maxime took off his beret and ran a hand through his hair. Basso stood there for a few long beats, hands on his hips, gazing out at the dead pigeon hanging from its tether in the distance. Personally, I was surprised this kind of thing didn't happen all the time; to me, a wild pigeon perched on a faraway tree branch looked not the least bit different from an appeau.

Basso wasn't one to dwell on unpleasant matters. A minute later, he was his old self again.

"No harm done, Francis," he said. "I'll spring for a new one. And I promise to have nightmares about dead pigeons for a week!" Then he climbed down the ladder and made his way to the shed to start getting lunch ready.

After Basso was out of earshot, Francis started complaining to Henri Michel. "He's a damn clown, that one. He's never serious."

Henri Michel just shrugged.

Francis sulked for a while, hands thrust into his jacket, but after a short time the friendly fire incident seemed to blow over. Francis bagged a pigeon on his next turn, and by lunchtime we had a handsome bouquet of eight dead birds, including the martyred appeau. Henri Michel bundled them together with twine and hung them from a nail—a rustic *nature morte* to serve as a backdrop for our midday meal.

At around one o'clock, Basso shouted from down below, "Send down the rope!"

Henri Michel got up from his stool and rubbed his hands together. "Lunchtime!"

He picked up a coil of green nylon rope and tossed an end out the door of the blind. I peered down. Basso was standing at the bottom of the ladder, an enormous black cast-iron cocotte at his feet. He took off his belt, looped the ends of it around the handles of the pot, and tightened the belt over the pot's lid. Then he tied the rope to the belt and gave Henri Michel the thumbs-up. Henri Michel hoisted the pot into the blind.

"Give me my belt," Basso said when he got to the top of the ladder, tugging at his jeans. "Unless you want to look at my ass while you're eating!"

I can say with some confidence that I will never have a better meal in a tree. Whatever transgressions Basso had committed that morning were redeemed by the lunch he laid out for us. We dragged our barstools over to the folding table, poured ourselves some wine, and enjoyed a banquet any earthbound Gascon would have been proud to serve: homemade foie gras, a squash-and-confit garbure, roasted potatoes, and—Basso's *pièce de résistance*—a civet of wild boar, which he'd started braising in the cocotte at home a couple of days before. The meat melted off the bone. For dessert Basso served a homemade lemon *tourte*. We ate it with crème anglaise from a supermarket Tetra Pak and spooned up the leftover cream from our paper plates like soup.

Any migrating pigeons that flew overhead between the hours of one and three that afternoon got a pass. After lunch, Maxime sat down in a corner, pulled his beret over his eyes, and took a nap. Francis went up to the spotter's perch and lazily repaired a piece of rigging. Henri Michel, looking supremely sated, a shaft of late-October sunlight falling on the side of his face, embarked on a philosophical disquisition about Gascon dishes cooked with blood:

boudin, sanguette, chitterlings made with pig's blood and cornmeal. This led to a far-ranging discussion with Basso about pork offal: how to season the pancreas, how to stuff the bladder, how to cook the lungs and spleen, how to use lard to shine your shoes.

As the sun continued its downward arc, Basso dictated to me his recipe for the civet, which called for a bottle and a half of Madiran (and knowing how to bag a wild boar). This prompted Henri Michel to divulge a family recipe for chicken fricassee and then, with no segue at all, to hold forth for a while about the cultivation and use of spring onions. For this he produced an actual specimen, a freshly sprouted bulb he had been carrying in his jacket pocket. He held it delicately between thumb and forefinger as he spoke lovingly of the flavors of the allium and described how best to plant and harvest it.

Basso concluded our impromptu cooking symposium with one final recipe, for a dish called boiled crow:

Take one crow. Add it to a pot of boiling water with a big rock. Simmer. When the rock is tender enough to pierce with a fork, the crow is done.

SOMETIME AFTER THREE, BY SOME unspoken consensus, the hunting resumed. A few more birds were bagged. More jokes were groaned at. More cigarettes were rolled. At around four thirty, another *bon paquet* of birds was spotted coming in from the north. Basso dispatched the volants. Maxime worked the appeaux.

"Two big ones just landed!" Henri Michel whispered, peering through a peephole.

Suddenly Basso pressed his twelve-gauge into my hands. "*Vas-y! Vas-y!*" he said. "Take my turn!"

He nudged me alongside Henri Michel, who was already draw-ing a bead on his target through one of the holes.

I heard Francis ask Basso, "Does he know what he's doing?"

"Yeah, yeah," said Basso. "He goes hunting all the time."

"Actually, I—"

But there was no time for clarifications. Basso had his hand on my shoulder and was pointing through a peephole.

"You see them?" Basso whispered.

I didn't.

"They're right in front of you, *nom de dieu*!" he said. "In the dead oak!"

There were a lot of dead-looking trees to choose from.

"Hurry up!" Henri Michel wheezed, gun at the ready. "They're not going to sit there forever!"

Finally, I made out two dove-shaped silhouettes on a leafless branch. I took aim at the one on the left as best I could, but I couldn't keep sight of the bird through the peephole while the barrel of the gun was occupying it. This was a rather major flaw in the design of the palombière, I thought.

Francis counted to three. I pulled back gently on the trigger. A gun discharged. It wasn't mine. I pulled the trigger a little further. Nothing. Then a bit further. Finally, *ka-blam!*

A suffocating silence fell. Henri Michel collected his spent shell and, without uttering a word, went down to retrieve his bird.

Basso took his gun back. "Don't worry about it, *mon brave.*"

Francis was scratching the side of his face and staring at his feet. His teeth were clenched, and his jaw muscles were bulging. He turned to Basso and unleashed a tirade. The Gasconized French came so fast and furious that I could catch only bursts of what he was saying: "Always playing the fool! . . . look like a bunch of amateurs! . . . isn't a game! . . . you said he knew what he was doing!"

Basso leaned an arm on the spotter's platform, looking unper-
turbed. "Eh oh, Francis, *calme-toi*."

I flashed Maxime a confused look.

"He'll get over it," he said out of the side of his mouth.

"Get over *what*?" I said. "That I missed?"

"You fired too late," Maxime explained. "You both have to fire
at the exact same time, on the count, or else the second bird will
hear the first shot and take off. And it's illegal to shoot a palombe
when it's flying."

So *that's* why they fire on the count of three.

I felt like an idiot.

"It's no big deal," said Maxime after Francis had emptied himself
of invective and retreated to the spotter's perch to brood. "The only
thing my dad cares about is his pals in the next blind overhearing
two shots—*pim! pam!*—and thinking we're up here getting drunk
and shooting at whatever moves."

I didn't say so, but that's actually what I'd pictured pigeon hunting to be like.

Later, as we were taking down the appeaux and getting ready to
head home, I apologized to Francis. He looked more embarrassed
than angry.

"*Pas de souci*," he said in a pinched voice—no worries.

I felt a little sorry for him. He'd poured the entirety of his leisure
time into a single hobby, but it didn't seem to make him that happy.

On the drive back to Plaisance, Basso was as upbeat as ever.

I thanked him for taking the heat for my screwup.

He slugged my shoulder with the back of his hand. "Twenty
more days up in that tree, and you might get the hang of it!"

I told him that after twenty days in a tree house I'd be as uptight
as Francis.

"Eh oh!"

I realized just then that Francis had been right about one thing: Basso was *never* serious. At first I'd thought his nonstop bonhomie and wisecracking was an act. No one could naturally be like that all the time. But now I was convinced this was just his default setting.

Out of the blue, I asked Basso if he had a family. He said he had a wife and kids and a lot of dogs. Then I asked him if he was from Plaisance.

He shot me a wily look.

"I'll tell you my dark secret," he said. "My family is originally from Italy!"

I told him he seemed pretty Gascon to me.

Basso dropped me off just as the sun was sinking behind Plaisance's rooftops. Henri Michel had given me four pigeons to take home. Feeling I hardly deserved them, I'd tried to refuse, but to no avail. Now I left the birds on the doorstep and went in to tell Charlotte and Michele I was home and unharmed. When I came back outside, there were only three. A cat from the village had dragged the fourth away and was making a bloody feast of it down by the stream. I snatched the remaining pigeons and took them into the kitchen.

"Are those birds dead?" Charlotte asked.

"Very," I said.

"You're not keeping them in here, are you?" said Michele.

"Well, I can't keep them out *there*," I said.

Honestly, I wasn't quite sure what to do with them. It dawned on me that I had no idea how to pluck, clean, and prepare freshly shot wood pigeons.

"Maybe you should call Nadine," said Michele.

I was already reaching for my phone.

THE NEXT MORNING, I FOUND myself hunched over Nadine's kitchen counter with a plucked pigeon in my hands, trying with considerable difficulty to detach the digestive-tract membrane from the bird's anus so that I could pull the pigeon's guts out the neck hole in one piece without rupturing the intestines and spreading their contents all over the place. Nadine had demonstrated the procedure on the first bird and made it look as easy as peeling a banana. With a similarly breezy savoir faire, she had shown me how to locate the bird's heart and liver amid the bloody viscera so that the organs could be washed and added to the sauce. She also demonstrated how to separate the jacket of usable tissue in the gizzard from the fibrous core. Notably, none of these delicate tasks were mentioned in Palay's recipe, which began simply with the line "Clean the birds."

Nadine, predictably, had scoffed when I told her over the phone that I intended to make a *salmis de palombes* using the old Béarnais's cookbook. With the calming authority of a nurse, she had instructed me to put the dead pigeons in a plastic bag in the bottom of my fridge and to bring them over promptly the next morning so that she could instruct me in the proper way to make the dish.

Now, with the gutting and cleaning of the birds complete, Nadine and I proceeded with the rest of the preparation, which I found to be pleasurably straightforward. From a cursory examination of the birds, she had determined that they were young, and thus wouldn't require a long cooking time. Young birds, she said, called for nothing more than a quick browning in the oven and then a low simmer in wine with a hash of vegetables and ham hock, enriched by the birds' giblets and roasting juices, and darkened with a couple of caramel-extract pastilles. As a last step before letting the birds cook for a while, she slid the tough skin of the ham hock, which another cook might have discarded, into the bottom of the saucepan to infuse the sauce with extra flavor from the bottom up.

"Nothing wasted," Nadine said, and then winked, as she was wont to do when imparting a bit of wisdom.

When the pigeons were done, Nadine transferred the birds to a baking dish. Then she puréed the hachis and strained it several times, producing an ink-black sauce so glossy it was almost luminous.

After that, she poured the sauce over the birds, covered the dish in foil, and sent me on my way.

We had the salmis de palombes for dinner that night. It is a dish that calls for, and indeed insists on, the companionship of a very rude tannat. Fortunately I had a bottle of old-vines Madiran on hand that could cut through anything. I poured a couple of glasses and sliced into one of the birds, cloaked in its dark, glimmering sauce. The flesh released a musky scent that caused Michele and Charlotte to wrinkle their noses. And yet the perfume disappeared the moment I took a bite, subsumed by the salmis' all-enveloping richness.

Before going to bed, I flipped through Palay's book again, studying its many game-bird recipes. I hadn't noticed it earlier, but there was actually a recipe for crow. It suggested cooking the bird in wine. No rock required.

18

Noble Spirits

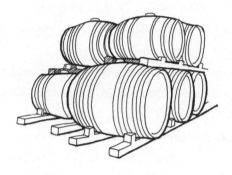

Here's a factoid that visitors to Gascony are likely to hear eventually. The quantity of Armagnac produced in any given year is equivalent to the angel's share—the volume of spirit lost to evaporation—of a year's production of Cognac. I've never crunched the numbers, but have been assured by several Armagnac makers that this observation isn't far off the mark. Whatever the exact ratio of this disparity between Armagnac and Cognac, the overall message to take from it is that the shadow cast across Gascony by that *other* white-grape brandy, which hails from the Charente, is very long.

In fact, over the years many Gascons have gotten into the habit of defining Armagnac simply by listing the ways it is *not* like Cognac. For one thing, they'll say, Armagnac is distilled only once, not twice, meaning it retains more of its aromatic character and *terroir* and, as a rule, requires longer aging to soften the rough edges. For another, Armagnac is produced in small quantities on family estates, not in massive industrial distilleries that have, in the eyes of Gascons at least, created a monstrous global thirst for cheap, young brandies. Also, Armagnac's origins go farther back than Cognac's by nearly 200 years, the spirit having been invented in the early Middle Ages, when it was valued as a cure for everything from tonsillitis to fistulas. (In the fourteenth century, Charles the Bad, King of Navarre, allegedly suffered a gruesome death when his bedclothes, soaked for medicinal purposes in eau-de-vie, caught fire.)

The vocabulary deployed by writers and sommeliers to describe Armagnac's aromas and flavors is vast and—as is the case with tasting notes of all kinds—occasionally ridiculous. An incomplete list of the descriptors I found in a book about Armagnac by the French restaurateur and wine expert Frédéric Lebel includes: *pear, kirsch, fig, sloe, blackberry, violet, apple blossom, bracken, tree moss, hay, fennel, linden blossom, vanilla, cinnamon, gingerbread, cloves, licorice, civet, fur, leather, meat juice, musk, almond, peanuts, prunes, mandarin, grapefruit, lemon, coffee, cocoa, flint, toast, tar, rancio, oak, pine, ethyl acetate, butter, beeswax, hot sand.*

Similarly, enthusiasts have come up with colorful if not always illuminating metaphors to describe the distinction between Cognac and Armagnac. In the preface to Lebel's book, the master sommelier Gérard Basset writes, "Armagnac is to Cognac what the Rolling Stones were to the Beatles." Paula Wolfert quotes a Gascon friend of hers who characterized Cognac as "a pretty girl in a freshly laundered smock carrying a basket of wildflowers" and Armagnac as "a tempestuous woman of a 'certain age,' someone you don't bring home to Mother . . ."

I've been a lover of Armagnac, if not tempestuous women, since 2002. That's the year Michele and I honeymooned in the Dordogne and, during a meandering drive one afternoon, dipped unknowingly into the northern fringes of Gascony's Armagnac-making country. Small arrow-shaped signs started cropping up at crossroads, advertising *Dégustation Armagnacs et Eaux-de-Vie*, and we'd followed one of them down an unpaved road to a somber-looking gray house flanked by a few farm buildings that had seen better days. I rang a bell, and we waited a long time until an oldish woman wrapped in a shawl emerged from the house and led us, without a word, to a frigid, cement-floored room lined with shelves of bottles. There, in the company of the woman's fidgety lap dog, we tasted a dozen Armagnacs, each of a different age. They were beguiling brandies, in hues of amber and topaz and old gold, fiery but soft, too, with all kinds of toasty and caramelized aromas, and flavors that shimmered weirdly around the edges with suggestions of fruit and spice. We bought three bottles for what seemed like an unjustifiably small sum and were offered, again with barely a word, a fourth as a parting gift.

Sadly, though I remember perfectly well the name of the woman's dog—Noisette—I have forgotten the name of the estate itself. But those first tastes of Armagnac made an impression, and as my Gascony infatuation flowered in the years that followed, I educated myself as best I could about the distilled spirit. I toured distilleries big and small (rather, small and smaller). I interviewed cellar-masters and barrel-makers. I had the workings of the copper column stills, known as alembics, explained to me in exhaustive and sometimes exhausting detail. I sat for marathon tastings. I carried home bottles in my suitcase so that I might spread the gospel of Armagnac to friends back home.

The one thing I had never managed to do, though, was to witness the distillers in action. *La distillation*—which begins after the last of the fall harvest has been turned into weak distilling wine, and lasts anywhere from a couple of weeks to several months, depending on the size of the estate—is invoked by Gascons in reverent terms.

The descriptions usually include stoic men standing vigil day and night in unheated sheds, tending to their chugging copper stills as eau-de-vie trickles into charred-oak casks, where the clear new-born brandy will mature to golden mellowness in moldy *chais*, as the aging sheds are called.

In truth, what interested me more than the distilling itself were the meals that attended it. Because the alembics have to perform their work continuously until the last of the season's *petit vin* is used up, the distillers eat where they work. And because this is Gascony, where you don't just unwrap a sandwich on your lunch break, the circumstances have given rise to a distinguished tradition of feasting.

ONE DOES NOT JUST SHOW up for a *repas distillation* as one might for a village cookout. One has to be invited. Knowing this, I cast a wide net, apprising everyone I knew of my desire to take part in such a meal. In the end I snagged three invitations.

The first came from one of the Esbouhats. Luc Périssé was in his forties and sported longish hair and a scraggly salt-and-pepper beard. He made a habit of slapping me on the back and shouting "Whassuuuuuup!" whenever he saw me, perhaps (though I never confirmed this) because he mistakenly believed that this was how men of my generation greeted each other in America. Luc had, by his own account, been raised by the Esbouhats, to whom his dad, one of the club's founding members, had entrusted his son's care during long absences for work. Luc described himself as a *négociant* who traveled around the region to buy and sell wine and *produits du terroir*.

Luc and a group of friends gathered each year at the estate of a young distiller named Jean-Christophe for what Luc characterized as a distillation dinner of Falstaffian dimensions. The meal, Luc said, went very late, was attended exclusively by men, was provisioned with nothing but meat, and was irrigated with great quantities of wine and Armagnac.

I did not hesitate to accept the invitation, though I confess that I felt a certain apprehension at the prospect of being stranded in the hinterlands of the Gers at the mercy of hard-parying Gascons.

When Luc picked me up on the night of the dinner, I asked if we might take two cars.

He shook his head and laughed. "You'd never find your way back."

Indeed, the domaine of Jean-Christophe was about as lost in the hills as one can get in the Gers. I remember quickly losing track of where we were as Luc drove us north out of Plaisance in the darkness along a series of ever narrower roads that cut through unfamiliar villages, the car's headlights illuminating crumbling stone fences and snarled hedgerows.

After a half hour or so, we arrived in an empty gravel courtyard surrounded by barn-like buildings. Light seeped from the entrance to one of them. I followed Luc inside and found myself in a cold, cinder-block-walled room gazing at a formidable assemblage of riveted copper that was belching smoke into a vent hood and shuddering rhythmically, *ka-chug ka-chug ka-chug.* This alembic—the first wood-fired one I'd seen—looked not unlike an old-fashioned train locomotive, and wasn't that much smaller. Luc went to look for Jean-Christophe, which gave me a chance to study the contraption. One part of it consisted of an iron firebox attached to an oblong receptacle—which I took to be the boiler—topped with a five-foot sectioned column. To the right of that was a single, fatter, and much taller column made of smoother and shinier copper. The two columns were connected by two copper pipes, one of them straight, the other goosenecked. A thicket of rusty valves jutted from the middle of the big column. From one of those valves emerged a curving length of copper tubing. Clear liquid was trickling from the tube into an oak cask that had been propped on its side.

Luc came back into the room with a gray-haired man in a flannel shirt and oval glasses: Monsieur Dutirou, the night-shift alembic-tender. The others hadn't arrived yet.

Dutirou slid a few pieces of wood into the firebox, dusted off his hands, and beckoned us over to the cask. He filled three plastic shot glasses from the end of the copper tube.

"*Santé*," said Dutirou, and we threw back the eau-de-vie. It left a trail of pure fire, with a trace of fruitiness fighting through the burn.

Dutirou looked admiringly at the alembic, which, he said, had been made in Agen in 1945. "She's a beauty, *non?*"

While Luc kept checking his watch, Dutirou proceeded, with the earnestness of a science teacher, to describe how the alembic worked. Of the many tutorials on this subject I'd received over the years, his was by far the most lucid. Here is a distillation, if you will: To begin with, the season's freshly fermented weak white wine—all Armagnac makers must first be winemakers, *forcément*—travels from a stainless-steel *cuve* into the taller of the alembic's two columns. As the wine flows upward through the tall column, it passes around condensing coils. In an ingenious symbiosis, the cold wine from the cuve causes the warm vapors traveling down through the coils to condense as they descend, even as the heat from those same vapors warms the wine as it rises. The now-warm wine, having performed its condensing duties, passes from the tall column over to the shorter column, where it flows down through a series of platforms on its way to the boiler receptacle at the bottom, getting hotter as it goes. Once the wine boils, its vapors bubble back up through the plat-formed column, picking up fruity and floral aromas from the wine that's flowing downward. (Here, Dutirou strayed into a discussion of esters and congeners; this was the only point at which he lost me.) Finally, the vapors migrate over to the taller column via the goose-neck pipe, travel down through the condensing coils, and become limpid, throat-scalding eau-de-vie, which trickles out of the spout and into the cask. The cask, in turn, will impart to the brandy, over the course of years and even decades, pleasing color, flavors, and aromas.

"Now," Dutirou said, raising an index finger, "it is in the aging where the real story of Armagnac begins." At that moment, to Luc's evident relief, the lesson was interrupted by the arrival of Jean-Christophe and the first of the evening's other esteemed *convives*.

The guests, eight or so of them, were in the food-and-wine business, like Luc. One was a gregarious restaurateur in his late twenties, another was a middle-aged, pot-bellied foie gras buyer who, according to a whispered aside from Luc, did a clandestine side trade in ortolan, the banned but delicious songbird. There was also a dapper wine négociant who arrived with two cases of very fine-looking bottles.

One of the attendees looked familiar to me. After a minute, I realized it was the friendly counterman from Boucherie Cugini. He seemed as flabbergasted to see me in this out-of-the-way place as I was to see him. He'd come bearing dinner wrapped in bloody waxed paper: six enormous and extravagantly marbled rib eyes.

Our host, Jean-Christophe—his neck mummified in a thick wool scarf in that fussy French way—excused himself frequently to perform adjustments to the alembic, confer with Dutirou, take temperature readings from the eau-de-vie, and make notations in a yellowed ledger. He seemed distracted and distant, though he did, admittedly, have more-immediate concerns than the rest of us.

The festivities began, in the accepted tradition of Gascon male bonding, with a ridiculous quantity of charcuterie—boudin, andouillette, Ibérico ham, saucisson, pâté de tête—and two enormous slabs of foie gras. With this we consumed many glasses of what the wine merchant called the "small stuff": a couple of Languedocs, a Chinon, a Nuits-Saint-George, a juicy Châteauneuf-du-Pape. We ate and drank standing up, off plastic plates, with the alembic throbbing away next to us, infusing our clothes with wood smoke. For a while, the men engaged in shop talk. The foie gras buyer lamented the renewal of the ortolan ban. The restaurateur talked about a shortage of oysters in the Arcachon Bay. Luc complained about the rising price of Basque wines. But as bottles continued to be emptied, the banter got looser and faster, and soon had escalated to a full-bore gasconade, bristling with put-downs and dirty jokes.

At around ten o'clock, Jean-Christophe flipped shut his ledger and stood up. In an unexpectedly macho flourish, he grabbed a shovel that had been leaning against the wall, opened the hatch of the firebox, and, releasing a dazzling shower of sparks, shoveled a pile of hot coals onto the room's stone floor. Over the spread-out coals he laid a grill grate. Then he threw on the rib eyes. After sixty seconds or so, he flipped them. Sixty seconds after that, he took them off. The thick steaks had fraternized with the coals just long enough to color the meat's exterior and soften the fat; inside was cool, crimson, uncooked flesh. This, the young Cugini butcher told me emphatically as we repaired to a long dinner table at the room's far end, was as it should be.

We were too distant from the alembic for its heat to warm us, so we ate dinner in coats and scarves. The steaks tasted deeply of tangy, bloody aged beef. As the meat disappeared, the wines got older: a 2008 Vacqueyras, a 2001 Saint-Julien, a 1982 Haut-Médoc, and, as we were mopping the juices from our plates, a 1964 Saint-Émilion Grand Cru, its label mostly rotted away. It was a musty artifact, shot through with skeins of dark fruit and a distant echo of tannins. Dessert was store-bought chocolate truffles. We ate them like peanuts, tossing the foil wrappers onto the bloody steak platter.

Never once did the machine-gun chatter slow down. After a while, I stopped trying to follow along, though the others took no account of this—every few minutes, someone would toss a non sequitur my way as if I'd been listening the whole time:

"You've got to fry the bird whole!"

"Never trust a Béarnais!"

"I didn't even get her name!"

"Whaaaassuuuuuuuuup!"

At length the Armagnac came out: a half-dozen bottles, each a different vintage and a different blend. I wish I could remember how they tasted. But it was late, and my palate had given up the ghost. The restaurateur, who was sitting next to me, took a sip of one, closed his eyes, and said: "Like Baby Jesus in a velvet suit."

Now it was three o'clock in the morning and Jean-Christophe was standing at the head of the table with a long glass pipette in his hand.

"Me first, doctor!" someone shouted.

We followed our host outside into the frosty night. Our feet crunched across the gravel, and we entered the damp darkness of the chai. Jean-Christophe flicked on a light. Four rows of wood casks marched off into the indiscernible recesses of the stone-walled shed. Jean-Christophe extracted a straw-colored liquid from one of the casks and dispensed a little of it into each of our glasses: an Armagnac in gestation, a foretaste of the nectar it would become.

Sometime before dawn, Luc deemed himself sober enough to drive us back to Plaisance. His engine wouldn't turn over, so he got three of his friends to push the car down the tree-lined dirt track so he could pop the clutch. We rolled through all the stop signs on the way home.

IT MAY COME AS A disappointment to some, and as a relief to others, that not all Armagnac-distillation feasts call for swilling wine and brandy until the wee hours. The following week, Henri stopped by to deliver an embossed card requesting the pleasure of the recipient's company at this year's *repas distillation* at the Domaine Baronne Jacques de Saint Pastou, in the village of Monguilhem. Henri told us that Saint Pastou was a very old Armagnac-making family with roots in Gascony's noblesse. The lunch sounded fancy, but Henri assured us it was really quite *mondain*, by which he meant lots of tiresome small talk and air-kissing.

"Monique doesn't go anymore," he said. "It bores her to tears."

Henri also mentioned that the Saint Pastou family was a little bit famous even outside of Gascony, because Pierre de Saint Pastou, the estate's young heir, had been a contestant on a recent season of *L'Amour Est Dans le Pré*, a reality-TV series that matches lonely bachelor farmers with potential mates. (The series name—literally, "the love is in the field"—is a play on the title of the rom-com set in Condom.)

Henri said that Pierre's brief turn as a TV personality had worked out well: The couple got married, and business had been very good ever since.

The Saint Pastou domaine was one of those demure French farmsteads that could have been conjured in the mind of a painter or a movie-set designer. At the center of the property, which was surrounded on all sides by picturesque vineyards, stood a perfectly square manor house with two skinny stone chimneys rising from a pyramidal roof. Keeping the house company were a few pristinely maintained farm buildings and an immense, high-ceilinged chai sheltered by a steeply pitched tile roof with deep eaves. The estate was accessed via a long, narrow white-gravel drive. The day was sunny and unusually mild, and as we approached the house, with

Charlotte and Michele in the backseat in pretty dresses, and Henri at the wheel relating some interesting fact about an old rail line that once served the area, I decided, mondain or not, that this looked like a fine place to spend a Saturday afternoon.

A few dozen guests were already milling around a long table in front of the house. A thick-set young man with a cherubic face, dressed in a cable-knit sweater, was standing behind the table, serving drinks and making conversation. This was the scion, Pierre de Saint Pastou.

Among those in attendance, there was an unusual preponderance of tweed and corduroy. More than a few guests were wearing hunting jackets—the old-fashioned kind with the padded shoulders and elbow patches. One fellow was sporting knickers, which he had paired with bright-red wool socks pulled up to the knees. Cashmere seemed to be favored among the women. Almost everyone, male and female, had a scarf draped over their shoulders, including the local *curé*, who was standing at the edge of the crowd in his cassock and collar. It seemed every living member of the local nobility had descended on a single patch of farmland for the day.

As if to confirm this impression, I ran into Irène Pinon, the mother of our friend Agnès, while I was waiting for a drink. Wearing her customary oversize sunglasses and gripping a snifter of Armagnac, she looked me over and, by way of greeting, asked, "Who are you with?"

I pointed to Henri, who was a short distance away, chatting with Michele.

Surely seeking a brighter star in the social firmament, Madame Pinon made to leave but was delayed by a balding, tweed-clad man of wide girth. He kissed Madame Pinon on the cheek.

"My son, François-Xavier," said Madame Pinon.

François-Xavier grinned and shook my hand.

"Agnès has spoken of you in her e-mails!" he said, showing a more cheerful mien than his mother. He insisted we join him at lunch, and asked me to call him Feex.

Feex was interesting company. Seated at one of the refectory tables that had been set up in the chai, with a bottle of Madiran and plates of grilled magret in front of us, we talked at length about his sister. Feex spoke with unguarded candor about how hard it had been for the siblings to get their mother to accept Agnès back into the family, and about how he admired his sister's independence.

"Agnès forced us out of our aristocratic torpor," he said.

Parting with Gascon tradition, I asked Feex what he did for a living. He said, somewhat obliquely, that his line of work was *le networking*.

Toward the close of the meal, after ceremonial glasses of new eau-de-vie, the elderly patriarch of the Saint Pastou family, Jacques-Henri, stood in front of the alembic with a microphone and led an eight-man choir in the singing of a Basque ballad called "Itxatxo." This was a moment of unexpected, arresting beauty. So splendidly harmonized were the men's voices, so resonantly did they carry through the vast, stone-walled chai, so haunting was the song's melody, so mournful its intonations—though I couldn't understood a word—that I found myself suddenly choked with emotion.

It was a clever bit of timing. No sooner had the song ended—with more than a few guests wiping their eyes—than Jacques-Henri thanked everyone for coming and invited the attendees to make their way to the ad hoc boutique that had been set up near the door of the chai. With that, everyone rose from their seats and began queuing up at a high wood counter, behind which stood Pierre de Saint Pastou. Grinning broadly, he accepted fistfuls of cash in exchange for bottles of Armagnac, which the guests tucked under their arms as they strode out into the waning afternoon.

THERE ARE FOUR MAIN KINDS of grapes used for making Armagnac: ugni blanc, baco, colombard, and *folle blanche*. Of these, the least-used is folle blanche, which goes by different names in different parts of France, including *fol, fou, enrageat, plant de madame, dame blanche, gros plant, picpoul, taloche, came braque, mendic, mendik*, and *mondic*. Folle blanche (crazy white) accounts for just 4 percent of the total surface area under cultivation in the Armagnac-making zones of Gascony. Most estates grow just a little of it, to add some backbone to their distilling wine. This is because folle blanche, from a grower's perspective, is *emmerdant*—a pain in the ass. It falls prey easily to gray and black rot and various kinds of insects, and requires lots of extra care and attention.

Almost no one makes Armagnac exclusively from folle blanche. Those who do are for the most part considered stubborn eccentrics. If there is a cult figure among this small coterie of distillers, it is a woman named Martine Lafitte.

"She is *pur et dur*," André Dubosc said when, on one of our excursions, we paid Martine a visit. He accompanied that description with a knuckle-rap to the skull, a gesture he reserved for the most irascible Gascons. Dubosc explained that bottles of folle blanche Armagnac from Domaine Boingnères, as Martine's estate is called, fetched hundreds of euros apiece, but that because the yield from the grape was so poor, Martine had never parlayed her cult status into a wider success.

"When it comes to folle blanche," said Dubsoc, "her motto is *plutôt mourir que trahir*." "Sooner die than betray."

The entirety of our visit with Martine that day took place in the foyer of her house, standing up, while she stroked her cat. Glancing at me from time to time through thick-lensed glasses, she seemed wary of her foreign visitor. Looking to be in her sixties, she had dark bangs and a stout frame packaged in a tight leopard-print top and black slacks. After she and Dubosc chatted for a while, Martine cut the conversation short, saying she had business to attend to. When I inquired about the distillation, she extended a vague invitation to visit the domaine.

I was surprised when, not long after, she actually called me—and, moreover, sounded put out that I hadn't phoned her first. She said that I should visit the estate as soon as possible, as they were almost finished distilling the season's harvest of folle blanche.

The next morning, I was parked in front of a schoolhouse in a village called Le Frèche. Martine had instructed me to call when I got there so that she could send someone to fetch me: Finding the place on my own would be *compliqué*. I phoned the number she'd given me and spoke to a gravel-voiced man who told me to stay put.

Soon a white van pulled up and flashed its brights. I followed it down a series of country roads. A thick fog had moved in, and I couldn't see much in front of me beyond the van's taillights. Eventually, though, I could make out rows of vines on either side of the road, their leaves a late-autumn yellow. We pulled into a wide courtyard and parked under a cluster of leafless plane trees that had been pruned to the knuckles. They looked like bony hands reaching up from the underworld. A shuttered farmhouse stood a short distance away—the old family manor, no longer occupied, it seemed. Opposite that was a plain, plaster-walled structure. I guessed that this was the distillation shed, because a pipe sticking out of the side of the building was discharging a steaming liquid into a cistern, filling the air with a rotten-fruit smell—this was the *vinasse*, the alembic's unevaporated runoff.

The van's driver got out. A fireplug of a man with a pug nose perched at a great distance from his upper lip, he resembled a caricature from a nineteenth-century political cartoon. He said his name was Claude.

He explained that Madame was running late and had asked him to show me around the vineyard.

I grabbed a scarf from the backseat of my car. With resignation, I'd taken to wearing one, Frenchman-style, because Gascony's particular variety of damp autumn chill had a way of getting right down my shirt collar. I followed Claude along a muddy path separating two vine plots, and then into a row of vines. He crouched by one of them and pointed at tiny holes in its trunk.

"Insects," he said. "Worse every year."

We walked a little farther.

He crouched down again and plucked off a handful of shriveled, unharvested grape carcasses, which disintegrated in his hand. "Black rot."

Claude excused himself momentarily to urinate behind a tree. He continued to speak as he did so.

"Growing folle blanche is hardly worth it anymore," he called out. "But Madame, she is set in her ways."

As we walked back toward the distillation building, Claude divulged that Madame Lafitte was planning to sell the estate. She had no children, he said, and she would soon be too old to run the place.

He revealed that there had already been an offer on the property, but Madame Lafitte had turned it down because the buyers weren't interested in keeping the domaine going, and had indicated that they would uproot the vines.

For a fleeting, ridiculous moment, I fantasized about buying the place myself and becoming a gentleman-farmer-distiller. Alas, I lacked both the funds and even a fraction of the horticultural aptitude required of a grower of folle blanche.

Domaine Boingnères's alembic was much shinier and newer than the ones I'd seen previously. It was gas-fired, and its boiler and twin columns were perched on brick pedestals. Otherwise, though, it was the same basic scene: *ka-chug ka-chug ka-chug*, firewater trickling into a barrel. Claude went over to the still to check the temperature of the eau-de-vie with a glass thermometer and then consulted a well-thumbed book—titled *Guide Pratique d'Alcoolmétrie*—that was lying on top of some newspapers on a linoleum-topped table.

This distillation shed had a peculiar feature: a full kitchen. I could see it through a doorway at the far end of the room. Inside, a skinny, apron-clad woman was adding pieces of vine wood to a hearth. I asked Claude if I could go in and introduce myself. He looked at me funny.

"Not much to see," he said, "but be my guest."

The cook had a long, sallow face and appeared to be infected with the same gloominess as Claude. I was beginning to think spores of it were floating in the air. When I asked what she was making, she seemed surprised that I could possibly be interested. She pointed to a platter of plucked wood pigeons and told me they were going on the grill. All I could think of was how long it must have taken her to clean them.

The cook told me she prepared all the meals during *la distillation*. "Lunch and dinner, every day for twenty days—*ouf*," she said. "But it's easier than it used to be. Before Madame added the kitchen, the meals had to be carried all the way from the house."

At one o'clock, lunch was served at the linoleum table. Martine had arrived—same bangs, same black slacks, same leopard-print top—in the company of an elderly cousin and the cousin's middle-aged son. Claude joined us, as did Martine's two other alembic-tenders, taciturn men in rugby shirts whose names were never shared.

The energy at the table was less than effervescent. As we sipped our aperitifs while awaiting the first course, the conversation remained at the lowest simmer, mostly gossip and bits of local news, the kind of chitchat made by people who spend a great deal of time in one another's company.

A platter of oysters came out. What little talking there'd been ceased as the bivalves were eaten with an every-man-for-himself urgency. I was beginning to wonder why Martine had bothered inviting me.

When the grilled wood pigeons arrived, accompanied by toasts topped with a flambéed hash of the birds' hearts and livers, I ventured a conversational foray, asking about the aperitif Martine had served.

She described the drink as a Pineau.

Before I'd thought better of it, I let slip that I thought Pineau was usually made with Cognac.

At the utterance of the *C*-word, Martine looked like she'd swallowed a horsefly. "The original Pineau was made with Armagnac!" she said. "The Charentais stole the idea from us."

I started in on my grilled palombe and listened to the others talk for a while. Soon enough, though, my foot was in my mouth again. I mentioned to Martine that more than a few of my American friends, on tasting Armagnac for the first time, had likened it to a fine Scotch. I realized instantly that I'd uttered another dirty word.

Martine choked down a bite of food and made a sour face. "Armagnac can't be compared to whiskey!" she said. "Armagnac is a nectar of the vine."

Her laugh was tinged with bitterness. "You cannot put the date of the harvest on a spirit made from mashed-up grains!"

I decided to change tack and asked if Martine could tell me about the different Armagnac-growing areas. She seemed to warm to this. Pouring herself another glass of wine, she explained that there are three official appellations and proceeded to list them in ascending order of esteem. On the lowest rung is Haut Armagnac, in the south and east of the Gers; the brandies made there are simple and usually drunk young. The Armagnacs of the Ténarèze, covering the center of the Gers and a sliver of the Lot-et-Garonne, are often harsh and require long aging. And finally, straddling the border of the Gers and the Landes, is Bas Armagnac, home to tawny-sand soils that produce brandies of unparalleled depth and richness.

"I presume that's where we are now," I said.

An index finger went up. "Where we are now is in the *heart of the heart* of the Bas Armagnac," said Martine. "We are in the Grand Bas Armagnac."

It seemed she had waged a long battle, as yet unwon, to gain official recognition for this fourth, ultraprestigious appellation, which had been coined by her and the owners of a handful of nearby estates.

"We are not allowed to put *Grand Bas Armagnac* on our labels," said Martine. "It's idiotic. But of course the lesser houses are always happy to see their fortunes lifted by the great ones."

Martine went to fetch something from the kitchen. I looked around at the others, who were gnawing at the bones of their pigeons. I was suddenly overcome by the feeling that I'd stumbled onto a lost world, or rather had been summoned to it so that I might bear witness to its final throes.

Martine returned to the table with a half-full bottle of a deep-hued Armagnac and poured a round. I read the bottle's sepia-colored label. It was printed in old-fashioned gothic lettering:

Bas Armagnac
Folle Blanche
1986
Domaine Boingnères

I imagined Martine in her bottling room with a quill and ink-well, writing *Grand* at the top of each label.

Everyone warmed the snifter in their hands before taking a sip. I did so, too, then drank. Nothing special happened at first. The brandy was compact, a little hot. I chewed on it for a second or two. Then something did happen. The Armagnac effloresced with flavors, crazily and in so many different directions at once that I couldn't quite get a handle on what they were—flowers and dried fruit, maybe, and certainly vanilla and some kind of warm spice, plus all kinds of nutty and fire-tinged notes, and many lovely things in between that made me wish I had that sommelier's word list handy. Then the whole, mad explosion resolved itself in a kind of symphonic chord.

I hardly realized it, but I'd had my eyes closed. When I opened them, Martine was watching me. She smiled for the first time all day.

"*Ah oui*," she said, a little wistfully, "*la sacrée folle blanche.*"

Before I left, Martine showed me her cask cellar. There were vintages going back to the 1960s that had yet to be bottled. On our way out, she pulled a bottle off a shelf and handed it to me. It was another 1986 folle blanche.

She gave it a gentle pat. "A little gift to remember us by."

19
Aux Armes, Citoyens!

As late as the 1860s, on the eve of the Third Republic, virtually none of the *communes* in the Gers were French speaking. The Gascon dialect of Occitan was the lingua franca, and even that tongue had its variants within the département. "The old dialectical world was fragmented in the extreme," writes Eugen Weber in *Peasants into Frenchmen*. "Dialect might change from one valley to another, from high ground to low, from one riverbank to the next, if physical barriers made communication difficult." As was the case with much of southern France, rural Gascony and its sub-regions were essentially countries unto themselves almost until the twentieth century: loose assemblages of isolated and self-sustaining peasant communities conducting their daily life almost completely outside the purview of the French national identity. Weber cites the account of a British visitor to the western fringes of Gascony in the

1860s: The people there, the visitor wrote, "'live on French soil, but cannot be called Frenchmen. They speak a language as unintelligible to a Frenchman as an Englishman; they have none of the national characteristics—little, perhaps, of the national blood.'"

Weber's book is packed with surprising anecdotes about the insularity of the Southwest of France. Until the mid-nineteenth century, for example, no one had bothered to build a bridge anywhere along the length of the Garonne River—Gascony's northern frontier—between Bordeaux and Toulouse. Similarly, when a representative of the French government proposed constructing roads connecting Gascony to its adjacent provinces after the Revolution, "the people of Auch, bourgeois and common folk alike, protested: 'We have all we need to live well.'" For many generations, Weber notes, any villager who made the difficult journey north to Paris was, upon his return, referred to forever after as a *"Parisien."*

One of the best parts of *Peasants into Frenchmen* is a short history of "La Marseillaise." According to Weber, France's national anthem—born as a battle hymn in Strasbourg in 1792 to rally the Army of the Rhine against Prussian and Austrian invaders—did nearly as much as roads and bridges to bring far-flung peoples like the Gascons into the French national fold. Weber does not fail to point out the irony of the fact that the song's name—coined in honor of the Marseille Battalion, whose soldiers embraced the hymn with a particular fervor—refers to "a city whose people did not speak French" at the time. And yet, Weber avers, in very short order the song became an incredibly effective vector for the spread of the national language and of Frenchness in general.

What's fascinating to me about all of the above is that, while I've heard "La Marseillaise" sung in other parts of France, I have never seen it accorded more respect and solemnity than I have in Gascony. Nowhere has that hymn made me feel more firmly rooted in

French soil, or more unreservedly respectful of the French national ideals. It seems that somewhere along the line the Gascons, though they remain quite happily a nation unto themselves in certain ways, became model Frenchmen.

THE EVENT THAT SPURRED THIS particular revelation was Armistice Day, an anniversary that's largely yawned at in the United States but is still a big deal in France—the First World War having been a lot deadlier for Frenchmen than the Second. Public commemorations take place all over the country, in cities, bourgs, and bourgades alike. In preparation for the ceremonies in Plaisance, Charlotte's class had been practicing "La Marseillaise" daily, and with a diligence that I thought was impressive. It seemed I was hearing the verses emanating from the classroom windows every time I passed by the school. For two weeks, Charlotte had been reciting the song at home, sometimes with a school-issued lyric sheet in front of her and sometimes just idly, while going about her usual business. One morning, I found her in her room dressing a stuffed animal in a toilet-paper gown while repeating the lines "Form your battalions!" and "Let impure blood water our furrows!"

I'd never realized how violent France's national anthem was until I studied Charlotte's lyric sheet. Throats are slit, mothers' breasts are ripped, warriors are struck down by mercenary phalanxes. The song paints a violent scene. (Here's an interesting fact I learned later: In the 1990s a coalition of activists, including France's first lady at the time, Danielle Mitterand, started a campaign to change the lyrics. The movement gained steam after a ten-year-old French girl sang an a cappella version of the anthem at the Albertville Winter Olympics, shocking quite a few non-French viewers who were following along to the subtitles. The campaign ultimately failed.) I confess I was a little taken aback by the lyrics, but not terribly surprised. The French don't, on the whole, sugarcoat bloody episodes in their national history for the benefit of their children. Indeed, Charlotte was having nightmares about some World War I photos she'd seen with her class during a field trip to the local *médiathèque*. The exhibit wasn't pulling any punches. There were pictures of bodies piled in the trenches and portraits of the gruesomely disfigured faces of mustard-gas victims. It was enough to give a grown-up bad dreams, too.

The day of the commemorations dawned damp and gray. Over breakfast, I helped Charlotte practice the song one last time. She'd been tripping over the line "Against us tyranny's bloody banner is raised!" Then, at ten o'clock, the three of us walked up to the esplanade, where townspeople were assembling in front of the war memorial—a white-marble statue of a bare-breasted heroine with an upraised sword, set atop a plinth bearing three marble plaques inscribed with the names of Plaisance's war dead.

The mood was somber. Members of the town council, dressed in dark suits, had lined up alongside the mayor and the president of the *conseil général*, all of them wearing serious expressions. Four veterans—of which war I wasn't sure—took their place as flag-bearers; they wore white gloves and had medals pinned to their chests. A few gendarmes from the local *caserne*, in their flat-topped kepis and dress uniforms, were there, too, as was a good cross-section of the village, with most of the attendees crowded around the perimeter of the esplanade. In my immediate field of vision, I could see Coscuella, Alphonse, Lorette, the butcher from the new bastide, the baker from the old bastide, Doudou from the school cafeteria, and at least a dozen other familiar faces. I received a few tight-lipped smiles and nods of the head—subdued greetings appropriate to the tenor of the day.

Charlotte joined her classmates on the esplanade. I could see

Charlotte in front, horsing around with her friends, looking not the least bit nervous or out of place. The Maîtresse got the kids settled down, and the crowd fell silent.

Now a marching band—a mix of high-school kids and adults, maybe fifteen musicians in all—rounded the corner down by the town hall, playing a military tune. We made way for them as they trooped past and installed themselves next to the war memorial. The band stopped and it was quiet again. A thin, slouching man wearing a ski parka over a suit approached a dais draped with red-and-blue bunting. He picked up a microphone, tapped it, and announced that the ceremonies would begin with a rendition of "Le Soldat" by the singer Florent Pagny, as interpreted by members of the local junior-high-school choir. Nine kids of wildly varying heights filed onto the esplanade. A young teacher played a chord on a portable electric piano, and the students' quavering, pubescent voices rose up. Michele, who has been known to cry at Halloween parades and school band concerts, palmed away a tear.

Next, the mayor, accompanied by three students, laid a wreath at the foot of the memorial. A town council member gave a short, poignant speech about how war binds nation and family together. Then, one by one, the names of Plaisance's war dead were read aloud. After each name, the entire crowd—babies and toddlers excepted—responded in unison with an incantatory *"Mort pour la France."* This funereal call-and-response took quite a while. I counted more than seventy names in all, starting with a man named Ader and ending with someone named Touzy.

Now the band played a "Taps"-like tune. The man in the ski parka returned to the dais. "To conclude our commemoration," he said, "I invite you to lend your ears as the pupils of the École Primaire sing our *hymne national.*"

The children began to sing: *"Allons enfants de la patrie / Le jour de gloire est arrivé . . .*" They were out of tune, but they knew the words, every blood-soaked verse. Though I couldn't make out her voice, I could see Charlotte's lips moving, exhorting her fellow citizens to slay the foreign cohorts and vile despots. The crowd—reverent, standing rigidly as if at attention—mouthed along.

It was hard not to get swept up in the moment. Though I generally took a dim view of flag-waving and other nationalistic displays, standing there shoulder to shoulder with the people of Plaisance as "La Marseillaise" rang out, with the names of the dead still hanging in the air, I couldn't help but feel moved. A sense of inclusion and gratitude welled up in me. It was a sentiment that might accurately be described as *fraternité*.

After the anthem was over, the master of ceremonies invited everyone to the town hall to share *le vin d'honneur.* A nip seemed much needed, so we gave Charlotte a long congratulatory hug and proceeded together to the mairie. Plates of crackers and cups of sparkling wine had been laid out on plastic-covered tables in the *salle de réunion.* We sipped and snacked and chatted with Maîtresse Nathalie and the school principal; Alphonse and Lorette drifted over to say hi, as did Coscuella. The town council had mounted an exhibition of children's artwork on the theme of World War I. Charlotte's class had pasted Xeroxed photos of French infantrymen onto construction paper and written words and short phrases next to the photos: "hunger," "homesickness," "fear," "mud and lice," "dying too young." Charlotte showed us her contribution: "*beaucoup trop de morts.*" Her words were written in the perfectly uniform cursive drilled into every French citizen at an early age.

20

Chez Guérard

Elizabeth David, the famously opinionated British food documentarian of the postwar era, had little patience for Nouvelle Cuisine. In the third edition of *Provincial French Cooking*, she called that culinary movement—which in the 1970s became France's herb-flecked answer to rich béchamel sauces and heavy things cooked in aspic—an "affectation." She went on to say: "Everyone who has experienced it in restaurants where it is practised . . . has his or her own story of the five green beans sitting lonely on one side of a huge white plate, three tepid chicken livers *avec quelques feuilles de salade* nine inches distant on the opposite edge." Presumably to David's dismay, Nouvelle Cuisine eventually went mainstream, becoming the model for posh restaurant food the world over, and for more-radical culinary experimentation yet to come.

The principles of Nouvelle Cuisine—smaller portions, lighter

sauces, faster and more-direct cooking methods, artfully deraci-
nated presentations—would appear to be patently un-Gascon. And
yet Gascons are quick to claim as their own one of the movement's
founding fathers. I feel obligated to point out that this chef, Michel
Guérard, is not a Gascon, at least not by birth. He hails from the vicinity of Paris, and earned his stripes there at a restaurant, long gone,
called Le Pot au Feu. But since the 1970s he has made his home, and
sealed his reputation as one of France's best-loved culinary *person-
nages*, in a village in the Landes called Eugénie-les-Bains.

Guérard has the dual advantage of being a naturally great cook
and also having married well. Guérard's father-in-law was Adrien
Barthélémy, the founder of an immensely successful chain of ther-
mal spas. Barthélémy's daughter and heir, Christine, helped Guérard transform Eugénie-les-Bains—formerly a run-down spa station
once frequented by Napoléon III's wife, the Empress Eugénie—into
a culinary and wellness empire.

Though Eugénie-les-Bains lies only forty minutes or so from
where we lived, it is the anti-Plaisance: a showpiece of impeccably
restored buildings lining immaculate sidewalks decorated with ceramic planters. An old convent and handsome stone farm buildings,
painstakingly renovated, have been put into service as guesthouses
and restaurants for spa-goers. Guérard's fief also includes a culinary
institute devoted to the chef's trademarked Cuisine Minceur (slimming cuisine), which is an even lighter offshoot of Nouvelle Cuisine, designed specifically for the kinds of Parisians who routinely
travel hundreds of miles for a mud bath and a massage. Cuisine Minceur begat a line of popular cookbooks during the 1980s and earned
Guérard a feature in *Time* magazine.

The jewel of Guérard's realm is Les Prés d'Eugénie, a fancy
restaurant—certainly the fanciest in all of Gascony—that received
its third Michelin star in 1977 and, in an impressive feat of staying

power, has hung on to it ever since. From what I'd gleaned, the restaurant—Nouvelle Cuisine's daintier aspects notwithstanding—was an haute-cuisine temple of the unabashedly decadent kind. (Though a "slimming menu," I'd been told, was available on request.) Among my Gascon friends, the place was talked about in terms of degrees of separation—so-and-so knew someone who knew someone who ate there—but the reports that trickled down were never less than ecstatic: truffled this-or-that, opulent *déclinaisons* of foie gras, an ambiance of unparalleled refinement. Invariably, such secondhand accounts would wrap up with that reliable cautionary coda: *C'est très cher.*

Personally, I didn't have much interest in eating at Les Prés d'Eugénie. For one thing, it was way out of our price range. For another, though Gascons welcomed the cachet it had brought to the region, the restaurant didn't seem to have an organic connection to Gascony. And anyhow, high-end dining didn't really agree with me. I almost always seemed to get seated next to someone unpleasant, and there's something about fancy restaurants that makes me self-conscious.

But sometimes one is called upon to put aside one's prejudices.

ANDRÉ DUBOSC LAUGHED AWKWARDLY WHEN, under the totally legitimate pretext of not being able to afford it, I declined his invitation to have lunch with him and a colleague at Les Prés d'Eugénie.

"Ah, but you misunderstand," he said over the phone. "*Je vous invite.* You will be our guests."

I said I couldn't allow it.

Dubosc took a conspiratorial tone, explaining that Guérard was an old friend, and that the wine cooperative was seeking new business with him.

"It will look more sociable," he said, "if we go *à quatre*." Of course, he added, it was expected that I'd bring Michele.

He went so far as to offer his wife's babysitting services. She had already dined *chez Guérard*, he said, and had volunteered to watch Charlotte before he'd even asked.

"You see," said Dubosc, "all of our grandchildren are boys."

I told him I'd check with Michele. When I did, she stared at me with an expression of flabbergasted disbelief that I'd hesitated to accept.

And so, that Saturday, she and I put on our nicest clothes and dropped Charlotte off at Dubosc's house. His wife, Françoise, wrapped Charlotte in her arms as if the two were already fast friends. Then she gave Charlotte a chocolate and stroked her hair appraisingly, in a sign that some serious braiding might be in their future. When it comes to spoiling other people's children, Gascons are not to be outdone.

We arrived at the restaurant at half past eleven and were waved past a gatehouse by a uniformed guard. We parked at the edge of an expanse of topiary-hemmed gardens laced with trim, bowered paths. The restaurant's lobby, which doubled as the reception area of the adjoining hotel-spa, was a placid sanctuary of white plaster moldings and classical statuary. As we waited for Dubosc's colleague, a couple of svelte women in flowy outfits swished past us, heading toward the spa and trailing a scent of roses. A telephone trilled softly somewhere down the hall. We'd entered a distant, un-Gascon universe.

Our fourth arrived. Olivier Bourdet-Pées was Dubosc's young successor at the co-op. The new *directeur* had a tennis-player's build, a receding hairline, black-rimmed glasses, a French-guy scarf— Dubosc a quarter-century ago. If I hadn't known otherwise, I'd have pegged him for Dubosc's own son. This impression was enhanced by the fact that Dubosc's body language around Olivier was that of a jocular mentor. In lieu of the gentle arm touches Dubosc reserved for me and Michele, it was shoulder-drapings and back slaps for Olivier—to which the younger man reacted like someone listening politely to a stale joke.

Dubosc had arranged to meet with Guérard before lunch to discuss a few matters of business, so after announcing our arrival to a willowy hostess in a chic black dress, we installed ourselves on two Empire-style settees beneath an immense crystal chandelier in an extra-tranquil corner of the lobby. A black-tied server, unbidden, brought coffee and candied fruit on a silver tray.

Dubosc, holding his demitasse decorously over its saucer, glanced behind him and then leaned forward slightly so that he might speak to Michele and me in confidence. "Guérard's wife designed every inch of this place," he said. "She treats it like the Louvre—you're not even allowed to take photos."

This made me very badly want to pull out my phone and start doing just that.

Before I could act on the impulse, Guérard appeared. I hadn't noticed him walking over, but now suddenly here he was, standing before us.

We stood up to shake his hand. Guérard was close to a foot shorter than me. Dubosc introduced us and mentioned that my wife and I were from Chicago.

Guérard beamed. It was the unflappable smile of someone who's been photographed a lot. "Ah, the Obamas' hometown," he said. "I've extended an invitation to the First Lady to come visit the *institut*. She and I share much the same mission."

We retook our seats, and Guérard went on to lament, albeit in the most diplomatic language, the global spread of McDonald's and its offspring, *le fast food* being a perennially popular punching bag of French chefs. In my experience, when the topic came up, the

American in the room was cast, willingly or no, in the role of fast-food apologist so that the Frenchmen in the room might have a ready target to assail. But Guérard made the gentlemanly gesture of changing the subject.

For a short while, he reminisced about being a child in northern France during the war. "I have lived through hunger and fear," he said. "I am grateful for this."

Then he changed the subject again, speaking nostalgically of the decline in the hallowed tradition of culinary *apprentissage*. "Today," he said, "young chefs seek celebrity before they seek wisdom."

Guérard spoke a mannered Parisian French, his talk devoid of rugby and bullfighting metaphors. He closed his eyes as if trying to remember something, then quoted several verses from a Paul Valéry poem. They had something to do with a master and his protégé.

Conversation turned to more pressing affairs. The three men discussed hectoliters and wholesale prices for a while, Olivier doing most of the talking, leaving Dubosc to contribute the occasional droll remark.

Finally, business having been concluded, Guérard brushed a bit of lint from his trousers and rose from his chair. He extended his hand to each of us. "Now I must leave you," he said. "I'm needed at the stoves."

As suddenly as he'd appeared, he was gone.

We were led by the willowy hostess to the restaurant's salon: a baroque fantasia of a sitting room with three crackling fireplaces, deep leather couches, and gilt-framed oil paintings, including a softly lit and nearly life-size portrait of Eugénie herself. We were seated at a burnished-wood coffee table and served pre-lunch snacks of tiny house-made white boudins skewered on toothpicks. For an aperitif, we drank a copper-colored 1973 Jurançon that Olivier had brought from his own cellar. It was decanted and poured by a bird-faced sommelier in a waistcoat and lavender tie, and tasted of chestnuts and candied fruit.

At twelve forty-five, we sat down to lunch. The dining room was airy and flooded with light. Our table, covered in fresh white linen, could have comfortably accommodated eight people. With the exception of a few well-polished silver serving carts, no functional elements of a working restaurant, right down to electrical outlets, were anywhere to be seen.

We placed our order with a young captain who evinced a carefully calibrated mixture of warmth and fawning and, like Henri, never once during the meal gave the appearance of haste or exertion. The sommelier returned and engaged Olivier, who had been half hidden for some time behind a thick, hardbound wine list, in negotiations. Moments later, a Chablis Grand Cru was brought to the table. It was crisp and vivacious and spurred the appetite. A silky, dried-blood–colored Saumur Champigny soon followed.

What did we eat? A staggering amount of food, even by Gascon standards. And it couldn't have been remotely slimming. I remember black Périgord truffle—that most coveted and expensive of fungi—shaved onto a vichyssoise; more slices of that truffle, delicately white-veined and tasting of damp earth, strewn over the top of some kind of blini; morels in an ethereal emulsion that tasted like the essence of a million freshly foraged mushrooms concentrated into a small pillow of foam; a soft-cooked egg with a top hat of caviar, each spoonful a surge of salty, creamy richness; oysters concealed under different-colored citrus foams; tender pieces of some cosseted breed of chicken served in a ragoût made with cockscomb and *rognons de coq*, which, Dubosc explained with a mischievous smile, were rooster testicles; and a square of crisp-skinned sea bass, alone on the plate in nothing but its own cooking juices. There were scallops, too—grilled, as I recall—served on a slick of melted sea salt butter. After that: a halved lobster tail smoked in a stone hearth with candied onions, then a rare-cooked medallion of beef wrapped in a leaf. I know there were cheeses, but I regret to say I can't call to mind what they were. By the time they'd shown up, we'd been at the table for a couple of hours, and I was nearly overcome with the urge to dash out for air. But I resisted it and held on through dessert—mille-feuille, rhubarb ice cream, peach melba—and then through coffee and digestifs.

By four thirty or so, it was done. Dusk was preparing its advance across the sky. Guérard came to the table and basked in our praise for a minute or two. My faculties dulled by the excesses of the meal, I found myself unable to summon anything more poetic than "*C'était très, très, très bon.*" Guérard smiled his practiced smile, shook our hands, and took his leave.

The meal had indeed been very, very, very good, and an interesting hybrid, too. Many of the hallmarks of Nouvelle Cuisine—none of them *nouvelle* anymore—had been in evidence: the hearth-cooked dishes, the spare presentations, the elegant sauces. Showy flourishes of more recent vintage had found their way into the lineup, too—the foams, the leaf—as had luxe touches from the classical era: the caviar, the black truffle, the blini. There'd even been a nod to rustic Gascon food: namely the ragoût with its rooster testicles.

Overall my memory of the lunch is a fine one, not least of all because Dubosc seemed so pleased to have exposed me and Michele to the glow of Gascony's beacon of three-star luxury. Oddly enough, though, what I remember most vividly about the day is the funny sensation of returning to the mill after all that fancy treatment. The living room was damp and dark and smelled of cold ashes. I built a fire and recall sitting with our backs to it, eating leftover soup for dinner, and, in spite of it all, feeling happy to be home.

21

Le Saint Cochon

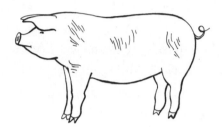

Champion of duck that I am, I don't take great pleasure in saying this, but for much of history, the animal that played the most vital role in the day-to-day sustenance of the Gascon paysan was the pig. For corroboration I will turn to my three sages.

Weber: "If bread stood for plenty, bacon or lard was a symbol of wealth. The hog was the real patron saint of the countryside—Sent Pourquî in Gascony—a miraculous animal, every bit of which was good for something . . . and which almost everybody could afford to raise."

Wolfert (echoing the bread comparison): "There is a mystical feeling about these beasts on the farms of the South-West, similar to the way bread is regarded in some other parts of France."

Palay (cue the fanfare): "It is the pig, in our land, that constitutes the carnal portion of our diet. Every household feeds and fattens a pig or two that will, with few days excepted, provide the bacon, the ham, the sausages, the confit, the meat that appears regularly on our tables."

For generations, pigs were slaughtered on the family farm, sometimes by the farmer, sometimes by an itinerant butcher. The season's first tue-cochons, as the killings were called, awaited the arrival of cold weather, as the slaughtered animal was usually left to hang outdoors overnight before the *découpage*, the salting, and the sausage-making began.

Gascons' love of charcuterie runs deep. At any worthy Gascon market, one will find a chorus line of air-cured and salted pleasures: hams, saucissons, chorizos, and more, alongside pâtés, coppas, terrines, and, most prominently, boudins, made with pig's blood. I can remember Nadine, during one of her sentimental journeys into the past, going on at great length about the making of boudin when she was growing up. The day after the slaughter, she said—and sometimes the day of—women from several families gathered to make the wine-colored sausages, toiling over a mixture of blood, lard, and trimmings, adjusting the seasonings just so and then inviting the menfolk to taste the raw filling before it got stuffed into the casings. Gascons make incredibly good boudin.

While it's not uncommon even among bourgeois Gascons to buy a whole pig from a farm—or go in on one with a neighbor—and have it brought to a *charcutier-traiteur* to be cut up and made into various delicacies, not many families in Gascony kill their own pig anymore.

That said, there are still a few butchers roving the Gascon countryside who will do the job.

I found this out when I ran into my historian friend, Alain Lagors, in town one day. He informed me excitedly that a hard freeze had been forecast.

"What's the bad news?" I said.

Lagors gave a puzzled laugh. "As you may know, the weather must be cold for a pig slaughter."

In light of the weather, Lagors said, his neighbor, a traveling butcher named Jean-Pierre, had scheduled the season's first tue-cochon for two days hence.

"Jean-Pierre is a piece of living history," Lagors said. "*Hélas*, most people nowadays buy their chops and boudins from the Inter-marché."

The inaugural killing would take place at Jean-Pierre's home, outside Plaisance. The pig had already been chosen. Her name was Mimi.

JEAN-PIERRE'S HOUSE AND THOSE AROUND it were of recent construction, located in one of several small tracts that had sprouted from the flat expanse of farmland between Plaisance and Préchac. The neighborhood had a vaguely suburban feel that seemed unsuited to the business of pig slaughtering, and I said so to Lagors as we pulled into Jean-Pierre's driveway.

Lagors said that the neighbors complained only rarely. "Usually when it's a squealer."

Jean-Pierre hadn't returned yet from collecting the condemned animal from a nearby farm, so Lagors and I loitered in the house's small yard, which was enclosed by hedges. A cauldron of water had been set over a wood fire. On the grass next to that sat a crudely fashioned wood trough that reminded me of a pauper's coffin. A folding table covered with a plastic sheet stood against one of the hedges.

Lagors, who'd never met a silence he couldn't fill with a history lesson, began talking—prompted by what, I don't know—about

how officers of Lord Wellington were said to have begun the tradition of fox hunting outside Pau, the capital of the Béarn, after passing through the region during the Napoleonic Wars.

Before Lagors could delve too deeply into the subject, a mud-
spattered hatchback pulled into the driveway and came to a stop a
few feet from us. It was hauling an open-topped, metal-sided trailer.
In it sat an enormous pink sow, also mud-spattered. A bald, ruddy-
faced man got out of the driver's seat. He had the potbelly of a bon
vivant. This was Jean-Pierre.

He bounded toward me and squeezed my hand hard. Like Basso,
he had the permanent half-smile and deep crow's-feet of an invet-
erate joke-cracker.

Jean-Pierre led me over to the trailer. "Meet Mimi!"

He leaned over and gave the pig a slap. "Sorry, girl! We couldn't
find a priest for the last rites!"

Two more men arrived in a second car. One was young and
skinny and the other was old and round; the latter had a toothpick
in the corner of his mouth.

On the way over, Lagors had explained that a traditional tue-
cochon was at minimum a five-man operation: four men to hold
each of the pig's legs, and a fifth to wield the knife. Today's killing,
however, would be done the "modern" way, with four men and a
tractor. Presently, said tractor rumbled up the drive. It was an old
John Deere with a forklift attachment on the front and a buzz-cut
Gascon named Olivier at the wheel.

Mimi's executioners were now assembled.

The men got to work with barely a word. They had obviously
performed this ritual together many times before. Jean-Pierre flipped
down the gate of the trailer and tied a rope around each of the sow's
front hooves while the skinny fellow tied another around its snout.
Mimi obstinately laid herself down. Jean-Pierre and his two help-

ers began pulling mightily on the ropes while Olivier shoved the animal from behind. There was much grunting from the men but not a sound from Mimi. She refused to budge.

At that moment, I noticed a man in city clothes walking up the driveway. I guessed it was a neighbor coming to complain preemptively. But the man strode up and shook Jean-Pierre's hand—I recognized the newcomer as the village pharmacist. "I was afraid I'd missed it!" he said.

"You're cutting it close!" said Jean-Pierre.

Eventually, the men cajoled Mimi out of the trailer and with continued yanking and shoving moved her into the yard. The tractor's front wheel had been positioned over a thick wood plank. The men situated the sow in front of the plank, and Jean-Pierre tied ropes around her hind legs and secured the other end of the ropes to the tines of the tractor's forklift. He gave Olivier a thumbs-up, and, with the two other men holding her front legs steady, Mimi was slowly hoisted into the air, hind end first, until her head was a foot above the ground. Jean-Pierre took the rope attached to the animal's snout, looped it through an eyelet screwed into the plank, and pulled it taut. Mimi was fixed in her death pose—a pig in mid-swan dive.

Something compelled me to study Mimi's face. I suppose it's the mark of a city dweller to seek signs of emotion in a farm animal's countenance, but that being so, I could find none. Her eyes were unblinking and blank. I couldn't tell if she was frozen in fear or merely indifferent.

Jean-Pierre noticed me gazing at the sow. "Don't worry," he said, "this one won't squeal."

He got down on one knee and placed a plastic bucket in front of the pig. "You're a brave one, aren't you, Mimi?"

In his right hand Jean-Pierre held a thin-bladed, wood-handled knife, the kind my mom uses for slicing cucumbers and carrots.

Without further ado, he plunged the blade into the middle of the pig's throat and made a swift upward cut. Blood thundered into the bucket with shocking force. Mimi jerked faintly and emitted a gurgling sound.

When the flow had slowed to a trickle, Jean-Pierre stuck his hand into the bucket, the contents of which looked for all the world like raspberry purée, and swished the froth around vigorously to prevent the blood from coagulating. When his hand emerged, it was painted crimson to the wrist.

"That's going to make some fine boudin," he said.

Olivier maneuvered the deceased pig into the wood trough. Then the men poured buckets of scalding water, retrieved from the cauldron, over the carcass, filling the air with the scent of boiled pig. With impressive speed and vigor, they scraped off the animal's hair using wallet-size squares of metal that, according to Lagors, had once belonged to the blade of a scythe. The hair came off in wet tufts.

Jean-Pierre had one rubber-booted foot inside the trough, the other on the ground. "The Basques use old sardine cans," he said, smiling at me and Lagors over his shoulder, his hands flying back and forth across the carcass. "But we Gascons are more high-tech."

Now Olivier raised the pig again, and Jean-Pierre removed the hard-to-reach pockets of hair using a propane torch, adding an acrid edge to the air's perfume.

The gutting began. With the pig hanging upside down in front of him, Jean-Pierre made an incision down the center of the belly from tail to head. The abdomen opened like a curtain, the sow's bulging, pinkish-gray entrails flopping out and releasing tendrils of steam into the cold air. Jean-Pierre removed the intestines to a bucket. Then out came the stomach, the liver, the heart, and the lungs. Each went into its own bucket. The older man, toothpick still in his teeth, carried the entrails and stomach over to the plastic-covered table and began cleaning them—a fragrant task I preferred to witness from afar.

The innards removed, Jean-Pierre used a bow saw to halve the pig lengthwise right down the spinal column, finishing the job by splitting the skull and hard palate with three tremendous whacks from an enormous cleaver. Now the two sides of the animal hung from the forklift tines, rib cage exposed to the air, each half a picture of the pork cuts to be.

After inserting an iron hook between the bones of each hind leg, right above the hoof, Jean-Pierre wrapped his arms around one of the carcass halves and shouted at Olivier to unloop the rope from the forklift tine. Then Jean-Pierre performed a two-part maneuver that could only be described as balletic: As the 130-pound side of pig was released from the forklift, the brawny butcher did a plié while gripping the bottom third of the carcass, and then pirouetted deftly so that it flopped, skin side down and perfectly centered, onto his shoulder.

Lagors shouted "Bravo!" and clapped loudly. The pharmacist and I clapped, too. It was an unexpectedly delicate culmination to the day's bloody work—though, in fact, there'd been just as much grace and precision to everything Jean-Pierre had done.

Now the carcass halves were hanging from the ceiling of the garage, where they'd rest for a spell before Jean-Pierre began breaking down the animal and making his chops and charcuterie. The boudin would get done straightaway, as would the andouille, that most fragrant of French encased meats, made from the animal's stomach and intestines. The tender, little-worked muscles of the loin would be frozen and, later, sectioned into chops. The tougher but tastier shoulder and butt would be transformed into roasts that would eventually be larded with strips of the pig's back fat and then smartly tied in the prim French manner. More fat, from the cheeks and neck, would go into various pâtés, terrines, and rillettes. The feet would probably get cooked, pickled, and, possibly, encased in aspic. The immense upper part of the hind legs—future hams— would be salted and then hung for many months to cure. The legs' knobby *jarrets*, or hocks, would almost surely find their way into the family's garbures, where they would in all likelihood keep good company with pieces of the pig's fatty belly.

Finally, his work done, Jean-Pierre washed his hands and opened a bottle of rosé. His cheeks were red and his eyes glimmered. He poured us all a round and raised his glass.

"To Mimi," he said.

"To Mimi!" we shouted.

22

Foie Gras

Residents of the Gers eat foie gras, on average, twice a week. If this seems excessive, consider that fattened duck or goose liver, a foodstuff regarded by much of the world as an indulgence—even a sinful one at that—is as widely available in Gascony as cold cuts. It's produced in the late fall and early winter on family farms all over the Gers—year-round on bigger ones—and eaten in every season. At home, Gascons mostly consume foie gras *en conserve*, which means "preserved in sterilized jars." Sometimes they spread it on pieces of baguette or toast; sometimes they eat it on its own, sliced into medallions or squares, possibly with some coarse salt or pink peppercorns sprinkled over the top. Gascons also eat foie gras in the form of terrines and pâtés and, at its most elemental and delicious, pan-seared. Occasionally they eat it raw. To the fullest extent of my knowledge, they do not eat foie gras on lollipop sticks, freeze-dried and broken into shards, or encrusted with Pop Rocks—a few of the many ends to which American chefs have employed the ingredient in recent years.

Gascons react with confused dismay when the subject of banning foie gras comes up. During the time I resided in Gascony, Californians were living under such an embargo, since lifted. My hometown of Chicago, too, had enacted its own short-lived ban. Both had the vociferous support of animal rights activists, who, I suspect, viewed the force-feeding of ducks and geese as something akin to a giant bull's-eye. The fact that most people in the United States consider foie gras to be something rich people buy—like mink coats or Rolexes—certainly didn't hurt the activists' cause.

No one is certain who first had the idea to force-feed waterfowl, but the ancient Egyptians were the earliest enthusiastic adopters of the practice. The watershed of the Nile was a popular wintering ground for geese, and the Egyptians figured out that if you hand-fed the birds moistened grain, a little more every day, they got fat very quickly. This is because geese, like ducks, are predisposed to do exactly that in preparation for their long migrations, storing the valuable fat in their skin and in their hepatic tissue. The Egyptians force-fed geese in order to generate lots of fat, which they used for cooking, medicinal purposes, lamp fuel, and the like. The engorged livers were most likely considered a happy by-product. The Romans, who fed geese figs instead of grain, were the first to document the delectation of the fatty liver, which they preferred to cook whole.

In his book *Foie Gras: A Passion*, the American foie gras expert Michael Ginor probably irked a few Gascons by diverging from the French party line, which has long held that the practice of gavage took root in Western Europe thanks to resourceful Gallic farmers, who'd learned the practice from the Romans and kept it alive through the Dark Ages, in what is now southwestern France. "A more likely guardian of the foie gras–making arts," Ginor writes, "were the Ashkenazi Jews of Western and Central Europe. . . . A long trail of literary evidence linking the Jews to foie gras begins in the eleventh century with the earliest reference to fattened geese in medieval Europe."

Whatever the history, today the Southwest of France is to foie gras what Wisconsin is to cheese. This owes partly to the fact that the Gers, the Landes, and especially the valley of the Adour River constitute France's corn belt, and corn is the present-day feed of choice for gavage. (Not long after arriving in Gascony, while driving down a farm road outside Plaisance, I was stunned to see a sign for DeKalb seed stock, named for a town in northeastern Illinois just west of where I grew up.) In the postwar years, after an easier-to-breed variety of the moulard was developed, and after André Daguin wowed the world with the splendors of rare-cooked duck breast, ducks overtook geese as the preferred source of foie gras in France and throughout the world. Though large-scale duck farms have cropped up in other parts of southwestern France in order to meet global demand for canned foie gras products, in the Gers gavage remains for the most part a farmhouse chore like any other—though one that requires extra finesse.

The task has traditionally fallen to women. The first time I witnessed gavage was on a farm in the northeastern Gers, my host a winsome *fermière* sporting designer jeans and blond highlights. I'd watched as Christine poured a cupful of white corn into a feeding funnel, corralled one of her white-feathered ducks, placed the duck between her knees, tilted back its head, and lowered the funnel's tapered spout into the animal's throat. As she did this, she explained that a duck's esophagus is keratinized—lined with fingernail-like bristles—and does not have sensation, though I can't say the procedure looked particularly pleasurable. Quickly, she activated the funnel's electric auger in order to send the corn down the tube and into the duck's crop, which filled like a beanbag. The funnel slid out, and the duck waddled over to a trough and took a drink. The other birds waited their turn without any noticeable excitement.

The force-feeding lasts several weeks, Christine had told me, at the end of the ducks' four-month-long life, which is spent mostly outdoors. Proper gavage must be performed by the same person each day—usually once in the morning and once at night—as the ducks are very sensitive to changes in routine. Christine proved an articulate defender of gavage, pointing out that a duck's entire anatomy is designed for gorging and that a fattened liver is not diseased—as is sometimes claimed in anti–foie gras circles—just fat. She became defensive only at the end of my visit, when I'd asked about the origins of the technique. She admitted reluctantly that while Gascons frequently liked to assert that they'd been the sole guardians of the practice in Europe for centuries, and even went so far as to say they'd invented it, neither claim was true.

That first encounter with gavage had taken place outdoors on a sunny morning. My second one—at the home of my Esbouhats hunting buddy Henri Michel—fell on a black December night, in weather so foul that I considered staying home. In the end, I bucked up and drove to his house in the Madiranais through gusty, pelting sheets of rain, windshield wipers thwacking on their fastest setting. After a couple of wrong turns in the dark, down muddy lanes, I pulled into a rutted, steeply sloped gravel driveway. I opened the car door, and a large dog with mud-caked paws leaped halfway into my lap. I could hardly blame it for seeking shelter. The dog led me up the drive to a farmhouse with a light in the window. Through a sliding door, I could see Henri Michel sitting at a table with his wife, sipping floc and eating nuts. I tapped on the glass hesitantly, fearing I might be mistaken for an intruder.

"Ah, good, you're here," Henri Michel said, letting me in. "It's almost feeding time."

He handed me a dainty stemmed glass. "Drink that down and we'll go out to the shed."

The shed in question was really more of a lean-to, lit by a couple of bare bulbs. Rain hammered on the corrugated-metal roof. A dozen moulards were milling about on a raised platform covered with straw. Henri Michel, his glasses glazed with rain, climbed onto the riser, sat down on an overturned bucket next to a vat of corn, reached for the funnel, and began his work. With wind blowing in through gaps in the shed's wood-plank walls, the scene felt slightly macabre. But Henri Michel performed his task with good cheer, recounting how he'd taken up gavage after retiring from his job with the railroad a few years back.

"The old-timers called it a woman's chore," he said. "But I got the hang of it right away."

I told him it seemed like a lot of work: dawn and dusk feedings every day for weeks, no matter the weather. I asked him why he didn't just cure ham as a hobby, like Alphonse.

"I cure ham, too," he said.

Henri Michel explained that in a few days he would take the fattened ducks up to his garage, kill them, pluck them, and, over the course of an afternoon, with the help of his neighbors, perform the découpage: removing the livers, the breasts, the legs, the wings, the necks, and all the rest—some of it destined for canning, some of it for the freezer, and some of it for immediate enjoyment.

"When we're done," he said, "we have a big feast."

Naturally.

ON BEHOLDING A WHOLE FOIE gras for the first time, a person unfamiliar with the delicacy could be forgiven for refusing to believe that the organ had resided inside a duck. A fattened moulard liver, which consists of two elongated, putty-colored lobes and can weigh as much as three pounds, is an immense and formidable repository of lipids, iron, and protein. Foie gras is creamy, smooth, and dense in much the same way frozen custard is, and it's almost as quick to melt on the tongue. Fresh foie gras that's browned in a pan is often said to taste like the caramelized fat on the edge of a grilled steak—except that seared foie gras is much finer than seared steak fat in both flavor and texture, with an even more concentrated and extravagant richness. Devotees have described foie gras as voluptuous, silken, satiny, and sumptuous. I would not contest any of those words.

Throughout our stay in Plaisance, we almost always had a jar of foie gras in the house. Nadine was a reliable source, to be sure; she had more foie gras than she knew what to do with. But as the season of gavage got under way, other people started giving it to us, too. Everyone we knew seemed to have an aunt or a *mamie* who raised ducks or preserved foie gras or both. A teacher from Charlotte's school sent her home with a jar, tied with a bow and accompanied by a note: "A homemade Gascon treat. Enjoy!" We added it to the jars we'd just gotten from Henri, Alphonse, and Diane.

And yet being able to eat foie gras with, say, a Monday lunch never stopped being a novelty. On the rare occasions when visitors made the long and somewhat taxing journey to Plaisance from abroad, I had a tendency to go overboard, as if to say, "Yes, we live off the beaten path, but we eat foie gras whenever we like!"

One weekend, our friends Liz and Dom came to visit from London. Liz and I went way back. We'd met as students in Aix-en-Provence and had bonded over a shared love of food, hitchhiking, the *Herald Tribune* crossword puzzle, and boozy sing-alongs, most often to the tunes of Jacques Brel. We had reunited while living in Paris two years later and had stayed close ever since. Liz and Dom were remorselessly dedicated eaters, so I wanted to fete them by packing as much foie gras and duck as possible into their short visit.

The day before they arrived, I went to Ferme Tomasella and bought a very large piece of fresh foie gras. I set aside part of it for pan-searing and used the rest to make a *mi-cuit*, which is a gently cooked terrine. I had never made a mi-cuit before. Nadine, who'd given me her recipe and even loaned me a ceramic terrine mold, had, as usual, made it sound easy. But as with the wood pigeons, I found myself stumbling over the first step: in this case, deveining the liver. This proved to be an unseemly business that required plunging my fingers deep into the pale, soft tissue to extract a slippery, *y*-shaped blood vessel. When I was finished, half the liver looked like mush. Dispirited, I called Nadine. She said not to worry—no one would notice once the foie gras was pressed into the terrine and cooked. Not for the first time, I wanted to bottle her reassuring voice. After that, I sliced the liver, seasoned it, and laid the pieces into the mold, then cooked it in the oven in a bain-marie before putting it in the fridge to chill overnight. For the pan-seared foie gras, I wouldn't have to do anything except slice it, season it, and try not to overcook it. The high heat would render the veins unnoticeable.

I'd decided that for the main course of our Saturday-night feast I'd try my hand at seared magret again. I'd been taking a break from it, consumed by the pleasures of braising and roasting, but we had only so much time left in Plaisance, and I wanted one more chance to get the dish right.

AS WE DROVE TO THE train station in Tarbes the next morning to pick up Liz and Dom, I tried to calculate how long it had been since Michele and I had seen them. Charlotte, I realized, hadn't even been born.

I touched my incipient bald spot and wondered how different we'd seem to one another.

Dom was, like me, a little softer under the chin, and Liz had cut her hair short, but by the time we'd gotten to the moulin and started lunch, I felt as if we'd picked up a conversation from the day before. We devoured the mi-cuit, which had turned out perfectly, as Nadine had promised, and polished off a few confit duck legs, a round of Époisses, and two bottles of Gaillac while we were at it. It was pleasantly strange to see these two faces from an earlier chapter in our lives in this old mill on the Arros.

After lunch, I showed our friends around Plaisance: the bakery, the school, the bullring, the Esbouhats clubhouse, the war memorial where Charlotte sang "La Marseillaise," word for disturbing word. I went on for too long about the history of Plaisance's two bastides, pointing out where the tanneries and workshops had once lined the river, where the medieval church had once stood, where the remains of an old dungeon tower rose from the courtyard of a block of houses. We stopped for a coffee at Le Plaisantin. The usual cast of men in paint-spattered jeans was there, sipping Stellas. So was Bernd, cigarillo in hand. When we returned to the house, our family of river rats made an appearance, as did the striped cat who'd absconded with one of my wood pigeons.

We napped. I got a fire going. Michele put on some music. I set out foie gras preserves on black bread, a plate of cut radishes with coarse salt, some olives, a bowl of fritons. I uncorked a bottle of floc. We made a toast. Charlotte and Michele sat in front of the fire and showed Liz pictures of our life in Chicago. Dom kept me company in the kitchen while I got dinner ready, taking care not to rush the magrets. I made a pan sauce with blackberry jelly, homemade stock, and Armagnac. Dom and I talked about aging parents and friends' divorces. Night had fallen, and soon our cozy moulin felt pleasingly cut off from the world outside.

After a time, we sat down to eat.

The rest of the long, wine-fueled evening comes back to me in a kind of jump-cut montage: Dom smacking his lips in a very British way as I bring out the seared foie gras, the medallions just shy of blackened on the outside, pale pink and lusciously smooth within; the platter of sliced magret, the skin crisp and melting, exactly as I hoped; Michele and Charlotte devouring every morsel, skin and all; Michele coming out of the kitchen with a homemade chocolate cake; me hauling in more firewood; Dom fetching the Armagnac.

Now it is late, and Liz and I are standing in the middle of the room, snifters in hand, bellowing along to "Ces Gens Là," the most mordant of Brel's songs, an aria of disdain for the rural petite bourgeoisie of his youth—the provincial matron with her "apostle's face," the drunk at Sunday Mass "as pale as an Easter candle," the burgher's family joylessly slurping their cold soup, *"flchss! flchss!"* Liz and I mimic Brel's every syllable and tic, straining to roll our *r*'s gutturally like the master. Michele and Dom have laid their heads on the table in an exaggerated display of annoyance. A couple more songs, and I am ready for sleep, steeped in good memories.

The next day, we had time for one more meal before Liz and Dom caught the train. I chose a place we liked in Marciac that had the rare distinction of being open on Sundays. Despite the indulgences of the night before, Liz and Dom showed no signs of flagging. Indeed, a certain *jusqu'au-boutisme*—literally "all-the-way-ness" but maybe better translated as brinksmanship—had taken hold, and so, at lunch, we did not hold back: pâté, oysters, pig's foot braised with garlic, a salad of *haricots Tarbais*, handmade *saucisses de Toulouse*, a soft round of boudin on a nest of frisée, all of it washed down with crisp beer from the Quercy.

Halfway through, I realized nobody had ordered foie gras. I was about to do something about that, but decided not to push it.

23
Confit

My culinary education in Gascony would draw to a close in much the same way it began: with a baptism by duck fat. The moment had finally come to make confit.

Foie gras and magret may have more widespread cachet, but confit is the true coin of the realm in Gascony, the mother ingredient, the foundation on which the entire cuisine has been built. Confit has survived the rise and fall of monarchies and empires and the vicissitudes of French gastronomy, from Escoffier to Cuisine Minceur. Confit is the purest embodiment of agrarian resourcefulness, a conduit to the foodways of antiquity. It is the soul of Gascon cookery.

Paula Wolfert, who was seduced by confit during her five-year vision quest in the Southwest of France, surmises that the practice of preserving lightly cured meat in rendered fat may have come from North Africa, where dried beef and lamb are given a similar treatment, but she acknowledges that it was in Gascony where the technique was perfected. Wolfert devotes lots of superlatives to the subject in her writing. Calling Gascons "the most extreme devotees of this splendid food," she goes on to declare: "So clearly has it left its stamp on great reaches of the South-West that one could construct an accurate map of culinary boundaries simply by the presence or absence of confit."

Duck confit is not deep-fried but, like a good braise, simmered slow and low for hours—usually just in duck fat, but sometimes with the addition of goose and pork fat—and allowed to cool gently before being transferred with its *graisse* to jars or crocks. Many visitors to Gascony who try duck confit have trouble believing that it was cooked and preserved in deep fat. A nicely aged and properly reheated confit duck leg, with its dark, moist flesh and carapace of crisp skin, is rich but not nearly as fatty and salty as lots of other kinds of preserved meat. Confit has a clean, nutty taste all its own.

Confire means simply "to preserve." For a long time in Gascony, the preserving was done by laying the simmered pieces of meat along with their cooled cooking fat in an earthenware vessel called a *toupin*, topping off the meat with more rendered fat, and then tucking the toupin away in a cool, dark place. In a testament to the miraculous preserving qualities of waterfowl fat, duck and goose put up in this manner have been known to keep for as long as a year. Toupins are still in use here and there: André Dubosc and I had lunch at the home of a winegrower whose mother-in-law responded to our impromptu visit by hauling a crock from her cellar, retrieving a couple of duck legs from the soft off-white fat, and crisping them in a skillet for our lunch. Nowadays, though, most home cooks transfer the cooked meat and its fat to jars, which they then seal and sterilize.

Duck confit is not the kind of dish a typical suburban cook might make for a weekend dinner party. For one thing, you have to have lots of rendered fat around. This is no problem in a land inhabited by 25 million ducks, most of them fattened on grain, but it's a considerably taller order in America, where cooking in animal fat has largely fallen out of favor and you can't just pop over to the neighbor's farm for a few jars of the stuff. For another, confit is meant to be made in large quantities—part of the age-old seasonal ritual of provisioning cellars and pantries for the winter.

Indeed, when I witnessed Gascon large-scale confit-making for the first time—at Nadine's house (where else?) on a frigid morning not long before we left Gascony—I felt I'd slipped out of the modern era altogether. And I couldn't escape the sense that all the grilling, searing, and braising I'd been doing for the better part of the past year had been building up to this moment.

Nadine was all business when Michele and I showed up at her house. There was a lot of confit to make, and little time for pleasantries. Aprons were donned, and we got straight to work. On the long table in her canning room—so cold we could see our breath—the following items had been laid out: an enormous aluminum bowl filled with duck legs, maybe twenty in all; another large aluminum bowl filled with duck wings and necks; one slightly smaller bowl filled with several dozen pinkish-brown goose gizzards, each resembling two ravioli fused together at the edges; and, finally, a couple of three-quart plastic tubs filled to the brim with duck fat that Nadine had accumulated during the year. The gizzards and duck parts had been salted and seasoned with black pepper and thyme the night before. They were ready for their long dip in hot fat.

To that end, an immense flat-bottomed kettle, three feet wide at the top, had been set over a propane burner. Nadine lit it, then raised an index finger and delivered her confit-making preamble:

"Confit," she said, "must be built from the bottom up. It must cook gently and slowly. If it cooks too fast, it's ruined."

Nadine issued our marching orders. I was to add the wings and necks to the kettle and let some of the fat render out from the skin. This, she reiterated, had to be done slowly, over gentle heat. Next I was to tip in a few heaping scoopfuls of the reserved duck fat, enough to nearly cover the duck parts once it melted. Then I was to stir the contents of the kettle gently to keep the meat from sticking to the bottom. The legs would go in a short while later, with more fat. The gizzards would go in last.

Michele was given the tedious job of scraping tiny stray feathers from the crook of some of the duck legs—a task that, to Nadine's chagrin, the duck farmer had failed to perform. Michele, who had a lifelong aversion to handling raw fowl, looked unnerved by her assignment.

After the wings and necks had cooked for twenty minutes or so, I added the legs, along with a baseball-size dollop of reserved fat.

Nadine took the spoon from me and added a slab twice the size of the one I'd just dropped in, scolding me for being too timid. The truth was, I found the sheer quantity of fat Nadine was using to be intimidating. For better or worse, fat was an ingredient that I, like many Americans of my generation, had been taught to use sparingly if at all, and even to regard as something bad or dangerous. So pervasive was the anti-fat dogma in contemporary American food culture that, despite my knowing full well that fat gives flavor and richness, and despite the gustatory rewiring that had resulted from my Gascony experience, I had apparently not extinguished a reflexive squeamishness when faced with cooking with many pounds of fat.

What's more, making confit is not pretty.

As the fat in Nadine's kettle liquefied, it became turbid, taking on a soupy brown tint. The skin and flesh of the duck pieces poking out at the top were covered in a gelatinous sheen. After a while, the thick liquid in the kettle became animated, percolating like a witches' brew. Enormous bubbles swelled and popped with a wet *blorp.*

Nadine came over to me while I was stirring. "Beautiful music, isn't it?"

She told me it was time to add the gizzards. I did so, and then put in a few more slabs of fat, which melted faster than the first ones. I stirred and listened as the music returned: *blorp, blorp, blorp.*

Just past noon, Jenny came in wearing a pin-striped apron and carrying a bowl of peeled onions and garlic cloves. She gave the bowl to Nadine and shook hands with me and Michele, smiling—we were familiar faces now. Nadine added the garlic and onions to the kettle, asked me to transfer custody of the wooden spoon to Jenny, and announced that it was time for lunch.

We ate roasted chicken stuffed with baguette ends, rosemary, and garlic. The bread had soaked up the chicken fat and the flavor of the garlic and turned spongy. This humble stuffing—one of the oldest paysan preparations in the book—was as delicious as the bird itself. It felt good to be out of the cold canning cellar, appetites awakened by our morning's work. We emptied a bottle of Madiran, and Michele and I listened to Nadine talk about the past in her fond and melancholic way.

When we returned to the arrière cuisine, Jenny was seated dutifully next to the burbling kettle, the wooden spoon held upright on her knee. A fine haze hung in the air, which was infused with the scent of cooked fat. It felt like a scene from another age—and yet one could find a similar picture in homes and on farms all over the Gers at this time of year.

It was nearly dark outside by the time we'd removed all the meat from the kettle, strained the cooking fat, and scraped out the gelatinous *fond* from the bottom of the duck-fat tubs—this Nadine would use to make her beloved graisserons. The duck parts would keep fine in the chilly canning room overnight, and Nadine would start putting them in jars tomorrow. Now she had the makings of months' worth of meals: The necks would be used for soups and stews, the gizzards for salmis and salads, the wings for garbures, the legs for unexpected company. As for the fat, she could use it again the next time she made confit. Duck fat was the ultimate reusable asset.

Nadine gave us a few duck legs, wrapped in foil, to take home. She expressed frustration that we wouldn't be sticking around Gascony long enough to wait until the duck's flavor deepened—confit, she said, doesn't really come into its own until it's mellowed for two or three months. Our imminent departure, in fact, seemed to cause Nadine more annoyance than sadness: Before we said good-bye, she rattled off a list of old-time Gascon foods she hadn't yet taught me how to make: sanguette, alicot, graisserons, rillettes d'oie. In Nadine's mind, Gascon cuisine was a gospel to be spread for the good of humanity, and she was clearly worried that her chosen emissary was going out into the world less than fully prepared.

That night I crisped three of the duck legs in the oven for dinner. I'm sure Nadine had been right about them getting better with age, but I can say without reservation it was the best confit I've ever had.

24

Apéro

I don't know if there's a meaningful irony in this, but it wasn't until the end of our time in Plaisance that I had the following epiphany: The most ingenious part of mealtime in Gascony is the beginning.

The Gascons have taken the quaint French tradition of the pre-meal apéritif and Gasconized it. Their *heures de l'apéro*—especially during the holidays—are long, extravagantly provisioned, and enlivened with ceremonial flair: decanters, serving trays, ice bowls, toothpick holders, cocktail napkins—all of it meant to convey that, upon taking possession of your glass of floc or pastis or whiskey, you have agreed to leave mundane cares behind and give yourself over fully to the sacramental rites of imbibing and feasting. It is not unusual in Gascony to be invited to a cocktail gathering—I use the word *cocktail* loosely, as the drinks are usually not strong—that's supplied with more food than a typical American family's dinner. Pâté, saucisson, homemade cheese puffs, crudités, nuts, crackers, cheese-stuffed olives, brandade-stuffed peppers, foie gras–stuffed duck hearts—these are a bare sampling of the vast panoply of Gascon cocktail snacks. A proper Gascon apéro (the word denotes both the ritual and the drink) can feel like a meal unto itself, and even when it's a simpler affair, an enveloping feeling of détente and good cheer prevails.

Our final week in the Gers was filled with a dizzying succession of holiday-season apéros—some more elaborate than others—to which our fast-approaching departure imparted a certain emotional charge.

The longest, and probably the most Gascon, apéro we attended was at Alphonse's. He lived in a renovated eighteenth-century farmhouse on the edge of town, just past Plaisance's retirement home. He and Lorette put out the biggest snack spread I'd ever seen outside a catered event: homemade *pâté-en-croûte canapés*, toasts topped with more homemade pâté, baked cheese tartlets drizzled with chile oil, sliced chorizo, sliced saucisson, pimiento olives, slices of smoked duck breast, cornichons and some other pickled things that escape my recollection, several kinds of nuts, and, in the center of the immense glass coffee table, resting on a length of cheesecloth, one of Alphonse's home-cured hams, its surface covered in a fine flowering of white mold, a knife lying next to it.

There would be no need for dinner.

Alphonse kicked off the evening by carving slabs of the ham, which he was quite proud of, for all of us to taste. With equal pride, he showed me his well-stocked bar. I studied the collection of spirits and liqueurs, then glanced over at the coffee table, my gaze falling on the bowl of pimiento olives.

I asked Alphonse to slide the ice bucket my way.

Borrowing a glass pitcher and a slotted spoon from the kitchen, I made two straight-up gin martinis. Alphonse took a sip of his, raised his eyebrows, and looked admiringly at the drink.

"Strong!" he said. "But sophisticated."

He'd summed it up nicely.

That evening's cocktail hour lasted three. Alphonse liked his martini so much that he asked for a second. I obliged him. Then he brought out the wine. By ten o'clock, the coffee table was covered with crumbs and balled-up napkins, and Charlotte was asleep in my lap. Michele, who'd been soldiering through a long conversation with Lorette and her visiting sister about baking, was looking ready for bed, too.

When we got up to leave, Alphonse boozily draped an arm over my shoulder. "We've gotten pretty used to having you in Plaisance," he said.

I told him we'd gotten pretty used to being there.

I exited before things could get mushy.

A few days later Alain Lagors invited us to join him for drinks at the home of Jacqueline Sanvert, the Anglophobic nonagenarian we'd met at the cookout in Préchac back in the summer. This apéro was the most elegant one I'd ever been to, in Gascony or anywhere in France.

Jacqueline lived by herself in a wide row house near Plaisance's town hall. She remembered all of us by name, and crouched down to plant a long, wet kiss on Charlotte's cheek.

"*Entrez*," she said, favoring the formal mode of address, in the accepted manner of the *haute bourgeoisie*. "The others are already here."

Jacqueline, short and sprightly and sporting a flame-orange cravat, led us into a spacious sitting room with an urbane, old-money vibe: pristine wainscoting, discreetly positioned reading lamps, contemporary furniture in taupes and beiges. Lagors was ensconced on a couch beneath a moody oil painting of a Spanish maiden playing a lyre. In an armchair opposite him sat a friend of theirs named Aline, who, when we approached, popped a cracker into her mouth, rubbed her fingers together to release some crumbs onto a napkin, and shook our hands with a deferential tilt of the head.

We took our seats around a marble-topped coffee table laid with a porcelain platter of homemade Parmesan tuiles and tapenade toasts. Next to this sat a gleaming two-handled silver serving tray that held a few heavy-bottomed drinking glasses, a bottle of Spanish gin, a bottle of tonic, a bottle of Banyuls wine, and a glazed ceramic decanter in the shape of a goose.

Jacqueline invited Charlotte to sit on the rug and gave her a game of pick-up sticks and an enormous candy shish kebab. These would keep her happily occupied for the remainder of the evening, which would go on nearly as long as Alphonse's soirée. Despite a few attempts by Lagors to steer the conversation toward subjects of a historical bent, the talk that night centered entirely, and without the least digression, on *la gastronomie*.

Jacqueline, a native of Pau, had traveled widely in her day, and now she spoke rapturously of dinners at the Carlyle and platters of *fruits de mer* at Le Procope, occasionally tilting her head back, eyes closed, and uttering a respectful "Mm, *dé-li-cieux*." Aline rhapsodized in a similar vein about the *bonnes tables* she'd dined at in the region: Les Puits Saint Jacques, La Table des Cordeliers, La Bonne Auberge. When I mentioned that Michele and I had recently had lunch at Les Prés d'Eugénie, Aline moaned and rolled her eyes ecstatically, and Jacqueline gasped, leaned back in her chair, and began fanning herself with her hand.

Infused with the holiday-cocktails spirit—not to mention the spirits of holiday cocktails—I ended the evening by inviting all of them to the moulin for drinks the next night. Michele looked a little startled by my impromptu proposal. But it seemed like the friendly thing to do. We had bought a small Christmas tree and had decorated it with festive lights, and (I'd nearly forgotten) I was in possession of a salt-cured duck breast that, if I'd marked my calendar correctly, was finally ready to eat. I decided I'd invite Henri and Monique, too, to liven the mix.

The next evening, I cut into the duck breast, which had been buried in coarse salt in the bottom of our fridge for weeks—I had been afraid to hang it, given the house's dampness and its resident population of spiders and mice. The duck had undergone a magical transformation in its salt sarcophagus. The red flesh had become firm, like prosciutto, and darkened to a deep garnet hue. The fat had become smooth and pearly. The magret had the salty, funky tang that all good dry-cured meats possess, but with an extra richness. I sliced the breast thinly, fanned out the pieces on a plate, and smiled upon my creation.

Michele had made a special trip to Aire sur l'Adour, a nearby bourg, to procure two other things for our cocktail gathering: some very good Basque chorizo from the town's covered market, and a box of savory puff-pastry petits fours from a patisserie Aline had recommended the night before with no small amount of euphoric eye-rolling. The two-bite cocktail snacks were of varying shapes and flavorings: mini quiches studded with bits of chive and *pimentón*; triangles of golden, flaky pastry folded around tiny squares of anchovy; macaroons flecked with caramelized shavings of Emmentaler and filled with creamy duck-liver terrine. The pastries were almost too pretty to eat.

Not that I should have been surprised, but our company arrived laden with gifts, making me feel badly that Michele and I hadn't thought to reciprocate. Henri and Monique gave Charlotte three French Christmas books. For Michele and me they'd brought a hand-embroidered dish towel from the Pays Basque and—in the cocktail-hour vein—a lacquered drinks tray inscribed with the words "It's Wine O'Clock." Aline and Jacqueline had gone in on a T-shirt for Charlotte; it had a photo of a kitten in a hat and scarf on the front. Lagors, who had gotten wind of my pigeon-hunting misadventure, presented me with a pen-and-ink drawing, made by an artist he knew, depicting a hunter climbing up to his treetop palombière.

I poured champagne, and we drank and snacked in front of the fire, wrapped in scarves.

The evening concluded with Charlotte singing the first few stanzas of "La Marseillaise." This got a standing ovation. On leaving, Jacqueline took my hands in hers and invited us to join her and her daughter for Christmas dinner. She looked let down when I told her we were departing the day before. Aline gave Michele a handwritten list of her favorite restaurants; it was two pages long.

Monique, on her way out the door, said something that has stuck in my mind ever since: "Thank you for bringing life to this old moulin."

I'M LOUSY AT GOOD-BYES. When faced with the prospect of a long separation, I tend to dissemble, joking and joshing and making promises of imminent reunions that have little chance of happening. Gascons, however, are not easily distracted from the sentimental gravity of a situation, and while they don't go in for lots of hugging, they do express their feelings with a disarming openness. As the holiday gatherings in and around Plaisance ramped up, this state of affairs began to test my powers of avoidance.

Parting ways with our expat friends—at a Christmas cocktail party thrown by Tim and Chloé—was easy enough, because, like me, they tended to keep the tone chummy and droll, in the British–

Northern European manner. But when Patrick, the only Gascon in attendance, gave us a book of his photos as a going-away gift, I clammed up, my jesting reflex suddenly disabled. The book was a collection of a hundred or so black-and-white portraits of the people of Plaisance: the butcher, the baker, the grocer, the pharmacist, the florist, the mayor. I paged through it and realized that I recognized almost all the faces.

The next afternoon was the elementary school's annual holiday pageant, held in Plaisance's municipal gymnasium. It was to be followed, as is the case with most large gatherings in Gascony, with *le verre de l'amitié*. There were skits performed in Occitan, poetry readings, and the singing of Christmas carols. The *spectacle* concluded with the principal taking the stage, microphone in hand, and asking everyone to join her in wishing a fond farewell to Charlotte, *notre jeune Américaine*, who would now be performing a special dance number with some of her schoolmates.

Michele and I had not been informed of this.

Charlotte and six older girls took the stage. Maîtresse Nathalie, standing in the wings, pressed a button on a boom box, and pop music echoed tinnily through the room. The girls began executing a series of pliés and arabesques, which were followed by some *Flashdance*-like business with folding chairs and then a few leaps and shaky relevés. As the music faded out, the other girls formed a circle around Charlotte and started chanting her name. Soon the rest of her classmates joined in. Then the whole room, parents and all. Charlotte held her ballet pose, a bewildered smile on her face.

After it was over, Michele and I remained in our seats, dumbstruck. Michele rummaged in her purse for a tissue. Eventually we got up and followed the other parents over to a long bar that was, as far as I could tell, a permanent fixture of the gym. We served ourselves cups of wine and shook hands with parents who came by to wish us a *bon retour*. Charlotte found us, and soon was surrounded by teachers from the school. Most of them, including the stoic Nathalie, were wiping away tears. I couldn't blame them.

The good-byes kept coming. André Dubosc invited me to his house for a midday apéro—not a rarity in Gascony—and persuaded me to stay for what he insisted would be a simple, improvised lunch. We ate homemade pâté, grilled quail, a zucchini-tomato tart, and a sorbet made on the spot from pears that Françoise had picked from the trees in the fall and frozen. All of this was whipped up with the nonchalance that an American might associate with the making of a ham sandwich. Dubosc also gave me a book to take back to the States: an illustrated catalog of all the known grape varietals of southwestern France. It was a hefty tome.

That night we had yet another farewell apéro, this one at Henri's. I was grateful for the invitation, though I'd been less than enthused at the idea of an evening of stiff conversation in the fussy upstairs salon. But when we arrived, Henri led us to their cozy living room on the main floor. The TV was on. A fire crackled in a wood-burning stove. We sat in comfy old armchairs. Henri opened a bottle of Pacherenc and brought out a bowl of nuts. Monique gave Charlotte a comic book to read. The couple's Springer spaniel snuffled around our feet, begging for snacks. Monique chattered about gardening, Henri chiming in from time to time to correct the exaggerations to which his wife was prone. It was spare as Gascon cocktail hours go, but it was one of the most relaxing, familial moments I can ever remember having in France.

Henri asked us to stay for dinner, and we did. As we were leaving, I remembered a dozen items of unfinished business at the moulin: returning the sleeping bag Henri had loaned me, locating the screws for the wobbly headboard I'd taken out of the master bedroom, giving back Henri's books. Henri stopped me before I could get halfway through the list.

He rested a hand on my shoulder.

"Don't worry," he said. *"Je m'en occupe."*

IN THE FACE OF SO much generosity and goodwill, I kept my composure as best I could.

The Friday before our departure, I made my final visit to the Esbouhats. It was their annual tapas night, the club's most popular event of the year: an apéro to end all apéros. The bodega was packed when I got there, and plates of food, contributed by various members, occupied every inch of counter space: scallop crudo, thin-sliced *jamón*, pieces of crisp-bottomed Spanish tortilla, curried chickpeas, bruschetta, plus the usual Gascon hit parade of pâtés and cured sausages and ducky things.

I found a spot at the bar. Doudou, the school cook, passed me a plate of his homemade samosas, and mentioned offhandedly that the club had raised funds so that he could fly back to Madagascar to visit his sick father.

Well-wishers migrated over: Bernd with his halo of smoke and a recipe for goulash he'd been wanting to give me; Henri Michel with a sampling of his homemade foie gras; Luc with an extra-long "Whassuuuuuup!"; Francis with an unexpected invitation to return to his palombière next year. Basso materialized, brandishing a bottle of Jameson's. He refilled my glass, raised his own, and bid me safe travels. I was certain I saw, for the most fleeting instant, his puckish grin disappear.

The evening rolled on. Someone topped off my drink again. Bernd offered me one of his cigarillos. For some reason, I smoked it.

I noshed, drank some more, chatted with some Esbouhats I hadn't previously met, and generally lost myself in the splendid conviviality of it all.

Now Alphonse was standing behind the bar, clinking a spoon against a glass. Suddenly the room was quiet and he was speaking. Heads turned in my direction. My face felt hot. Alphonse was saying something about bidding au revoir to "our American Esbouhat." I'm sorry to say I can't remember the rest, as my emotional defenses by this point had been reduced to rubble and I found myself in tears, in the middle of a roomful of rugby players, blowing my nose into a cocktail napkin.

25

Last Supper

For reasons no Gascon has ever satisfactorily explained to me, the denuded carcass of a duck—what's left once the breasts, legs, liver, and other parts have been removed—is referred to as a *demoiselle*. Gascons do not throw away the demoiselle. In fact, they take pleasure in grilling it and stripping off the remaining morsels of meat using their fingers, teeth, and, occasionally, a switchblade. A grilled demoiselle is the most irreducible of Gascon meals. It's what paysans ate after they'd sold off everything else. If you search among the profusion of posters and fliers for local festivals in Gascon villages, you'll probably find one or two for a *soirée demoiselle*. Such communal meals are also sometimes called, less euphemistically, *soirées carcasses*.

Our own soirée was nothing more than me, Michele, and Charlotte sitting in front of the fire on our final night in Plaisance, gnawing on duck bones, our chins shiny with grease. I had cut the hollow carcasses into quarters and grilled them on the hearth. We saved the *aiguillettes*—the tender strips of meat clinging to the duck's sternum—for last.

At some point while we were eating, I asked Michele and Charlotte if they were going to miss Gascony. The words came out in a loud dad-voice—I suppose I was fishing for affirmation.

Charlotte nodded *mm-hm* and continued attacking her duck. I decided to take this as a full-throated yes.

Michele wiped her hands and seemed to give the question due consideration. Then she smiled and said, "I really am."

After dinner I put on my coat, went outside, and sat on the banks of the stream so I could gaze at the bridge for a while. The Arros, glimmering faintly in the dark, flowed around the stone foundations and on toward its union with the Adour, joining the waters of thousands of Gascon brooks and streams.

I wondered when I'd be able to take in this view again. Suddenly I thought of Amandine. I'd said good-bye to her at the market a few days before and she'd informed me, in her laconic way, that she was selling her van and leaving the Gers to work as a nanny. The news had shaken me a little, disabusing me of the comforting but illusory notion that things in this sleepy corner of France would remain the same until I could return—same faces, same places, everything right where I left it. But Amandine's revelation had reminded me of an obvious truth: Change *does* come to the Gers.

Fortunately, it takes a while.

Acknowledgments

T hanks, first and foremost, to the Gascons who opened their doors for us, and to those who knocked on ours. I am especially grateful to Nadine Cauzette, a magnificent cook and a natural-born teacher, and to André Dubosc, the most knowledgeable ambassador for Gascony I could ever have wished to meet. Thanks also to Diane Caillard and her husband, Nicolas Kujawa, and to Patrick Fitan, a man for whom the phrase *joie de vivre* seems to have been specially coined. To Alphonse Caulier, Michel Basso, and the rest of the Esbouhats: If the spirit of the *mousquetaires* is alive and well anywhere in Gascony, it is in the bodega behind the old bastide. Thanks to Henri and Monique de Rességuier, whose patience and kindness would certainly meet the definition of *noblesse oblige*, and to Amandine Belmonte, who is wise so very far beyond her years. Special thanks to Paula Wolfert, who, unbeknownst to her, became my spirit guide during my first forays into Gascon cookery. Thanks, too, to Maurice Coscuella, Alain Lagors, Fred Poppe, Lut Goudleder, Tim and Chloé Wootton, Jean-Claude Dupuy, Colette Lasserre, Sandra Lemarechal, André Daguin, and his daughter, Ariane, who kindled my interest in Gascony with a phone call and a prediction: "This place will change your life." It did.

I owe enormous gratitude to my agent, Daniel Greenberg, who shepherded me through the book-making process with such aplomb. I'm equally grateful to my editor, Jonathan Jao, for peering into the thickets of my first draft and locating the true path, and to his colleague Sofia Ergas Groopman, whose line edits helped me do a rather un-Gascon thing: Trim the fat.

This book also benefited immeasurably from talented and insightful early readers. Mark Adams is preeminent among them: He is the most astute and sympathetic guide a first-time author could ever want. Thank you to Maura Fritz, who steered me away from so many writerly pitfalls, and to Alex Fischer, Melinda Blum, and the friends and colleagues who considered my first, inchoate ideas for the book and said, "Do it": David Brown, Bonnie Eldon, James Oseland, and Holly Dolce, among others.

Thank you to my parents, Jim and Susan McAninch, for their boundless love and support, and to Michele and Charlotte, for sticking with me, and for finding so much joy and beauty in places I'd never have thought to look.

Recipes

La Garbure de Nadine

Nadine's Cabbage and White Bean Soup

Serves 6 as a first course or light meal

There are meatier garbures to be found—the extravagant stew in
Paula Wolfert's *The Cooking of South-West France*, for one—but this
simple version from Nadine Cauzette is closer to the everyday garbures served in most Gascon homes. Dried Great Northern beans
are a fine substitute for haricots Tarbais, the kind of beans used for
garbure in Gascony. This soup tastes even better if made a day ahead
and allowed to rest in the fridge overnight.

> 4 confit duck legs
> 1 cured or smoked ham hock
> 10 medium waxy potatoes, cut into 1-inch pieces
> 4 medium carrots, cut into 1-inch pieces

2 small turnips, cut into 1-inch pieces

1 large leek, thinly sliced

1 medium onion, quartered

8 ounces dried haricots Tarbais or Great Northern beans,
    picked through, soaked overnight, and drained

1 head Savoy cabbage, cored and thinly sliced

6 garlic cloves, minced

Kosher salt and freshly ground black pepper

Remove the skin from the confit duck legs and set it aside for making cracklings. Warm the duck legs in a 350°F oven for 15 to 20 minutes until heated through. Let cool; pull the meat off the bones and tear it into chunks. Set the duck meat aside.

Add 5 quarts of cold water to a large pot along with the ham hock and bring to a boil. Reduce the heat and simmer the ham hock, skimming frequently, until the water starts to turn cloudy, 20 to 30 minutes. Add the potatoes, carrots, turnips, leek, onion, and beans and simmer over medium-low heat for 1½ hours, skimming occasionally as necessary. Add the reserved duck confit and the cabbage and simmer for another 20 to 30 minutes, skimming occasionally. Add the garlic and simmer for 15 minutes more. Remove the ham hock, strip off the skin, pull the meat off the bone in chunks, and return the meat to the pot. Discard the bone and skin. Season the garbure with salt and pepper to taste.

Magret de Canard à l'Armagnac et aux Mûres
Seared Duck Breasts with Armagnac-Blackberry Sauce

Serves 4

The name has a fancy ring, but this dish—one of dozens that pair magret with a sweet pan reduction—is as straightforward as can be.

> 2 skin-on moulard duck breasts (or 4 skin-on Pekin duck
>   breasts)
> Kosher salt and freshly ground black pepper
> 1 small shallot, minced
> 1 cup chicken or duck stock
> 1 ½ ounces Armagnac
> 1 ½ tablespoons blackberry jelly
> 2 tablespoons unsalted butter

Using a small, sharp knife, score the skin of the duck breasts in a crosshatch pattern, taking care not to cut into the meat. Season both sides of the breasts with salt and pepper and set aside for 15 minutes. Pat the meat dry with paper towels and place the breasts, skin side down, in a cold skillet. Turn the heat to medium-low and cook the breasts until most of the fat has rendered out and the skin is golden and crisp, 8 to 10 minutes. Flip the breasts and continue cooking for another 6 to 8 minutes until medium-rare.

(*Note*: If using Pekin duck breasts, cook over medium heat instead of medium-low, and reduce the cooking time by 2 minutes per side. Cook in two batches if necessary to prevent crowding the skillet.)

Transfer the breasts to a cutting board and tent them with aluminum foil. Pour off all but 1 tablespoon of the fat from the skillet, then add the shallot. Cook over medium heat until soft, about 1 minute. Add the stock, Armagnac, and blackberry jelly and stir to combine. Bring the mixture to a boil and continue boiling until it has reduced by a little more than half and has become lustrous and almost syrupy. Remove the sauce from the heat, swirl in the butter, and season with a little salt and pepper.

Pour the sauce into the bottom of a deep serving platter. Slice the duck breasts and place the slices on top of the sauce.

Daube de Boeuf
Red Wine Beef Stew

Serves 6

Like many Gascon dishes, this one takes time: a full night for marinating, and another to let the stew rest before it's degreased and
gently cooked a second time the following day. Most Gascons I know
use *poitrine de boeuf*, or brisket, for daube, but I recommend good-
quality chuck instead since American brisket isn't usually streaked
with fat in the same way French poitrine is. Also, adding tomatoes
isn't particularly Gascon, but they give a nice, subtle acidity to this
rich braise.

> 3 pounds beef chuck, cut into 2-inch chunks
> Kosher salt and freshly ground black pepper
> 1 large leek, chopped
> 2 bouquets garnis (each containing 3 sprigs parsley, 2 sprigs
>   thyme, 1 bay leaf)
> 4 garlic cloves, smashed, plus 2 more cloves, chopped
> One 750 ml bottle dry red wine
> 2 tablespoons all-purpose flour
> 2 tablespoons rendered duck fat or olive oil
> 2 large carrots, cut into 1-inch pieces
> 1 medium onion, roughly chopped
> 1 celery stalk, chopped
> 2 large plum tomatoes, seeded and chopped

Season the beef generously with salt and pepper and add to a cast-
iron Dutch oven (cocotte) along with the leek, 1 of the bouquets

garnis, the 4 smashed garlic cloves, and the wine. Stir to combine. Refrigerate, covered, overnight.

The next day, remove the chunks of beef from the marinade and pat the meat dry with paper towels. Strain the marinade using cheese-cloth or a fine-mesh strainer; discard the leeks, the smashed garlic, and the used bouquet garni. Divide the strained marinade between two bowls; whisk the flour into half the strained marinade.

Working in batches, brown the meat in the duck fat (or oil, if using) in the bottom of the Dutch oven over medium-high heat. Transfer the browned meat to a plate. Add the carrots, onion, celery, toma-toes, and chopped garlic to the Dutch oven and cook, stirring fre-quently, until the vegetables soften slightly. Return the meat to the Dutch oven along with the second bouquet garni and all the reserved marinade and stir to combine. Simmer, covered, over medium-low heat until the meat is tender, 2½ to 3 hours.

Remove the Dutch oven from the heat and allow the stew to come to room temperature. Refrigerate overnight. The next day, remove the congealed fat from the surface of the daube, and remove and discard the second bouqet garni. Allow the stew to come up to room temperature. Bring to a simmer again over medium-low heat and cook for 2 ½ to 3 hours.

Serve with steamed potatoes and plenty of crusty bread.

Poule au Pot
Chicken in a Pot

Serves 4 to 6

Finding a tough old hen like the one Nadine Cauzette used when we made this dish isn't easy in the States. This recipe, which includes the classic sauce gribiche accompaniment, has been adapted for a quicker-cooking roasting chicken.

For the sauce gribiche

> 1 hard-boiled egg, yolk and white separated, white part
>   chopped
> 1 ½ tablespoons white wine vinegar
> ½ cup olive oil
> 1 tablespoon minced capers
> 1 tablespoon minced fresh parsley
> 1 tablespoon minced fresh chervil
> 1 tablespoon minced fresh tarragon
> Kosher salt and freshly ground black pepper

For the stuffing

> ½ cup bread crumbs, soaked in milk
> 2 large eggs, beaten
> 4 parsley sprigs, leaves chopped
> 4 garlic cloves, peeled and chopped
> One 6-ounce piece dry-cured ham such as prosciutto or
>   jambon de Bayonne, chopped

Giblets (heart, liver, gizzard) from the chicken
Kosher salt and freshly ground black pepper

For the chicken

One 3 ½- to 4-pound roasting chicken with its giblets and, if
    possible, its neck and feet
Kosher salt and freshly ground black pepper
1 extra-large bouquet garni (6 sprigs parsley, 6 sprigs thyme,
    1 celery stalk, 1 bay leaf)
1 onion, pierced with 2 whole cloves
1 teaspoon white peppercorns
6 medium carrots, halved
2 large leeks, trimmed, halved crosswise, and tied with twine
    (so they don't fall apart during cooking)
2 large turnips, quartered
10 small waxy potatoes, peeled

Make the sauce gribiche: Mash the egg yolk in a bowl while slowly adding the vinegar, bit by bit, mixing constantly to create a smooth texture. Once the vinegar has been added, start adding the oil in a thin stream, stirring vigorously all the while, until the mixture becomes smooth and emulsified. Stir in the capers, parsley, chervil, tarragon, and chopped egg white and season with salt and pepper to taste. Refrigerate until an hour before serving time.

Make the stuffing: Drain the excess milk from the bread crumbs, transfer the soaked bread crumbs to a bowl, and stir in the eggs. Pulse the remaining stuffing ingredients in a food processor until they're very finely chopped; add them to the egg mixture and stir until thoroughly combined. Season the stuffing with salt and pepper and set it aside.

Stuff and cook the chicken: Season the chicken inside and out with salt and pepper. Fill the cavity with the reserved stuffing. Sew the cavity shut with kitchen twine and truss the bird. Bring 5 to 6 quarts of water to a boil in a large pot. Add the stuffed chicken and its neck and feet (if using) and let the water return to a boil. Skim any foam that rises to the surface, then reduce to a simmer over medium heat. Add the bouquet garni, studded onion, and the peppercorns and cook, covered, for 30 minutes, skimming as needed. Add the remaining ingredients and continue cooking, skimming occasionally, for another 40 to 45 minutes until the vegetables are very tender and the internal temperature of the chicken is at least 165°F. Taste and adjust the seasoning as necessary. Strain the broth and discard the bouquet garni, the onion, and the neck and feet.

To serve: Cut up the bird and transfer it to a large platter with its stuffing and the cooked vegetables. Ladle a little of the broth over the chicken and vegetables. Serve the remaining strained broth as a first course, if you like, and serve the bird and the vegetables with the sauce gribiche and some coarse salt.

Confit de Cuisses de Canard
Confit Duck Legs

Serves 4

Gascon cooks usually make confit in large quantities, in the fall, and preserve the meat in sterilized jars or cans, but you can make confit in small batches for more-immediate enjoyment at any time of year—if you're able to find enough rendered duck fat. Ask your butcher for some, or order a container of it from the specialty-foods purveyor D'Artagnan.

> 4 whole duck legs
>
> 4 tablespoons kosher salt
>
> 2 tablespoons minced fresh thyme
>
> 1 tablespoon freshly ground black pepper
>
> 6 cups rendered duck fat
>
> 1 bouquet garni (3 sprigs parsley, 3 sprigs thyme, 1 bay leaf)
>
> 1 medium onion, quartered
>
> 6 garlic cloves, peeled

Trim any excess skin from the duck legs and reserve the trimmings for cracklings. Mix the salt, thyme, and pepper in a bowl. Rub the seasoning mixture onto the duck legs. Cover the duck with plastic wrap and refrigerate for 24 hours.

The next day, rinse the duck legs and pat them dry. Place the duck legs, skin side down, in the bottom of a large cast-iron Dutch oven or heavy-bottomed pot. Turn the heat to medium and cook until some of the fat has rendered out from the skin, about 5 minutes. Transfer the duck to a plate, add the additional rendered duck fat to the Dutch oven, and let the fat melt. Return the duck legs to the Dutch oven, submerge them completely in the fat, and let the fat come to a steady simmer over medium-low heat, about 20 minutes. An instant-read thermometer inserted into the fat should read 200°F. Add the bouquet garni, onion, and garlic and continue cooking, covered, for another 1½ to 1¾ hours, stirring gently from time to time, until the duck is tender when pierced with a fork.

Remove and discard the onion, garlic, and bouquet garni. Let the duck cool in its cooking fat to room temperature, then cover the Dutch oven and refrigerate, making sure the duck pieces are covered completely in the fat. (You can also transfer the duck and its fat to another container, if you want.) The duck will keep, fully covered in fat, for up to 3 weeks.

When ready to serve the duck, remove the pieces from the fat and bake them, skin side up, in a 400°F oven until the skin is golden and crisp and the duck is heated through, 30 to 40 minutes.

Foie Gras Poêlé
Pan-Seared Foie Gras

Serves 4 as an appetizer

Searing fresh foie gras in a skillet is the simplest, and arguably the best, way to appreciate the delicacy. A dusting of sugar and *quatre-épices*, four-spice powder, enhances caramelization during cooking, and gives a sweet dimension to the foie gras's fatty richness.

> One 12-ounce piece fresh foie gras, cut into 1-inch-thick
>   pieces
> 1 teaspoon confectioners' sugar
> 1 teaspoon quatre-épices (four-spice powder), plus more
>   if needed (alternatively: ¼ teaspoon each ground
>   cinnamon, ground nutmeg, ground cloves, and ground
>   white or black pepper)
> 1 teaspoon crushed black pepper
> Kosher salt
> 2 tablespoons balsamic vinegar
> Coarse salt

Spread the foie gras pieces out on a baking sheet or large plate. Season both sides with the sugar, quatre-épices, crushed black pepper, and kosher salt. Cover the foie gras with plastic wrap and refrigerate for at least 1 hour and up to 12 hours.

Place a heavy-bottomed skillet over high heat. When the pan is very hot, add the foie gras pieces and cook, flipping once, until nicely browned, 1 to 2 minutes per side. (They will release a great deal of fat.) Transfer the foie gras to a serving plate and pour off the rendered fat. Add the vinegar to the pan to deglaze it; let the liquid boil for a few seconds, then drizzle it over the foie gras.

Sprinkle the foie gras with a little coarse salt. Serve hot.

Le Gâteau Basque d'Henri
Henri's Basque Tart

Serves 6

Of the many versions of this dessert that I've tried, Henri de
Rességuier's humble, unadorned one is my favorite.

For the dough

> 1 ½ cups all-purpose flour
> ½ cup sugar
> Pinch of salt
> 1 teaspoon almond flour
> 2 teaspoons baking powder
> 1 large egg, lightly beaten
> 8 tablespoons (4 ounces/1 stick) unsalted butter, melted and
>   allowed to cool

For the cream filling

> 1 cup whole milk
> 3 tablespoons sugar
> 2 egg yolks
> 1 tablespoon cornstarch
> 1 teaspoon Armagnac or dark rum

Make the dough: In a large bowl, mix together the all-purpose flour,
sugar, salt, almond flour, and baking powder until thoroughly com-

bined. Whisk in the egg. Add the melted, cooled butter and mix until a dough has formed. Shape the dough into a ball, flatten the ball, and separate it into two halves.

Make the cream filling: Heat the milk in a saucepan until steaming. Meanwhile, in a mixing bowl, whisk the sugar with the egg yolks until thoroughly combined, then whisk in the cornstarch. Slowly add half the hot milk to the bowl to temper the eggs, then pour the mixture into the saucepan and heat, stirring constantly, until the liquid boils and thickens, about 3 minutes. Let the cream filling cool to room temperature. Stir in the Armagnac.

Assemble and bake the cake: Preheat the oven to 350°F. Press half the prepared dough evenly into the bottom of a greased, 9-inch round cake pan. Pour the cooled cream filling evenly over the dough layer. Then begin cutting off small pieces of the second dough half, flattening them, and laying the flattened pieces gently on top of the cream layer until all the dough is used up and the cream layer is completely covered. Bake the tart until golden, about 45 minutes.

Fritons de Canard
Duck-Skin Cracklings

Portion size varies

One of the finest pleasures of duck cookery is also the simplest. To make fritons, just trim off the excess skin of a duck leg, duck breast, or whole duck, cut the trimmings into small pieces, and spread out the pieces on a baking sheet. Roast in a medium-hot oven, stirring occasionally, until golden and crisp, 20 to 25 minutes. Pour off and reserve the rendered fat, and transfer the cracklings to paper towels to drain. Sprinkle the cracklings with a little kosher salt, then toss them on a salad or—better yet—eat them as an apéro snack.

About the Author

DAVID McANINCH is the features editor at *Chicago* magazine and was an editor at *Saveur* for nine years. His writing has appeared in the *New York Times*, *New York* magazine, the New York *Daily News*, *Newsday*, *Rodale's Organic Life*, and *Departures*, among other publications. He lives in Chicago with his wife and daughter.